LISBURN

A History of the Catholic Community of the Parish of Blaris (Lisburn)

Pearse Lawlor

Published by
Clovercorry, Lisburn
Unit 17,
BT28 2UJ

Pearse Lawlor has asserted his right under the Copyright, Designs and
Patents Act 1988 to be identified as the author of this work.

LISBURN ARTS
ADVISORY COMMITTEE

© Pearse Lawlor, 2014

ISBN: 978-0-9931311

A CIP record for this title is available from the British Library

Printed by Trimprint Ltd, Armagh

CONTENTS

INTRODUCTION

This book is about the Catholic community of the Parish of Blaris (Lisburn) past and present. It is a history of Lisburn that has never before been recorded and as a social history links individuals with incidents, some long forgotten, some best forgotten and others not forgotten.

It traces the history of this community from the foundation of Lisnagarvey in 1609 and records the numerous events over the succeeding four-hundred plus years that have affected the lives of the Catholics of Lisburn.

This Catholic community is in many ways unique, moving from being ostracised by English legislation to being embraced by those of different faiths when, in 1786, the first Catholic church in Lisburn 'was built by donations from people of every religion in this country'. However local and national politics conspired to create division along sectarian lines and as groups and individuals exploited those divisions for political and personal gain sectarian conflict would be a feature which surfaced many times during the history of Lisburn.

This is not a book just for the Catholics of Lisburn, although it does provide a comprehensive history of the Catholic Parish of Blaris, but it will help readers understand how our past has shaped our present and probably our future. It is a study of how, from the beginning of this account, the Catholic Church was perceived to be a threat and how generation after generation this perception became embedded in the psyche of the Protestant and unionist community.

In conducting research for this book it was perhaps surprising that a Church as structured as the Catholic Church did not have comprehensive records held locally. While the Vatican does hold many records relating to the Church in Ireland, and I was privileged to be afforded access, it is a complex system with limited indexes.

Many of the references in the book are from other publications and from newspaper reports, which will have a nationalist or unionist bias depending on the publication. As this is a social history I have included the names of various individuals involved in various incidents. They have been included only where information about them is already in the public domain.

Written in diary form it encompasses the introduction of the Penal Laws, the 1641 rising, the 1742 rebellion, the creation of the Orange Order, the 1798 rebellion, the campaign for Catholic Emancipation in the 1840s, the Lisburn cotton famine in the 1860s, the Irish Home Rule movement in the 1800s to 1900s, the first World War, the sectarian riots of 1920 and 1931, the second World War, the 'Troubles' from 1969 and in recent years the crises facing the Catholic Church.

It is always difficult to know where to start but the Plantation and the founding of Lisburn as Lisnegarvey in 1609 is as good as any.

The English Crown in the 16th century had viewed Ireland as an area ripe for expansion; an undeveloped country where fortunes could be made. The Gaelic Irish and possible continental allies were also considered by the English Crown as a potential threat that had to be neutralised.

Attempts to conquer Ireland were repulsed by the Irish chieftains and reports that the Ulster chieftains were forming alliances with England's continental enemies provided a justification for the Nine Years War.

Economic and strategic interest was behind England's policy to expand and colonize.

When Hugh O'Neill and Hugh O'Donnell surrendered in 1603 part of the terms of surrender was that lands were to be held under English law. When these and other chieftains left Ireland in the Flight of the Earls in 1607 to seek help from Catholic Europe for further revolt, their lands were seized and distributed as a reward to those who had supported the English Crown during the war. The plan for the Plantation of Ulster was underway. One of the objectives of the plantation was to 'civilise and anglicise' the Irish Catholics.

The latter objective failed as we find three hundred and sixty years later, in 1969, the then prime minister of Northern Ireland, Terence O'Neill, in what was regarded by Catholics as a patronising interview, stating that, 'if you treat Roman Catholics with due consideration and kindness they will live like Protestants in spite of the authoritative nature of their Church.'

But back in the 1600s new landlords such as Sir Fluke Conway who settled in Lisburn and brought with him Protestant and loyal workers had other ideas. There was, by law, to be no Irish tenants on his land. The native

Catholic Irish were excluded. The 'them and us' had been created. They were seen as a threat and the official policy was subjugation.

The threat was realised when in 1641 the Irish gentry staged a rising to recover and drive the planters from their lands. A common feature of the rising was the brutal massacres carried out by both sides.

In Lisburn in November of that year the Irish forces were defeated as they tried to make their way through the town as they headed to take the port of Carrickfergus. Hundreds of their soldiers were slaughtered in the streets and as the defeated army retreated they set fire to the town. Protestant folklore recalls that they exacted revenge at Portadown when the planters were captured and put to death on a bridge in the town. It was believed that men women and children were thrown into the river from which there was to be no escape. This comes under the category of events not forgotten.

The rising progressed as the Confederate War and Catholics formed their own government - the Catholic Confederation. The war ebbed and flowed as English troops were recalled to deal with the English Civil War. It was only when Oliver Cromwell on behest of the English parliament landed in Ireland in 1649 to conduct a ruthless campaign, some historians describe it as genocide, was the war brought to an end. Hundreds of thousands had died in Ireland during this period. Catholic-owned land was confiscated and Ireland was firmly under English Protestant domination. This war was viewed especially by northern Protestants as proof that every Catholic, including their clergy, was engaged in a plot to exterminate all the Protestant settlers in Ireland.

Under the Penal Laws Catholics were required to pay tithes to the Anglican Church and Catholic churches were transferred to the Anglican Church of Ireland. Catholic priests, but not bishops, were initially tolerated but later were expelled from the country. Any priest discovered at that time was liable to summary execution. The Catholics of Lisnagarvey and the surrounding area were forced to worship in secret.

There was a ban on Catholics buying land under a lease for more than 31 years and they could not inherit Protestant-owned land. Under the Popery Act inherited Catholic land was to be equally subdivided between the owner's sons except where a son converted to Protestantism when he became the sole tenant.

In 1688 the English establishment became concerned when the wife of their Catholic king, James II, produced a male heir. This changed the existing line of succession and the prospect of a Roman Catholic dynasty in the kingdoms of England, Scotland and Ireland filled them with horror. They conspired to depose the king and put in his place the Protestant Dutch William of Orange who was married to King James' daughter Mary. In what became known as the Glorious Revolution William successfully 'invaded' England before turning his attention to the more problematic Ireland. In 1689 James, in a last ditch effort to regain the throne, engaged in a war in Ireland that was essentially Catholicism versus Protestantism. James was defeated at the Battle of the Boyne in 1690 and his forces finally defeated at Aughrim in County Galway in 1691. This comes under the category of events not forgotten. England, Scotland and Ireland, ruled by the Ascendancy dominated Irish parliament in Dublin, now became a Protestant nation.

However in Ireland there was a significant majority Catholic population and despite discriminatory laws to ensure that they were subjugated to the status of second-class citizens there was always a fear that someday they would retaliate.

Unrest continued in Ireland where land was owned by Protestant landlords, many absentee and many interested only in profit. Catholic and indeed Presbyterian tenants objected not only to having to pay tithes to the Anglican Church but to the rents they were being charged. Many Catholics, unable to survive on small holdings started to diversify into what was seen as a profitable but Protestant dominated industry of home weaving. Land for use as bleaching greens was an essential component of this industry and competition for land was intense. When a Catholic outbid a Protestant a riot was likely to ensue and matters seldom rested there. A skirmish between the two factions at the Diamond near Loughgall led to the formation of the Orange Order in 1795 which declared loyalty to the Crown, the country and the reformed religion. It was not so much what the brotherhood stood for as what they stood against. They adopted a strongly anti-Catholic stance and that would be the thread that ran through the Protestant community's relationship with the Catholics of Lisburn for years to come.

The two communities lived largely apart, with a few notable exceptions when they faced a common enemy. This was not just down to Protestant ascendancy or the attitude of the Orange Order prohibiting its members from attending services in a Catholic church or marrying a Catholic. Having said that Catholics, in the past, were not exactly encouraged to visit Protestant churches.

The position taken by the Catholic Church in Ireland in supporting, for example, Daniel O'Connell as he fought for Catholic Emancipation and later for the repeal of the Act of Union, firmly placed the Church in the opposing camp. The Church, always viewed with suspicion by northern Protestants and demonized because of its rituals, seemed to justify that suspicion. The notion that the Church of Rome was out to destroy the Protestant religion and to break the union with Britain took root and would be used over succeeding generations to unite the Protestant community in opposing any nationalist movement.

With the growth of the Home Rule movement in the 1800s the Catholic Church in Ireland viewed the movement as a serious threat to its power and influence, a view not held however by all the bishops and priests. Initially only three bishops out of thirty supported Home Rule but as the movement gained strength the inherent danger for the Church became the unity of its clergy and bishops. The parish priests in Lisburn during this period would have been regarded as Home Rule supporters.

The Catholic Church was divided on support for Home Rule and at the time of the 1916 Rising, while opposing the violence, found it difficult however to remain neutral but did later threaten members of the IRA with excommunication from the Church.

When the government of Northern Ireland was formed in 1921 the Church sought to protect its interests and remained hostile to the new government on matters including Catholic education. The new government adopted an anti-Catholic agenda and turned a blind eye to discrimination, gerrymandering of electoral areas and in the provision of housing for Catholic families. The attitude of the Church did not however remain neutral as violence erupted in the late 1960s and the actions of the IRA were frequently condemned.

All these events had an impact on the people of Lisburn, a relatively small population who worked together in factories and mills, often socialized together and had more in common than they would care to admit. They would however identify as separate communities but have demonstrated that they can peacefully coexist despite different ideologies.

The Catholic Community of Lisburn and the Parish of Blaris (Lisburn)

THE EARLY CHURCH

The Catholic presence in Lisburn is lost in the mists of time but an early record of a structured presence was the creation of the Roman Catholic diocese of Down and Connor in 1439 when the diocese of Connor founded in 480 joined with that of Down.

The newly formed diocese included the Parish of Blaris and the ancient parishes of Blaris, Drumbo, Drumbeg, Lambeg, Hillsborough, Magheragall, and Magheramesk.

It extended from a little beyond Moira railway station in County Antrim to within three or four miles of Comber in County Down. It included the following townlands which formed its border; Clontonkelly North, Knockbreckan South, Ballydolochan, Ballynavally, Ballynahatty, Edenderry, Ballylesson, Drumbeg South, Ballyskeagh, Lambeg, Lisnagarvey, Tonagh, Knockmore, Knocknarea, Moneybroom, Knocknadonagh, Ballyclough, Ballynadolly, Aughacarnan, Ballycarrickmaddy, Ballymave, Maheraliskmisk, Maghaberry, Magheramesk, Lisnabilla, Trummery, Inishloughlin, Creenagh, Gortnacor, Aughnatrisk, Ballykeelartifinny, Corcreeny, Taughblane, Aughandunvarran, Clougher, Tullynore, Ballyworfy, Cabra, Caracroy, Drennan, Drumra, Creevy, Ballycarngannon, Carr, Ballynagarrick and Carryduff.

There was undoubtably a Catholic presence in the area before the Plantation and this account relates to the Catholic community in what is now known as the Parish of Blaris (Lisburn) and the churches that make up the parish.

There is evidence that an ancient church was located at Kilrush, at the foot of Millbrook Street, Lisburn. The names in the old burying ground indicate that this was used by the Catholics of Lisnagarvey and Blaris and as the name Kilrush confirms there was a church on the site and it can be assumed that Mass was celebrated here at one time. Among the headstones is one, erected by the Irish Harp Society, to the memory of their pupil Patrick McCloskey, in consideration of his good conduct and proficiency. He died on 7 June 1826. (Ordnance Survey of Ireland - Parishes of County Antrim 1832-1838 Vol. 8)

In 'The Lives of Irish Saints' is a reference to a church at Blaris.

'Cathal Maguire states that Montan was venerated in a place called Blarus. We can only find one locality, in Ireland, bearing a denomination, at all corresponding. Within the county of Down lies the townland of Blaris and there may be seen an old graveyard, with very little of the ancient church remaining. Blaris or Lisburn parish being intersected by the River Lagan, belongs to both the counties of Down and of Antrim. In some old Inquisitions, it is called Bally-templeblarisses. It is denominated, on an old map, 'Blare'. The church and graveyard give name to this parish. Its etymological meaning may have been derived, from Blar, 'a plain,' or field, and Rus 'a wood' or perhaps, more probably, from Rus 'red,' for the soil everywhere around is of a red, sandy kind.

Montanus is classed as a disciple to the great St Patrick. He is said to have assisted the Irish apostle, in various ministerial labours. From his designation of Deacon we may fairly infer, that he was never elevated, beyond such an ecclesiastical rank, although Maguire, or his Scholiast, calls him a Presbyter.

(Much of this information was provided by Rev. David Mulcahy in a letter dated 8 August 1877. In that letter he stated that two of the holy water fonts are now in the possession of Mr P. Connery, Bridge Street, Lisburn. These were from the old church of Blaris. In another account ("An historical account of the Diocese of Down and Connor, ancient and modern") Connery's name is changed to Convery, which is probably the correct version.

In 1837 Thomas Fegan, writing about the Parish of Derriaghy, commented on an ancient church on the farm of Renny Boomer at Aghalislone (north of Lisburn) razed to the ground many years ago. Around it was a burial ground and on the site bones and pieces of earthen crocks were discovered. Nearby, on a farm owned by Daniel Partridge, a set of large square amber beads attached to a gold cross about four inches long were unearthed. The date of this church has not been recorded but it probably preceded the Plantation.

1306

The Deanery of Dalboyn in the Taxation of Pope Nicholas included the churches of Drumbo, Drumbeg, Derryaghy, Blaris, Magheragall, Glenavy, Magheramesk, Aghagallon, Aghalee, Ballinderry. There was formerly preserved among muniments of the See of Down a document, which purported to have been drawn up in 1210 from earlier documents, though as Dr Reeves remarks, it is much more recent. It states that Engusa MacMailraba, a prince who flourished in the time of Brian Boru and ruled over Dalbuine, gave to the Bishop of Down and to his successors the following churches and lands in that principality, Lambeg, Derryvolgie, Cluntarib (Clnnteriffe in Ballinderry), Aghalee, Rathmesge, Magheragall, Derryaghy, Drumbo and Blaris. (An Historical Account of the Diocese of Down and Connor, Ancient and Modern.)

A church once stood in the grounds of the old graveyard at Maghaberry and was known as the Church of Rathmesge. According to an ancient document drawn up in 1210 Engusa Mac Mailraba, who reigned in Clandermod and Dalbrime gave the Bishop of Down Rathmesge, the church with two caracutes (a unit of assessment for tax and is found for example in Domesday Book. The carucate was based on the area a plough team of eight oxen could till in a single annual season) in temporalities (secular properties and possessions of the Christian Church). The church was forty-five feet long by fourteen feet wide, had a high pointed window in the western gable and an entrance in the south side wall. A round tower stood nearby which was sixty feet high and five feet wide in the interior with a cupola- shaped roof. The tower collapsed in October 1828.

Before the Plantation Maghaberry was entirely Catholic but after the Plantation the church suffered the fate of many Catholic churches 'with its altar overthrown and its walls profaned.' (The Catholic Year Book St. Patrick's 1934.)

In the ante-Plantation days Magheramesk had its church in the old Trummery Cemetery. Beside it was a round tower. The ruin of the ancient Church of Magheramesk still stands in the townland of Trummery, close to the N.E. angle of which there formerly stood a round tower, said to have been 60 feet in height. In the adjoining townland was the fort of Innislochlin which commanded the Pass of Kilwarlin, said to have been garrisoned by an army in 1641. In the same year at Soldierstown, hard by where the Parish Church of the union now stands, there was a barrack for two companies of foot soldiers and a troop of horse. According to tradition it was these troops who destroyed the old Church at Trummery with field pieces, (Tradition has it that these soldiers used the ancient round tower at Trummery as a target for cannon fire), virtually demolishing it. and caused a great breach in the wall of the round tower, which was gradually enlarged, until, in 1828, the last remaining supporting stones were removed and the tower fell, leaving only its stump to mark the spot. (Dromore, An Ulster Diocese, E.D. Atkinson L.L.b. Archdeacon of Dromore - digitized and printed by G. Damien Kerr.)

1575

In 1575 Queen Elizabeth, daughter of Henry VIII, had been queen of England and Ireland for seventeen years. It was five years since the Pope had excommunicated her and a time of change and great difficulty for the Roman Catholics within her realm.

Henry VIII, a Roman Catholic, had parted company with the Pope when a request for a special Papal Dispensation to allow him to divorce Catherine of Aragon and remarry when she had not produced a male heir was refused. Henry went ahead with his plans and was excommunicated. He established himself as the Supreme Head of the Church in England and while England continued as a Catholic country the power of the Pope in England ended. Mass continued to be celebrated and the denial of the Real Presence, the physical body and blood of Christ in the consecrated bread and wine in the Mass, was a capital offence in Henry VIII's reign.

When his son Edward VI, aged nine, came to the throne the Church of England rejected the belief in transubstantiation, a belief that was punishable under law.

All that was reversed when his sister Mary who embraced the Roman Catholic faith became monarch. She revitalised and restored the Catholic religion in England but in doing so showed little mercy, executing those who disapproved by burning them at the stake.

Elizabeth, in turn, displayed equal brutality to bring the Catholic religion in her kingdom to an end. Priests who celebrated Mass did so in secret and in 1574 their number increased when they were joined by missionaries from Rome.

When members of the Society of Jesus, the Jesuits, were sent from Rome to minister to the needs of influential Catholics in England in 1580, followed by a number of secular priests, they knew that if discovered they would be tortured, hanged, drawn and quartered and they were. **The ultimate objective of the Jesuits was the restoration of the Catholic religion in England and Queen Elizabeth viewed the activities of the priests as much political as religious.**

Life for practising Catholics became increasingly difficult. Failure to attend Church of England services could result in the Crown seizing two-thirds of the offender's estate and sheltering a priest was punishable by death. Anti-popery became an ideology that was to dominate her life and policy and that of future monarchs until James II, who became a Roman Catholic and the last Catholic monarch to reign over the Kingdoms of England Scotland and Ireland.

Such were the conditions when Sir Henry Sydney, no stranger to Ireland a country which he 'cursed, hated and detested' returned in 1575 for a second term as Lord Deputy. Ireland had over the past forty years become a place where enterprising Englishmen could make a profitable career, enjoying office and status while acquiring property but the local Irish chieftains continued to be a problem.

In 1575 Con O'Neill, the Captain of Killultagh, was at the very zenith of his power and prestige. He acknowledged the sovereignty of none, native or English. Sir Henry Sydney, Elizabeth's Irish Viceroy (called Lord Deputy in those days) was making a tour of Ulster with his chariots, officers and servants - travelling, says one chronicler, like an Eastern potentate. On arrival at the Castle of Lisnagarvey he sent an equerry to announce that the Queen's Lord Deputy desired to pay his compliments to O'Neill. In accordance with protocol Sir Henry remained in his carriage outside the Castle. Had he entered it to pay his compliments that would have demeaned both himself and his Royal mistress.

The attitude of the Lord Deputy roused the Captain's native Irish blood because by waiting thus and expecting O'Neill to emerge to receive him he was placing the haughty chieftain in the position of a vassal. In reply to the message O'Neill sent this reply:

'Tell the Lord Deputy that the King of Killultagh is in his Castle where he will be happy to receive him but he would not cross his own threshold to meet the Queen herself.'

So with his tail between his legs, Sydney had to pass on his way, but reporting later to the Queen on his tour of Ulster Sydney wrote:

'I came to Killultagh which I found rich and plentiful after the manner of the country. The captain was proud and haughty. He would not come out of his castle to see me but he shall be paid for this before long. I will not remain in his debt.'

O'Neill was certainly paid in the coin Sydney had in mind, because within twenty years he had lost or been dispossessed of all his property which was handed over to those who had loyally served the Queen and her successor, James I, in the Irish wars which overthrew the armies of Hugh O'Neill, the Earl of Tyrone and head of the O'Neill clan.

An interesting feature of O'Neill's Castle in Lisburn was what was described as 'O'Neill's masshouse'. It was said to be within a few yards of the Castle wall and therein O'Neill's chaplain celebrated Mass for the Captain of Killultagh, his principal followers and the villagers. This building would appear to have stood near or on the site of the Cathedral. (In an extract of Reflection Lisburn Past and Present, the date of Sydney's visit is recorded as 1585 but Sydney's Irish career ended in 1578. He was in Ireland in 1575.)

17th Century

1609

30 June King James 1 granted the Manor of Killultagh to Sir Fluke Conway, originally from north Wales, as part of the Plantation. He established the town of Lisburn in 1622. There is an opinion that Sir Fluke Conway took over the already existing castle and church and adapted them to his own use. At the time he took over the Killultagh estate both the castle and church had fallen into disrepair because of the ravages of the war just ended. He had the place of worship repaired and enlarged for the use of the Protestant population which he had brought from England and had planted in or near the village as replacements for O'Neill's followers who had fled their homes after the defeat of the Irish or had been killed in the bitter struggle between Crown and rebels.

1641

28 November During the 1641 Rising when the Irish decided to take action against the English, Scottish and Welsh planters who had taken their lands there was a battle at Lisburn, then known as Lisnegarvey. Lisburn was defended at that time by Lord Conway's troops and his men led by his land agent George Rawdon.

Expecting to be engaged on a Saturday their forces took up position in Market Place (Square) and waited all nigh for the attack to begin. When it did not happen they sent scouts to investigate and found that the opposing force, located at Brook Hall about three miles outside Lisburn, was attending Sunday morning Mass. As there more than 500 men, (the number claimed to have been killed in Castle Street and Bridge Street and the surrounding area during the battle), it must be assumed that this was an open-air Mass.

The Irish were defeated and as they withdrew they set fire to houses, and the town, including the church, was destroyed. It was O'Neill's Castle but then owned by the Conways which was destroyed in 1641.

This is remembered as the first great fire of Lisburn. Sir George Rawdon's son Arthur is commemorated on Lisburn's coat of arms, as a cockerel perched on a crown. Sir Arthur Rawdon was known as 'The Fighting Cock of the North.' Another view is that the cockerel represents cock fighting and the fact that Lisnagarvey translates as 'fort of the gamblers'.

After their attack on Lisburn Sir Phelim O'Neill and Sir Con Magennis returned to Brook Hall/Brookhill. Remains of the old church, which was destroyed in the civil war (1641), exist near Brookhill, and have been converted into a stable: many human bones have been turned up by the plough; and silver and copper coins of the reigns of Elizabeth, James I., and Charles I., have been found on the estate of Mr. Watson, and are in his possession. (A Topographical Dictionary of Ireland, 1837.)

1664

2 July Lord Conway and Major Rawdon writing to the Earl of Ormond from Lisburn sums up their attitude to the Catholic church:

> *"Deem it to be their duty to communicate to the Lord Deputy certain intelligence herewith enclosed. ...*
>
> *The Popish Clergy are much alarmed by the late apprehension of certain Priests in the county of Cavan. In the belief of the present writers, "this poor Kingdom will never be at quiet, and in perfect obedience to his Majesty, till they be all removed out of it".* ... (Oxford University: Bodleian Library, Western Manuscripts.)

1670

A priest named Patrick Dornan returned by Oliver Plunkett, (later canonised in 1975) Archbishop of Armagh and Primate of All Ireland, is listed in 1670 as pastor of Crumlin, Hillsborough and Magheramesk.

1673

17 December Sir George Rawdon writes from Lisburn;

> *"I hear not of any priests transported nor is there shipping to carry them into foreign parts, so what his Excellency will do next I foresee not." His Excellency did the best he could in the circumstances pretend it was no affair of his to provide shipping. So, on 31st December, 1673, orders under the most stringest penalties were issued to the clergy registered in Dublin to quit the kingdom within fourteen days. A fortnight later it was reported to the Council that divers of the popish clergy were continuing about the port of Ross. Similar reports came from Galway, Limerick, Waterford and Cork. A further series of mandates was issued 12th January commanding them to depart before the 26th. Meanwhile some of the magistrates were showing activity."*
> (Irish Priests in Penal times 1660-1760.)

Secular priests, a priest who does not take the vows of chastity, poverty and obedience of the members of a religious order, but instead promises obedience to a diocesan bishop and to live a celibate life, could remain if they were registered.

1680

In 1680 there was a remarkable change in the attitude of Lord Conway to the Catholic church. In 1664 his view was that all popish clergy should be removed but in 1680 we find:

> .... About the same time, Lord Conway gave Priest Dornan part of a field that lay on the south side of the road opposite which is now called Antrim Street, on which he built a chapel, and very tiny was the extent of that place of worship. Each of those, buildings stood outside the borough boundary in that direction. The rector of the Cathedral, the parish priest, and the Presbyterian pastor, lived on the most friendly terms, and in times of death and scarcity of food, when the labouring classes suffered much privation, the three led the way with the laity in doing all in their power to alleviate distress. At that period the southern section of the town was said to end with the Sluice River, which ran unbridged across the street. The portion afterwards known as Bow Lane consisted of a few scattered houses; a footway on one side of the river served as the path for pedestrians. (An Extract of Reflection: Lisburn Past and Present (1887))

1691

The Penal Laws, passed after 1691 mainly by the Irish Parliament, were designed to restrict the religious, political and economic activities of Roman Catholics so that they would not have the means to threaten the Protestant (Anglican or Church of Ireland) monopoly of power. As a result Roman Catholics were excluded, for example, from political power at local and national level; from holding land on long leases and from many of the professions as well as the armed forces. However Dissenters, those Protestants who were not members of the Church of Ireland, were also affected by the Penal Laws. These were largely Presbyterians who formed a sizable proportion of the population in Ulster and were seen by the Established Church of Ireland as posing just as big a threat as Roman Catholics. Consequently, they too suffered from religious and political discrimination. Presbyterians, for example, could not be married legally except in a Church of Ireland church and the ceremony performed by a Church of Ireland clergyman. This prevailed until 1782. (PRONI.)

1697

Laws in Ireland for the Suppression of Popery were introduced - The Penal Laws.

Will III c.1 (1697):

An Act for banishing all papists exercising any ecclesiastical jurisdiction and all regulars of the popish clergy...

'Sec. 1. Whereas it is notoriously known, that the late rebellions in this kingdom have been promoted by popish bishops and other ecclesiastical persons of the popish religion, and forasmuch as the peace and public safety of this kingdom is in danger by the great number of said the clergy now residing here, and settling in fraternities contrary to law, and to the great impoverishing of his Majesty's subjects who are forced to maintain them, and said the clergy do not only endeavour to withdraw his Majesty's subjects from their obedience, but do daily stir up and move sedition and rebellion, all popish archbishops, bishops, vicars-general, deans, jesuits, monks, friars, and all other regular popish clergy shall depart out of this kingdom before the 1st day of May, 1698, and if any of said ecclesiastical persons shall after that day be in this kingdom, they shall suffer imprisonment, and remain in prison until transported out of his Majesty's dominions, wherever his Majesty or the chief governors of this kingdom shall see fit, and if any person so transported shall return, he shall be guilty of high treason.'

Records held in the British Museum of returns from each of the Excise districts show that in 1697 that, at least known to the government, there were 15 popish clergy in Lisburn. (Historical account of the Diocese of Down and Connor, ancient and modern Vol. 1 by James Lavery.)

18th Century

1704

The first priest registered as living in the Parish of Lisburn was Father Patrick Dornan. (There had been a previous Patrick Dornan in 1607). He was registered in the Government Register as popish priest in the year 1704. He had been ordained in 1678 by Oliver Plunkett, the Catholic Primate of All Ireland, who was the only Bishop then in Ireland. It appears he lived somewhere about Lissue.

Also in the year 1704, Nicholas Tren Lavery, aged 56, and resident in Ballinderry, was registered as popish priest of Ballinderry and Magheragall. He was ordained in 1669, at Navan, by Dr. Patrick Plunket.

1707

Sunday 20 April An accidental fire engulfed Lisburn destroying all the property in the town. It must be assumed that a thatched building in Bow Lane (now Street), used as a place for Catholic worship was also destroyed. Later reference to Catholics worshipping at this location would indicated that the house was rebuilt.

1713

Further evidence that a priest was resident in Lisburn is contained in a reference to the persecution of the Presbyterian Rev. McCracken who had refused to take the Abjuration Oath in 1703 - a law which was used against the Roman Catholics now was forced on the Presbyterians.

(I ..; Do abjure and renounce the Pope's Supremacy and Authority over the Catholic Church in General, and over my self in Particular; And I do believe that there is not any Transubstantiation in the Sacrament of the Lords Supper, or in the Elements of Bread and Wine after Consecration thereof, by any Person whatsoever; And I do also believe, that there is not any Purgatory, Or that the consecrated Host, Crucifixes, or Images, ought to be worshipped, or that any worship is due unto any of them; And I also believe that Salvation cannot be Merited by Works, and all Doctrines in affirmation of the said Points; I do abjure and renounce, without any Equivocation, Mental Reservation, or secret Evasion whatsoever, taking the words by me spoken, according to the common and usual meaning of them. So help me God.)

When Rev. McCracken was imprisoned at Carrickfergus before the end of 1713 this drew complaints that local justices, whilst engaged in this act of persecution, did not interfere with the nonjuring Roman Catholic priest responsible for the oversight of that denomination in Lisburn and he was permitted to carry on his pastoral duties undisturbed. (Presbyterianism in Lisburn from seventeenth century - First Presbyterian Church by W. I. Craig.)

1740

23 November The Most Rev. Dr Francis Stuart, a Franciscan friar, who was consecrated bishop of Down and Connor on 23 November, resided at Reilly's Trench, shortly after his consecration.

1742

Rev. Dr Stuart was driven from his home by the Royalists who burned the chapel at Reilly's Trench during sectarian "wreckings" opposing the move by the Catholic Bonnie Prince Charles' claim to the British throne which resulted in the 1745 rebellion. Mass was then celebrated under a tree standing at the road (now at St Colman's Hall). (The Catholics of Ireland under the Penal Laws in the eighteenth century (1899) - Patrick Francis Moran 1830-1911)

Dr Stuart was compelled to retire to a country house in Lissue and he died there in 1749 or 1750. He was succeeded by Rev. Patrick Taggart, a native of Gore's Island, Saul, who was appointed to Lisburn as parish priest. He died in 1769.

Dr Stuart was an adherent of the Pretender, to whose nomination he owed his appointment and his allegiance is sufficiently attested in two letters, which he wrote to the secretary of the Pretender and which are now preserved among the Stuart Papers in Her Majesty's library, Windsor Castle.

There has been a church at Reilly's Trench at least since the 1700s. Two other priests who officiated in Lisburn at this time were Rev. Patrick Burn and Rev. O'Hanlon.

Rev. John Magee succeeded Father Taggart in 1770 and lived at Knockmore and had a small farm (occupied by Robert Hall in 1906).

He in turn was succeeded by Rev. Roger Magee from Ballee who was later murdered near Tullynaskeagh in November 1799. Locals say it was because he officiated at a mixed marriage. He was buried in Kilclief graveyard. (Ros Davies' Co. Down Family History Research Site)

The Marquis of Downshire provided land and money to enable the church at Reilly's Trench to be rebuilt in 1805. There had been a major famine in the area in 1741.

1743

The following letter from Edward Hill of Hillborough, preserved in the Record Office, Dublin, refers to Dr. Stuart's residence in the parish.

"Sir,

I had the honour of his Grace's, the Lord Lieutenant's, and Council's order signified by you to me by this day's post; and in obedience to it I must inform you, that at present there doth not reside in my jurisdiction any Popish Archbishop, or Bishop. Lately a Popish bishop did reside near this place, but last year did leave it, and, as I am informed, lives now somewhere near Lisburn. There does reside in a neighbouring parish within my jurisdiction but one Popish priest, named Patrick Burn, who lives in the house of his brother, Edward Burn, who serves the Papists in this district, being not numerous, or at least nothing in comparison to the Protestants. Of any other Popish person exercising any jurisdiction here I know of none; and am. Sir, with all due respect,

Your obedient humble servant,

EDWARD HILL, Sovereign.
Hillsborough, March 5th, 1743."

1750

In the Diocese of Down and Connor, around this time, the Catholics of the districts around Lisburn assembled for Mass 'in some quiet corner between Blaris and the Maze near which their priests ventured afterwards openly to reside'. There is evidence that a Catholic church existed near the old graveyard at Blaris in the early 1600s but by the mid 1600s had become rather dilapidated and was too faraway for the people of Lisburn to attend regularly. An ancient holy water font was discovered close to where the former caretaker's house was before it was demolished. (Ralph Smyth family records, smythhist2b.htm)

1762

The Catholic inhabitants of Lisburn, when the opportunity arose, heard Mass in a private house. The first Mass said publicly in Lisburn was in an upstairs or loft in Bow Lane, now Bow Street exactly opposite Antrim Street. (In 1906 the site was occupied by Mrs. Bell's shop). This was known as the Mass House and Catholics even interred their dead in the garden. In the early 1900s an old man related how his relatives had heard Mass there before the chapel was built on Chapel Hill and recalled how the congregation coming out from hearing Mass were stoned as they went up Antrim Lane, now Antrim Street.

In a letter dated 1848 to Mr Hanna, Ballykinlar about the history of the parish Rev. Killen wrote:

'Before the erection of the present chapel in Lisburn Mass used to be celebrated on Sundays in a private yard in Bow Lane. Mr. Magee was a very bold man and at the same time, I understand he lived amicably with the Heretics, he resided within half a mile of the town on the Maze road and it is recorded of him that one night on his way to attend a sick call he leaped his horse over the toll gate near the town.' (Diocesan records)

The Rev. John Magee, was a popular curate from 1762, and parish priest from 1770. When the Presbyterian meeting-house in Market Square was in course of erection, he handed ten pounds to the building fund committee as his, and that of a few of his people's, contribution towards the good work. While zealously attending the duties connected with the creed of his fathers, he never interfered with the private opinions of those of other denominations. Priest

Magee delighted in cultivating social harmony with all around him, and he was held in special veneration by his own followers. He took much interest in the Volunteer movement, and, when leisure permitted, was among the spectators who usually assembled in large numbers to witness the parades of the local troops, as the men met for military exercise on Gough's Hill, now a portion of the Wallace Park. And at the tables of Poyntz Stewart, Commander of the True Blues; Thomas Ward, Captain of the artillery; as well as those of other Volunteer officers, Priest Magee was ever a welcome guest. With the popular rector of Lisburn and the Presbyterian minister, he lived on terms of the utmost, friendliness. (Lisburn Standard, 29 June 1917.) See also reference in 1768.

1766

5 March The House of Lords very much alarmed at the 'Increase of Popery,'

"Resolved, that the several Archbishops and Bishops of this Kingdom shall be, and are hereby, desired to direct the Parish Ministers in their respective dioceses, to return a list of the several families in their parishes to this House, on the first Monday after the Recess, distinguishing which are Protestants, and which are Papists, as also a list of the several reputed Popish Priests and Friars residing in their parishes." (Journal of House of Lords.)

The response included:

Hillsborough.— Sir,— In obedience to the order of the House of Lords, I inform you, that there are in the parish of Hillsborough, County of Down, 431 Protestant families, 95 Papist families. No Popish priest resides in the parish, but Mass is celebrated in it by Michael Morgan, who lives near Lisburn, the parish of Blaris.

Blaris. — Protestant heads of families, 1,068; Popish heads of families, 410. One Popish Priest, Michael Morgan ; two Popish schoolmasters, John Mulholland, and Henry Laverty.

Magheramesk.—Protestant families, 146; Popish families, 49. No Priest or Fryar.
(Historical Account of the Diocese of Down and Connor, Ancient & Modern.)

1768

The first Presbyterian congregation in Lisburn came into existence a few years after the Restoration, and the first meeting house was a plain building with a thatched roof in the Longstone area. This building was destroyed in the fire of 1707, and the next church was built on the present site of First Lisburn Church. In 1768 it was rebuilt to accommodate the growing congregation. It is noteworthy that, despite the religious dissensions of the times, contributions to the cost of the building were received from both the members of the Established Church and the Roman Catholic community.

The Church of Ireland Bishop of Down and Connor, Dr. Traill, and the Rev. Saumarez Du Bordieu, chaplain of the Huguenot community subscribed to the building fund, as did 'Priest Morgan on behalf of his flock' with a donation of £10. (Ulster Star Borough Supplement 27 June 1964.)

1786

The first Catholic church erected in Lisburn was built by Rev. Magee in 1786. The site, that of the present church, was donated by a wealthy Catholic merchant Luke Teeling, the father of Bartholomew, the martyr-patriot of 1798. Luke was an important linen draper in the town and also had a financial interest in bleach mills in County Down. He was an ardent liberal, a supporter of the Volunteers and was elected to represent County Antrim in the 1792 Catholic Convention. His son Bartholomew was among the earliest recruits to the Society of United Irishmen and participated in the French invasion of Ireland in 1798 for which he was later hanged in Dublin.

Bartholomew and his brother Charles were educated at Mr Dubourdieu's Classical School in Lisburn. (History from Headstones - Lambeg churchyard & The United Irishmen, their Lives and Times, R.R. Madden, 1846)

The original church was a plain oblong building with its entrance door in the right gable end. It had a small gallery. On the tower of the church was the inscription; '*Anno MDCCLXXXVI. This chapel was built by donations from people of every religion in the country. To preserve in grateful remembrance such Christian concord this stone was erected.*'

Prior to the construction of the church Roman Catholic clergy men were buried at the church at Lambeg, about a mile and a half from Lisburn. Rev. John Mullan, parish priest of Derriaghy and Belfast who died aged 80, on 15 September 1772 was buried there. The south side of the cemetery was reserved for deceased Catholics and this continued up to about 1807 when Catholics were forced to use a new burial ground which had opened at Hannahstown chapel. It was claimed that the Catholic practice of 'keening', a continuous crying lament, kept up at funerals was disturbing to locals and when funerals arrived in the vicinity of Lambeg they 'were insulted and abused by their dissenting neighbours, which uncouth treatment in a great measure induced them to change to a new burial ground'. (Ordnance Survey of Ireland - Parishes of County Antrim 1832-1838 Vol. 8.)

The Catholic Church discouraged keening and eventually the practice ceased.

Rev. William Teggart, born 1756 ordained at the first ordination held by Dr Hugh MacMullan was a curate in Lisburn before being appointed as parish priest of Glenarm in 1784.

THE SOCIETY OF UNITED IRISHMEN

The Society of United Irishmen, led by Theobald Wolfe Tone, Thomas Russell, Henry Joy McCracken and William Drennan was formed in October 1791 with the aim of achieving parliamentary reform of the Irish parliament and Catholic emancipation. For its goal to become a reality it was necessary to unite Protestant, Catholic and Dissenter in a common cause. Essentially a liberal organisation it was successful in bringing together persons not only from different religions but different social classes.

Influenced by events in France and the American revolution the United Irishmen began to take a more radical approach and its growth was viewed with concern by the authorities. The government fearful of a union of Catholics and radicalised Protestants introduced a number of bills repealing laws against Catholics but refused political enfranchisement.

When Britain declared war on France on 1 February 1793 any association with France was tantamount to treason and Britain heavily dependent on Irish soldiers could ill afford the development of a revolutionary force in Ireland and consequently outlawed the Society. Rome was happy to side with Britain following the French Revolution in 1789 when the Catholic Church suffered greatly with priests and nuns being massacred and the establishment of a secular state. In Ireland the Church was placated with the founding of Maynooth Seminary College from overtly supporting the United Irishmen.

The suppression of the Society only galvanized the United Irishmen to seek French support to end British rule in Ireland and to found a sovereign Irish Republic. Among those responsible for putting down this rebellion was Robert Stewart, educated at the Royal School Armagh, and now Lord Castlereagh, Chief Secretary for Ireland. He had close links with Lisburn. His mother was the daughter of Francis Seymour-Conway, 1st Marquess of Hertford. A supporter of Catholic Emancipation (and the abolition of slavery) he would have known the leading merchants of Lisburn. The Stewarts from Mount Stewart on the shore of Strangford Lough were Presbyterian merchants and many of their friends would have supported the ideals of the United Irishmen. He would also have known George Tandy from Bridge Street, Lisburn, whose brother James Napper Tandy was a prominent United Irishman.

His liberal and progressive views did not however prevent him from taking, often brutal, action to prevent an Irish/French alliance on England's western seaboard.

Lisburn would not be immune from his action and the rebellion of 1798 following the Battle of Ballynahinch left a lasting affect on the town. British forces led by Major-General George Nugent defeated the United Irishmen led by Henry Munro, a linen merchant and former churchwarden at the Lisburn Church of Ireland cathedral. Munro was later hanged outside his Lisburn home.

It is perhaps noteworthy that Wolfe Tone and Lord Castlereagh both met their deaths in a similar fashion - by slitting their throats.

In Wolfe Tone's case he was about to face the hangman in November 1798, having been found guilty of treason and it appears that he made a botched attempt to cut his throat so that he would not be hanged as a common criminal. His wound was bandaged but he bled to death. Lord Castlereagh in August 1822, when suffering from depression, cut his throat with a pen knife.

1792

28 November United Irishmen volunteers accompanied by Protestants of all denominations went to Mass in Lisburn as a demonstration of solidarity. Captain Alexander Crawford of the pro-British Lisburn Volunteers was in favour of the abolition of the restrictions on religious worship and to demonstrate this led his company to Mass in the Catholic Church on Chapel Hill.

The Lisburn companies paraded in full dress and marched to Mass, where a sermon was preached by Father John Magee and a handsome collection made to aid in defraying the debt on the Mass House. It is recorded that 'large numbers of other Protestants attended'. (Ulster Star 27 June 1964.)

He later wrote to them expressing his gratitude for their support for Catholic emancipation and for their 'liberality' in attending his church. (NAI, Rebellion Papers, 620/19/115.)

3 December Among the 233 delegates from all over the country who attended a convention of the Catholic Committee, 'the only power competent to speak the sense of the Catholics of Ireland', in the Tailors' Hall in Dublin's Back Lane, was Luke Teeling from Lisburn. In spelling out their demands in a petition to the King, Luke Teeling proposed that nothing short of complete emancipation should be demanded. (Catholic. Protestant and Dissenter, Wolfe Tone)

1795

A Sunday school was established in the Catholic Church on Chapel Hill. (Ordnance Survey of Ireland - Parishes of County Antrim 1832-1838 Vol. 8.)

1796

16 September Lord Castlereagh was on friendly terms with Luke Teeling, a prosperous linen merchant and bleacher in Lisburn. Luke and his family lived in a house (later occupied by Robert M'Call), on the south side of Chapel Hill, immediately adjoining the chapel).

Luke, and one of his sons Charles Hamilton and Castlereagh met early on the morning of 16 September outside Lisburn Castle, the home of the Marquess of Hertford, Castlereagh's uncle, and after chatting for a while were about to leave when Castlereagh raised his hand signaling for them to stop saying to Luke, 'I regret that your son cannot accompany you' and guided eighteen-year-old Charles through the outer gate of the castle. The gate was immediately closed and Charles was surrounded by a military guard. Castlereagh then read out a charge of 'High Treason' against young Teeling, a charge which carried the death penalty. Luke pleaded to be allowed to speak to his son but Castlereagh with whom he had been on the friendliest of terms moments earlier refused.

Castlereagh had been informed that Charles was one of a number of leading United Irishmen who had been in communication with the French to prepare for an invasion of Ireland. With Charles under arrest Castlereagh remounted his horse and accompanied by a military guard made his way to the Teeling home on Chapel Hill to search for evidence to support the arrest.

There he was met by Charles' fourteen-year-old-brother John and his mother Mary. As Castlereagh pressed a pistol into John's chest he conducted a search of the house taking with him a number of documents. Mrs Teeling made a tearful appeal to be allowed to see Charles but the request was denied. She said that he had no idea of paternal affection adding that 'your lordship is not a father'. The latter comment cut deep as Castlereagh, at twenty-seven, had been married for two years without issue. He turned on his heel and left.

As news of Teeling's arrest spread in Lisburn a crowd gathered outside the Hertford mansion demanding Teeling's release and threatening to assassinate Castlereagh when he returned. Teeling spoke to the crowd from the window of the room in which he was being held urging calm and not to seek revenge for his arrest. General Nugent, military commander in the area had Teeling removed to an inner room and extra guards posted.

Castlereagh returned safely to the Hertford residence in Lisburn about

9:00 p.m. after a very long day during which he had gone to Belfast to supervise the arrest of other United Irishmen. He had his evening meal with Charles Teeling, both sharing a bottle of wine, and assured Charles that he would be treated well. After pleasantries he explained that Charles would be escorted to Kilmainham Gaol in Dublin, along with other prisoners. After dinner Teeling surrounded by an armed guard was escorted through the crowd that had gathered outside and a path was cleared by the cavalry to the market square where those arrested were placed in a fleet of ten army carriages bound for Dublin. (Castlereagh - From Enlightenment to Tyranny, John Bew)

Castlereagh who was portrayed as having betrayed his friend ordered Charles to be released the following year on the grounds of 'ill health'. He was however imprisoned without trial in 1798, spending years in solitary confinement. He went on to become a journalist and established the Northern Herald and the Ulster Magazine in Belfast and the Newry Examiner in Newry. (irishancestryresearch.com/doc/Teeling_ancestry_report.pdf)

1797

13 March Two United Irish suspects John Kearns and Francis Walsh were detained when houses in Lisburn was searched by the authorities in an effort to disarm United Irishmen. Weapons had been seized at Lambeg, Derriaghy and Dunmurry. Walsh, it was claimed, was a Catholic and one of Henry Monro's aides-de-camps. Munroe, charged with treason and rebellion, would later be hanged and beheaded in Market Square on 16 June 1798. (Northern Star 20-24 March 1797.)

From the 1780s the authorities had watched with some concern the growth of radicalism within the Volunteer Movement which was the only defender of the Realm in Ireland. They hesitated to take action in the hope that attitudes would change but as we have seen the foundation of the United Irishmen had the opposite effect. The government considered that it had no other option but to disband the Volunteers and establish a Militia in Ireland, an army of Irish soldiers officered by Irish gentry. One such militia was the Monaghan regiment. There was some reluctance to include Catholics in the militia but as Catholics were already serving in British regiments throughout the world that argument was untenable although action was taken to exclude Catholics from senior ranks.

The United Irishmen set about persuading soldiers in the militia to support their objectives and as this became common knowledge the government placed informers at United Irishmen meetings. When the authorities learned that many in the Monaghan Militia had become members of the Society of United Irishmen they decided to make an example of four of these soldiers and to strike terror among the entire regiment and indeed other regiments. They were charged with mutiny and sedition and pleaded not guilty and forced to conduct their own defence. They sent a letter asking for clemency to General Lake but it was dismissed and with the decision to execute them already made they were taken in a public display from the New Barrack (New Lodge area) in Belfast to their place of execution, Blaris military camp.

16 May Daniel McGillain, Owen McKenna, William McKenna and Peter McCarron, privates in Monaghan Militia, who had been tried by a Court Martial in Belfast, were conveyed to Blaris Camp on cars, accompanied by two priests (Rev. John Magee and Rev. Peter Cassidy, C.C. Belfast) and by a strong guard of horse and foot, and shot at two o'clock. They seemed very sensible of the awful change they were about to make; and at the same time behaved with the greatest firmness, choosing rather to die than turn informers. (Northern Star.)

In what was the template for British action to suppress rebellion elsewhere in the world the various regiments in the Belfast area were brought to Blaris military camp to witness the executions. The four men waiting for their execution were ordered to kneel on their coffins while waiting to be shot. Following their execution the bodies were brought the short distance to Blaris cemetery and the assembled regiments were made march past the bodies which were placed on the ground in the churchyard prior to burial. They were buried in an unmarked grave close to the entrance gate and beside a laurel bush. Rev. Magee of St Patrick's, Lisburn and Rev. Cassidy of Belfast said prayers at the graveside. (The Monaghan Militia & the Tragedy of Blaris Moor, Brian MacDonald)

The laurel bush has long gone but to the left of the entrance an unmarked sward about sixteen foot long is still visible and this is probably the final resting place of the soldiers.

1798

11 June

An Orange Lodge was sitting in the front room of a house in Cross Row, Lisburn. Two members of the lodge who had come downstairs to look on the stirring scenes on the street were at the door, and while standing there they recognised the parish priest passing along on the opposite side. Both these Orangemen were well-known to Mr. Magee, and immediately on seeing that gentleman they rushed across the roadway, and, after apologising for stopping him, they added that such was the state of the town, and the excitement of party spirit, it would be very dangerous for him to attempt making his way home, 'Gentleman,' said the venerable clergyman, 'I have been out attending a sick call; one of my people, who lives at Plantation, became suddenly ill, and I have got so far on my return. It is exceedingly kind of you to give me the information about the unsettled state of affairs, but I hope to get on my way without molestation.'

'We cannot permit you to go alone,' replied the younger of the two; 'our lodge is sitting in Jemmy Corkin's, the business of the evening has been settled, and if you come over with us we will arrange for your safe convoy home.' It was then nearly seven o'clock: all was excitement in the Square, dragoons were dashing furiously round the Market House, and heavy artillery guns had been placed across the head of Bridge Street. After a few moments' hesitation, the priest said he would place himself in the hands of his friends, and on entering the lodge-room the Rev. gentleman was courteously received by the master and members. Having partaken of some refreshments, half-a-dozen stalwart men, well armed, rose and proceeded to escort Mr. Magee to his cottage home, which was situate about a mile distant on the Moira Road. It was nearly midnight when the party arrived at the priest's dwelling. A suitable entertainment followed, during which the hospitable host once again gratefully acknowledged the special attention that had been paid him; and, to the latest period of long life, the old clergyman was wont to relate the romantic story of his having been escorted to his home at Lissue by six Orangemen the night before the Battle of Ballynahinch. (This article was originally published in the Lisburn Standard on 29 June 1917.)

22 August During the 1798 rebellion the French army landed at Killala Bay, County Mayo to aid the Irish in their struggle against the British Crown. The aide-de-camp of the French General Humbert was Bartholomew Teeling, son of Luke Teeling, the linen merchant who lived in Chapel Hill, Lisburn (see above-1786).

His eldest son, Bartholomew - familiarly called Bartley - left his home in 1792 and went over to France, and some time after introduced himself to Napoleon, then First Consul, who appointed him lieutenant in his bodyguard.

Teeling landed at Killala with the French troops. The British Army met them at Castlebar, and the French invaders chased them out of town. The two armies met several times but at Colooney, Sligo, Teeling was taken prisoner and brought to Dublin. His get-up was perfect, as his six year's in Paris had acclimatized him, and he spoke the language like a native.

He was brought before Major Sirr, the chief military authority of the city who had been in command from 1793 till the time of Teeling's arrest. Sirr could not really assure himself that his prisoner was Teeling, formerly of Lisburn. He had him brought into his parlour, several soldiers in plain clothes being stationed in the hall to prevent any attempt at escape.

The Major, knowing that in Dublin Linen Hall were often to be seen merchants from Lisburn, sent his servant there to say that a gentleman of that town was eager see a Lisburn merchant. The late William Coulson, founder of the Damask Factory, came to Sirr's house, and at once recognised Teeling, and shaking hands with him, thus unquestionably proved his identity. It would appear that Coulson was tricked into identifying Teeling.

Teeling was immediately tried and found guilty, as several members of the English Army had seen him leading one wing of the French troops at Colooney. He was hanged next day at Arbour Hill, Dublin. (From the "Lisburn Standard' 28 December, 1895.)

His father Luke who had lived at Chapel Hill with his wife Mary Taaffe between 1782 and 1798 was imprisoned in jails in Belfast, Larne, Scotland and on a prison ship despite no formal charged having been made. His linen mill in Lisburn was demolished in 1798 by members of the Orange Order.

During the summer of 1798 Father Magee celebrated Mass at the United Irishmen Blaris Camp where soldiers of the Monaghan militia were stationed.

The solidarity that had been expressed in 1792 when Protestants had accompanied United Irishmen to Mass in Lisburn was not welcomed by all and in the political and religious agitation following the founding of the

Orange Order in 1795 all the Catholic churches (Derriaghy, Glenavy and Aghagallon) on the Hertford property were burned in 1798.

Rev. Philip Johnston, Vicar of Derriaghy, who was initiated into the Orange Order in 1798 and whose anti-Catholic speeches were blamed for inciting Orangemen to burn down Catholic chapels, incurred the wrath of Catholics. He denied the accusations and collected almost £60 from fellow Orangemen towards the repair of the chapels and promised to double that amount for 'the discovery and convictions of any person or persons who have committed these crimes.'

The Catholic priest in Derriaghy, Dennis Magreevy wrote on 7 April 1814

> ......*and also to show, further, the good intention of the Rev. Johnson, to do essential services to the Roman Catholics he commenced and promoted a subscription among the Orangemen and friends of that institution to assist in repairing the Roman Catholic Chapels which had been burned during the Rebellion, of which subscription, Mr. Devlin, then parish Priest of said parish, received twelve guineas, to assist in repairing the Rock Chapel of Derriaghy.* (Christ Church Derriaghy, A Short History of the Parish, W.N.C. Barr, Derriaghy Rectory 20 September 1974.)

Rev. Johnston survived a number of unsuccessful attempts on his life. He was severely wounded on 8 October 1796 when he was ambushed while riding from Lisburn to his home at Ballymacash. (Orangeism - The making of a tradition, Kevin Haddick Flynn Wolfhound Press.) Rev. Johnston would feature later in riots in 1825.

(Philip Johnson resided at the historic Ballymacash House which was originally built in the 1600s by Philip's grandfather, Ralph Smyth. The house may have been burned down or partially destroyed in the 1641 rebellion and Ralph Smyth, as High Sheriff of Antrim in 1680 'built himself a substantial residence at Ballymacash House'. According to the 'Hearth Money' taxes for 1669, apart from Lord Conway's castle, this was the largest house in Lisburn. It was then rebuilt by Philip Johnson in 1791. Ballymacash House remained in the hands of the Johnson family up to the 1940s when it was bought by Mr. Ernest Green, owner of Green's grocery shop in Bow Street, Lisburn. It now belongs to the Drayne family and is the headquarters of Drayne's Dairy.) (Lisburn.com. and Smyth family records.)

19ᵗʰ Century

1801

Rev. John Magee served in Lisburn until 1801 when he went to Ballee. He was a long time in the parish because it was said that he baptised the child and its grandparents. (Rev. Killen letter 27 April 1848)

Rev. Edward Dempsey P.P. lived on a farm near Blaris graveyard and was the last of the parish priests to reside outside Lisburn town. There is still a road named Priest's Lane at Blaris. Born in the parish of Bryansford in 1750 he studied in France after his ordination and on his return he was appointed to the curacy of Lisburn, before serving in Saintfield. He was appointed parish priest of Lisburn in 1801 and served the parish for 31 years. He died on 12 February 1832 aged 82 years. His remains were interred in Lisburn old church and are still under the cover of the present church. (A historical account of the Diocese of Down and Connor - James O'Laverty.)

Some years before his death Rev. Dempsey deposited £2,000 in the Bank of Ireland so that two daily Masses might be offered for his intentions, one of which to be said in Lisburn, for which £30 was paid annually. (Rev. Killen letter 1848)

This would subsequently cause some concern for a future parish priest Rev. Edward Kelly and would lead to prolonged correspondence with Rome.

(The Rev. George Dempsey was born in the parish of Maghera, or Bryansford, County Down and was ordained by Dr McMullan in Downpatrick, on the 11 March, 1811. He retired on a pension at Easter, 1848, and went to reside with his relatives at Blaris where he died on 11 February, 1850. He was interred in the grave of his uncle, Father Edward Dempsey, in Lisburn Church).

1805

There had been a large population of native Irish in Kilwarlin until the war of 1641 and the old chapel at Reilly's Trench, commonly called Kilwarlin

Chapel, was of considerable antiquity. It was burned down by the 'Royalists' between 1742 and 1745. The Catholics, however, continued to assemble at the site of the ruined chapel, and Mass was celebrated under the shade of an old tree until Father Dempsey erected the present chapel in the year 1805. The date was commemorated on a slab in the interior of the church.

Reilly's Trench Church, situated about half a mile from Hillsborough on the Moira Road was dedicated to St Colman. With a floor partly boarded and partly mud it could accommodate a congregation of up to 300 persons (per a Government report 1834). The chapel is described as a 'stone roughcast whitewashed building with a painting of a crucifix over the altar.' ('Hillsborough - A Parish in the Ulster Plantation' by John Barry.)

In a record of Lisburn written in 1803 it reported that, in addition to the Quakers who had an elegant meeting house there was also a large body of Presbyterians and Methodists who each had an elegant meeting house, some Roman Catholics had a good chapel. The town had water piped from Castlerobin and the streets were wide well paved and lighted with globe lamps at proper distances.

1811

The agitation among the Catholic population, which had remained largely silent for years, for the repeal of the Penal Laws resulted in a coalescing of Catholics under the repeal banner. Now identified as a united body they were perceived as a threat to Protestant ascendancy. It should be noted however that at a meeting of the Catholics of Ireland on 9 July 1811 they resolved 'to persevere in petitioning the legislature for a total and unqualified repeal of the penal laws which aggrieve and degrade the Catholics of Ireland'. Among those 'noble lords' thanked for supporting their cause in the 'house of peers' was the Marquess of Downshire. (https://archive.org/details/jstor-30072884.)

12 July The Protestant children who attended a mixed school of Catholics and Protestants in Lisburn were encouraged to join in the parade in the town. This was seen, from a Catholic perspective, as an attempt to perpetuate prejudices to succeeding generations and 'to poison the mind with the worst of passions'.

The school, which was not named, was a school for boys conducted on the Lancastrian plan 'where Catholics and Protestants were indiscriminately educated and where Catholics had not shown the smallest disinclination to send their children'.

This was seen as proof that Catholics had no objection to their children receiving instruction as long as there was no attempt to influence their religious opinion.

'To do good in Ireland, education must be kept quite separate from all attempts to proselyte, Catholics will repeal (sic, rebel?) and bigotry will be raised in opposition to bigotry.'

For several days after the procession, the bitter fruits of party prejudices were excited, and were to be noticed among the children of the town where this ill judged exhibition took place. (Monthly Retrospect of Politics-the Belfast Monthly Magazine, July 1811.)

1812

A school was kept by Mrs. Sweeney at a house in Chapel Hill, Lisburn. Amongst the pupils there was Francis McNamara, who emigrated to Barbados, and rose to wealth and eminence as a sugar planter. (Lisburn Standard, 28 December, 1895.)

1813

The issue of Catholic emancipation occupied parliament in February 1813 with numerous petitions being presented respecting the claims of the Roman Catholics and opposing the claims. Among those opposing were the Protestant inhabitants of Lisburn. (Hansard HC debate 24 February 1813)

Relations between Catholics and Protestants in Lisburn were not improved when it was claimed that an Orange certificate had been found in the wallet of Thomas Walker, a pedlar from the village of Poleglass, when he died suddenly while selling his wares in Drumbo. The certificate, it was claimed, stated that Walker, a member of Poleglass Orange Lodge 170, had refused to take the Extirpatory Oath which, it was alleged, included the words; ....
'and I do further swear that I will use my utmost exertions to exterminate

the Catholic of Ireland'. Historians dispute if this ever existed in the early days of the Order and it was vehemently denied by the Orange Order. This may well have been a propaganda exercise to discredit the Orange Order but would have been accepted as true by many Catholics. ('Orangeism-The Making of a Tradition', Kevin Haddick-Flynn, Wolfhound Press.)

1814

Close to the church at Reilly's Trench were a National School and the teacher's home. The school was built there in 1814 but was not used until 1829. ('Hillsborough - A Parish in the Ulster Plantation' by John Barry.)

1816

Due to an increase in the Catholic population of Lisburn the church on Chapel Hill was enlarged. An aisle and two galleries were added.

1821

Sunday 9 December The Ballymacash Yeomanry, with Captain Mathew Francis Johnston at their head, marched to church to the tune of 'The Protestant Boys.' They were celebrating the departure of Mr Grant (Chief Secretary for Ireland) from Ireland. This corp had been placed on permanent duty on the understanding that it would be impartial and co-operate with all religious persuasions but 'the most exasperating party tune' was played on the way to the 'Temple of Peace'. This action was considered to render the Yeomanry who should be guardians of the community 'odious and disgusting'. The Marquis Wellesley was asked to put a stop to these practices. (Bristol Mercury 29 December 1821.)

In 1821 the Lord Lieutenant of Ireland, based in Dublin Castle, asked the Chief Secretary's Office to write to John Coulson, the Lisburn damask manufacturer, requesting him to report on the parish priest of Lisburn, Rev. Edward Dempsey.

In his undated reply sent from Linen Hall, John Coulson wrote;

Sir,

On my return home this (?) day I had the honour of receiving your letter requesting information respecting the Rev. Edward Dempsey for his Excellencys information.

I beg to acquaint you Mr Dempsey is a loyal respectable member of society he has been parish priest of Lisburn (— —?) of 30 years a number of the workmen employed by me in our Damask manufactory are of his persuasion which gives us an opportunity of knowing more of him and we have at all times found him actively endeavouring to promote sobriety honesty and general good conduct. His chapel has long been in a very wretched state as his parishioners are all of the poorest description he can get no assistance from them there is not one person of wealth or property among his flock.

I have the honour to remain Sirs
Your very obedient
Humble Servant
John Coulson

Linen Hall
Monday Evening
(National Archives Ireland Ref CSO/RP/1821/70.)

DANIEL O' CONNELL
AND CATHOLIC EMANCIPATION

1823

Daniel O'Connell, a Dublin lawyer, established the Catholic Association to press for Catholic Emancipation. All Irish citizens were encouraged to join and to pay 1d per month which was collected after Sunday Mass.

Daniel O'Connell, from a fairly wealthy family, dispossessed of its lands, in Cahirciveen County Kerry became a prominent barrister in Ireland. He had been an advocate for political and religious equality in Ireland at a time when discriminatory legislation was used by the government in Ireland 'to repress the people and to maintain the ascendancy of a privileged and corrupt minority'. He campaigned for Catholic Emancipation, including the rights for Catholics to become

members of the Westminster Parliament and the repeal of the Act of Union which joined Ireland and Great Britain.

Because of his opposition of the use of violence to achieve his objective of Catholic Emancipation it was only natural that the Catholic Church would be supportive. However his later campaign for repeal of the Act of Union and the Church's association with O'Connell would be one of the most significant factors in creating a political and religious divide in Ireland.

The introduction of Catholic Emancipation was seen as an erosion of Protestant ascendency and was bitterly opposed as was the plan to recreate Ireland as a self governing independent kingdom albeit with Queen Victoria as its queen. Many of the landed gentry and the clergy of the established church joined forces in opposition to what was seen as a plot to establish Rome rule in Ireland. The Marquess of Downshire however supported the repeal of the Penal Laws. The Orange Order was also active in opposition and the Rev. Henry Cooke, the Presbyterian leader in Belfast who was as gifted an orator as O'Connell, preached to the Protestant working class in Belfast about the threat of the Roman Catholic Church to their religion and the link with Great Britain.

1824

It was recorded that the Catholic Chapel in Lisburn had a plain external but the interior had a neat pleasing appearance.

The priests listed under Roman Catholic Chapel were Rev. Edward McCarten and Rev. Hugh Dempsey. (City of Dublin and Hibernian Provincial Directory 1824.)

The following notes were written by J. Glassford during the course of several journeys, undertaken 'for the purpose of examining the state of Education in Ireland as conducted in the various schools and seminaries supported, in whole or in part, by grants from the public revenue, and among these, a more especial manner, the elementary and common schools for the people at large, including the operations of those societies which are occupied, in that country, with the important work of popular education.'

'Proceeded to Lisburn; visited the free school connected with Capel Street Association for discountenancing vice; 180 on roll, of whom 99 Church of England, 65 Presbyterians, the other 16 Roman Catholics. The Scriptures read once a week by all the children. A circulating library, furnished by the Kildare Street Society, is kept in the school for the use of the pupils.' (Records of Old Lisburn printed in the Lisburn Standard 27 April 1917.)

In Belfast the Magistrates of Belfast District came to a determination to withdraw the license from any public house where, in future, Orange Lodges are held. In Lisburn 'a few ragamuffins paraded the town, decorated ribbons, that once appeared to be Orange and a profusion of Orange Lilies'. (Freeman's Journal 14 July 1824.)

1825

12 July   There were riots in Lisburn after Lisburn magistrates took steps to prevent a procession which was deemed illegal under the Unlawful Societies (Ireland) Act. (The Act had been introduce to ban O'Connell's Catholic Association but it also had an impact on the Orange Order.) When they ordered the Orangemen to disperse they were challenged by Rev. Philip Johnston, Vicar of Derriaghy, who marshalled the Orange band and led the procession. The town was kept 'in a state of alarm' during the whole of the day. The impact this had on the Catholic population of the town was not recorded. (Hansard 29 March 1827.)

1827

In 1827 Elizabeth Fry, the prison reformer who opposed capital punishment, was invited to advise the authorities in Ireland on matters concerning their penitentiary institutions. During her travels she was accompanied by her brother Joseph John Gurney, a recorded Quaker minister who wrote of their visit to Lisburn;

'The public meeting at Lisburn was remarkably interesting; many Roman Catholics there: and my doctrine, as I supposed very anti-papistical, but the report made by one of their own community was that I preached the same thing as their own priest!' (Quakers in Lisburn, Arthur G. Chapman. p36)

Elizabeth Fry's humanitarian work was recognised when in 2001 her image was depicted on the reverse of Bank of England £5 notes. Shown reading to prisoners at Newgate Prison, the design incorporates a key, representing the key to the prison awarded to Fry in recognition of her work.

29 March Orange processions in Lisburn and the Roman Catholic question were discussed in the House of Lords in relation to correspondence between the Lord Chancellor and others and Rev. Philip Johnston about the twelfth of July parade in 1825. Mr Peel expressed his entire disapprobation of the silly and irritating exhibitions, saying that he had always recommended rather to put a stop to them by discussion and example, than by the employment of harsh measures. (Caledonian Mercury 2 April 1827)

The matter was raised later in the House of Commons when Mr. Brownlowe stated that while Orange processions were banned the Roman Catholic Association 'exercised power and was in full vigour'. (Derby Mercury 4 April 1827.)

Included among the signatures to an anti-Catholic petition of the Protestant noblemen, gentlemen and landed proprietors in County Antrim were; P. Johnston J.P. D.D. Governor of the County of Antrim, Ballymacash, Lisburn, Anthony Traill D.D. Archdeacon of Connor, Lisburn, John Cocker, landed proprietor, Ingram Cottage, S. Cupples, Rector of Lisburn and J Stannus, Vicar of Ballinderry. (Freeman's Journal 7 April 1827.)

1828

26 January About 50 Catholics (a posse of Papists, per the 'Belfast News Letter') held a dance in a house near the Rock Chapel about four miles from Lisburn. A number of Protestant neighbours had been invited. It appeared that there was a number of Ribbonmen present and as the drink took hold the Protestants were quietly advised to leave.

(The Ribbon Society, a secret group of rural Catholics, had been formed to prevent landlords changing or evicting their tenants and supported the political separation of Ireland from Great Britain. This brought them into conflict with the Orange Order. What is significant in this report is the Catholics invited their Protestant neighbours to join them. Which faction actually started the fight may be disputed).

When it was discovered that some were leaving they were pursued and badly beaten. Their companions rushed out to help them and in the darkness there was pandemonium. One of the pursuing Ribbonmen fell and was mistakenly attacked and killed by his comrades who smashed his head with stones. At his inquest a verdict of willful murder was returned against John and Robert Jordan but they had absconded.

In another incident Charles Lavery, a Catholic from Broomhedge stabbed John Collins, a Protestant, in the stomach with a shoemaker's knife after 'a trifling dispute'. Collins survived and Lavery was committed to Carrickfergus for trial. (Belfast News Letter 29 January 1828.)

The Committee of the Lisburn Catholic Sunday School received the sum of £5 from John W. Fulton, London. It was his fourth donation to the institution. (Belfast News Letter 5 September 1828). John Fulton was an Irish Protestant gentleman connected with the India trade in London. He also contributed £200 to a national tribute to Daniel O'Connell. (The Atlas 1828.)

1829

On 27 January a meeting, chaired by Bishop Crolly, was held in the chapel in Donegall Street, Belfast to maintain pressure on the British government to ensure the introduction the Roman Catholic Relief Act. Among those attending were liberal Protestants including the Rev. Henry Montgomery from Dunmurry, near Lisburn. When invited to join the various speakers at the altar he was greeted with enthusiastic cheers as everyone in the church stood to welcome him. Here was a Presbyterian minister standing on a Catholic altar beside a Catholic prelate 'with whom he lived on the most friendly terms' and although he differed so widely in his religious sentiments he was prepared to support 'those glorious principles of civil and religious liberty'. This was evidence on a continuing strand of Presbyterian liberalism reaching out the hand of friendship to their Catholic neighbours but others in Lisburn took a different line. (The Life of Rev. Henry Montgomery - www.forgottenbooks.org)

Maintaining control of the electorate in Lisburn was an important issue.

The petition of the noblemen, gentlemen, clergymen and inhabitants of Lisburn was raised in the Commons on 12 March and in the Lords on 23

March probably by MacNaghten, the county Member, and Lord O'Neill, respectively. John Croker, Hertford's friend and agent, informed Peel that month that, 'Lisburn is in the hands of the Protestants at present', and urged him to alter the £5 franchise in order to prevent lower class Catholics coming to dominate the electorate. (The History of Parliament: the House of Commons 1820-1832, ed. D.R. Fisher, 2009.)

April The Catholic Emancipation Act was passed by Wellington's ministry allowing Catholics (and Presbyterians along with members of other Christian faiths) to sit as MPs at Westminster and be eligible for certain public offices. The downside was that in Irish county elections the 40/- freehold qualification was raised to £10 which reduced the number of peasant voters.

The introduction of the Catholic Emancipation Act was not welcomed by northern Protestants; a Catholic gain was seen as a Protestant loss. When the 12 July parade in Belfast was banned there was widespread rioting there and in other towns.

This violence was not condoned by the landlords in the Lisburn area who were holding out the hand of friendship to the Catholics of Lisburn. Equally, despite the animosity which existed, people of all denominations contributed towards the cost of building a house for the parish priest. It would appear that the disturbances organised by the banned Orange Order did not have universal support in Lisburn. The relationship between Rev Smyth and his counterpart in the Church of Ireland in Lisburn was extremely friendly and courteous and both enjoyed conducting conversations in French. Further evidence of this liberal attitude to the Catholics of Lisburn was demonstrated by the Marquess of Hertford.

1830

A plot of land in Longstone was provided by the Marquess of Hertford as a gift along with a subscription of £20 to help build a parochial house. Rev. Stannus, agent for the marquess, helped the parish priest Rev. Denvir select a site for a house and garden and assured him that he should have as much land 'as may be requisite for his further accommodation'. It was said that 'such acts of disinterested liberality are naturally calculated to promote the peace and happiness of our country and we are convinced that they will long be remembered by the Catholics of Lisburn.'

The house was very small and even with improvements made later it was scarcely capable of accommodating two priests. It was eventually extended by Rev. Mark McCashin by adding to each end of the building, providing accommodation for four priests. The site was on Longstone and the entrance to the house was from Priest's Lane.

The house, two and a half story of stone and lime, slated and measuring 35 and a half feet by 22 feet outside, was built in 1830, with good office houses and an enclosed garden The cost, about £400, which including Lord Hertford's gift was raised by subscription from benevolent persons of all denominations within the parish. Information provided by Rev. Hugh Smyth and others in 1835. (Ordnance Survey of Ireland - Parishes of County Antrim 1832-1838 Vol. 8)

1831

The Marchioness of Downshire provided land to be used as a graveyard at Reilly's Trench church. The oldest headstone is dated 1831.

In the 1831 census the population of Lisburn was 5,745. The Municipal Corporation Boundaries (Ireland) Report on the proposed municipal boundary of the Borough of Lisburn mentioned a conspicuous house which is the permanent residence of the Roman Catholic clergyman (this house situated north of Long Stone Street and east of Magennis Lane.)

1832

12 February Rev. Edward Dempsey died aged 82 and was succeeded by the famous doctor priest Father Hugh Smyth. Born about 1759 he was a student in the Irish College in Paris at the time of the French Revolution. He had to leave the college and began to study medicine. He returned to Ireland in 1794 and served in Kilcoo, Ballymoney where he erected a church. He resigned from Kilcoo following a dispute with some of his parishioners which led to him being assaulted. He then went to Newtownards in 1814 and later went to Lisburn. While in Lisburn Priest's Lane used to be crowded with vehicles of the sick who came from all parts to consult him. Rev. Smyth was also an accomplished violinist and children from the parish would come to hear him play the violin in the parochial house.

1833

Rev. Smyth was appointed as a member of a committee to superintend the building and management of the fever hospital in Lisburn.

(The fever hospital was completed in 1833 at a cost of about £800 and stood south of Bow Street contiguous to the Dublin Road. It stood three stories high and was slated. It could accommodate sixteen patients,'with each bed designed for one patient.' There was a good running spring a few yards from the front door.)

Along with the clergy from other denominations he was also a member of the committee of the Lisburn Charitable Society which had been formed in 1832. The reverend gentlemen were placed at the head of the committee as a matter of courtesy and because they were subscribers to the funds of the society which took care of the poor of the borough. (Ordnance Survey of Ireland - Parishes of County Antrim 1832-1838 Vol. 8)

1834

The following is one of the letters written to the Ordnance Survey Office, which are now preserved in the Library of the Royal Irish Academy: —

" Lisburn, March 21st, 1834.

Dear. Sir, — I called this evening on the Rev. Mr. Smyth, Roman Catholic priest of this district of Lisburn, which comprises eight Protestant parishes around the town of Lisburn. He is a very old man, who was educated in France, and I was struck with the amazing difference between the ease and refinement of his manners and the hauteur of petty county landlords. When I told him what I was about, he said, ' Sir, I shall be happy to lend all the assistance in my power to promote your object; but, in this part of Ireland, it is often difficult to ascertain the correct names of places, I am afraid you are one hundred years too late.' He showed me his little parlour, and then commenced to tell me about the kindness of the Marquis of Downshire towards him in giving him one acre and a half, free of rent, to erect a chapel and burial-place, and some money to assist in its erection. He never asked what religion I was of. He wished I would call to-morrow to see his chapel. His venerable appearance and square velvet cap reminded me of the old patron saints of Irish churches. He is of opinion that the round towers were for some ecclesiastical purpose, ...”

In 1834 it was assumed that snakes would not survive or breed in Ireland. This was probably linked to the story of St Patrick driving the snake out of Ireland.

When in June 1834, following snakes being introduced to Ireland at Milecross near Newtownards and being found to survive and breed, Thomas A. Larcom then head of the Ordnance Survey, directed John O'Donovan to investigate the matter. Among the people he spoke to was Father Smyth of Lisburn. When he told Rev. Smyth that snakes were in abundance in the neighbourhood of Downpatrick the priest said that he was much inclined to doubt the truth of that report but recommended that he consult his nephew Dr Smyth of Downpatrick who was well acquainted with zoology. (Belfast Irish Weekly February 1904.)

'Whatever be the cause, this sect of Christians residing here, (and indeed in the surrounding districts,) have always been remarkable for their peaceable conduct and moral behaviour, being greatly divested of that antipathy to Protestants, and that bigotry and intolerance which distinguish those of Dublin, Cork and other large cities.' (Topographical & Historical Account of Lisburn - Henry Bayly 1834.)

1835

The church was described, as follows, in the Ordnance Survey Memoirs of 1835.

The Roman Catholic chapel of Lisburn is slated, stands one and a half storey, built with stone and lime, corners and base of cut stone. The front or long aisle stands east and west and measures 60 by 27 feet outside and stands 15 feet high, plastered and imitation cut stone on the north side wall. There is an aisle attached to the south side which measures 25 and a half feet by 26 and a half feet outside, height as above, walls 2 feet thick. Doors on chapel 4, windows 7, arch and two square. The floor is part made of clay and part of board. Pews on the ground floor 14, single seats 25, which averages 10 and a half feet in length each, including seat ends, and will hold persons each 7, allowing 1 and a half feet to each sitting, total 175. No seats in the back aisle; in it stands a baptismal font of cut stone 2 feet 10 inches high, and also detached from it a vestry room, slated and stands on one storey. The altar and pulpit are erected in the middle of the front aisle and against the north side wall. They are well finished and stands elevated some feet above the floor and over the altar a large framed picture representing Christ nailed to the cross, and at the foot of it some of the Holy Family represented in an attitude of prayer. Above the picture stands a dove and a small cross. The entire is neatly executed.

Fronting the altar in the ground floor is a tomb on which is inscribed the following memorial:

'Sacred to the memory of the Reverend Edward Dempsey, P.P. of Blaris, who as pastor of that parish for 31 years, and during that period his conduct uniformly evinced the zeal of a sincere Christian, the manners of a gentleman and the benevolence of a worthy member of society. He departed this life on 12 February 1832 aged 82 years.'

There is a gallery on each end of the chapel, stairs or passage to them separately and inside the chapel; west gallery 15 feet by 23 feet, seats on it 6. They are divided into small pews, but averaged 20 feet in length each of the 6, and will hold each seat persons 14, total 84. East gallery 16 and a half feet by 23 feet, seats 6 averaging the above length and description and will accommodate 84 persons. South gallery 21 by 22 and a half feet seats in front 3, divided as above but averaging the same length and will accommodate 42 persons. The choir box stands on this gallery, has three seats, 9 and a half feet long and will accommodate total persons 19. Accommodated with seats on the 3 galleries 229, accommodated on the ground floor 175, total accommodation with seats in the chapel 404.

Above one-half of the congregation are standing on the ground floor and galleries in the absence of seats for their accommodation.

In the north side wall and front of the chapel stand a marble stone on which is cut the following inscription:

'Anno MDCCLXXXVI. This chapel was built by donations from people of every religion in this country. To preserve in grateful remembrance such Christian concord, this stone is erected.'

The chapel stands on a handsome elevation south and at the west end of Bow Street. The yard is 80 feet from east to west and about 160 feet from north to south. The front adjoining Bow Street is enclosed by a stone and lime wall 3 and a half feet high, topped with cut stone over which stands iron rails 3 feet 8 inches in height. This, together with 3 iron gates encloses the above 80 feet, which together with a good quantity of young and grown forest trees in front of the chapel, gives the site a handsome appearance from Bow Street (now Chapel Hill). The remainder of the yard is enclosed by a stone and lime wall varying in height from 3 to 7 feet. No burials in the yard. (Author - The latter statement is at odds with a headstone dated 1831) (These Hallowed Grounds Vol. I.)

The south aisle was built to the Roman Catholic chapel of Lisburn, 1816, at the expense of 300 pounds and the east and south galleries put on with other improvements at the same period and included in the above amount. A lease of the site of the chapel was given in trust in 1795 to Mr Luke Teeling, merchant, Lisburn for 3 lives renewable etc. at 1s sterling money per annum by the late most noble Francis, Marquess of Hertford, for the sole use and benefit of the Roman Catholic congregation of the parish of Lisburn alias Blaris.

The lives inserted were those of the late George III, then King of Great Britain, France and Ireland, and 2 other members of the Royal Family and their survivors. (Ordnance Survey of Ireland - Parishes of County Antrim 1832-1838 Vol. 8)

Average attendance at the Roman Catholic chapel of Lisburn on Sundays about 1,200. There is a collection made in the chapel on Sundays. The proceeds averages for each Sunday the sum of 8 shillings. One-half of this collection goes to defray casual repairs on the chapel from time to time and the other half distributed among an average of 25 persons of both sexes and of all denominations who indigence obliges them to apply for aid. (Ordnance Survey of Ireland - Parishes of County Antrim 1832-1838 Vol. 8)

4 May A large number of Orangemen came into Lisburn that evening to escort individuals who had been discharged from Carrickfergus gaol after being imprisoned for rioting in Lisburn on the night of 17 January last. With drums and fifes they paraded through Bow Street to Chapel Hill and played 'The Protestant Boys' and 'Croppies lie down'. Outside the church they shouted 'To hell with the Pope.' A police constable, James Donaldson, provided sworn evidence, dated 19 May 1835, that the assemblage provoked animosity between His Majesty's subjects of different religious persuasions and tended to disturb the peace of the town of Lisburn.

(A number of Orangemen had been summonsed the previous July for marching in a large Orange procession on 12 July which had been banned by the government.)

(house of lords the sessional papers orange lodges, associations, ... - books.google.co.uk/books)

1836

Rev. Hugh Smyth and curate James Killan were in Lisburn at this time and were among the original subscribers to the newly established Lisburn News-Room. (Lisburn Standard 28 December 1895)

Mr. Daniel Lavery was the teacher at Reilly's Trench National School.

1837

24 March Rev. Smyth, parish priest of the parish of Blaris and Hillsborough received an average annual income from his charge of £52 of which the Rev. Richard Killan, his curate, gets one-third as his proportion, together with a collection made yearly in Lisburn chapel and another chapel belonging to his charge, the proceeds of which collection amounts to about £9 annually, making in whole for the curate £26 6s 8d and free lodgings in the chapel house. This arrangement leaves the parish priest a net income of £34 13s 4d per year and a good house and garden for the time being.
(Ordnance Survey of Ireland - Parishes of County Antrim 1832-1838 Vol. 8)

Commenting on the character of the people of the Parish of Blaris (Lisburn), the Ordnance Survey Memoirs 1832-1838 recorded;

> Though there are eight different religious sects in the parish and that each regards their own as the best, yet as far as temporal affairs are concerned all live in good neighbourhood with each other and all, equal to their means, equally contribute to charitable purposes unlimited, save Quakers and Methodists. The latter limit their gifts chiefly to the poor of their own creed.

Rev. Smyth was the superintendent of the Sunday school held in the chapel.

There were ten male and ten female teachers catering for 280 male pupils and 220 female pupils, 180 of whom were exclusively Sunday school scholars. (It would appear that in addition to religious education an element of general education was included.) The Sunday school operated from 3:00 p.m. to 6:00 p.m. during the months from May to November. The Catholics of Lisburn did not attend the Sunday school in the chapel exclusively. A number attended Sunday schools operated by other denominations in Lisburn and the rural areas. (Ordnance Survey of Ireland - Parishes of County Antrim 1832-1838 Vol. 8.)

1839

Relationships between the Catholic Church and Christ Church Cathedral in Lisburn were extremely good at this time. A minute held by Christ Church Cathedral records that a Court of Vestry was held in the Parish Church of Lisburn in and for the Parish Church of Lisburn alias Blaris on 13 May 1839. Among those present were James Stannus, rector of Lisburn and Hugh Smyth, parish priest. (Article in Ulster Star 22 July 1972.)

18 November Rev. Hugh Smyth died on 18 November 1839 (not 1840 as recorded on his headstone according to Rev. Mark McCashin) aged 84 years.

28 November Rev. John McCourt, ordained in Belfast by Dr. Crolly on 30 July 1833, was appointed curate in Lisburn.

Rev. William Reeves, born in Charleville, County Cork in 1815 was ordained curate for Lisburn in 1839. He was later appointed to the perpetual Curacy of Kirkinriola (Ballymena) in 1841. (Journal of the Armagh Diocesan Historical Society.)

ST CLAIR MULHOLLAND

1 April St Clair Augustine Mulholland (later General Mulholland) was born in Lisburn.
The old graveyard in Kilrush carries in its headstones a wealth of

information on the Mulhollands. In one corner of the graveyard there is an old damaged grave which had once been a very prestigious family memorial.

Here lieth the remains of
Hugh Mulholland of Lisburn merchant
who departed this life 30th May 1833
aged 73 years
His wife Elizabeth who departed 1818 aged 45
their daughter who died March 1816,
Also Ann wife of Henry Mulholland Bridge Street
who died 22nd June 1835 aged 34 years
and their daughter Eliza 27 years
also their grandaughters
Margaretta Mulholland died 17th May 1899
Jane Eliza Mulholland died 31st August 1901
and their grandsons
Hugh Mulholland died 7th February 1874
Joseph Richardson Turtle Mulholland
Died 16th Oct. 1916 also
Also John Rogers Millar died May 1891
Anna Mulholland born 5th Jan 1828 died 13th April 1925

St Claire's grandparents were Hugh Mulholland, born c1760 and his wife Elizabeth Richardson most certainly Protestant, born c1773. Hugh died May 1833 and Elizabeth 1 October 1818. Hugh and Elizabeth had 10 children and one of them Henry Mulholland was born on 19 November 1796.

This was St Claire's father. It would appear Henry was a Catholic and his wife Anne Turtle Protestant and their children raised as Catholics. Henry was to marry twice, first to Ann Turtle born about 1800. With Ann Turtle, Henry had 14 children between 1818 and 1835, nearly a child per year. Some, if not all, of their children were baptised as Catholic by leading Catholic clerics in the area at that time, two named as Rev. Denvir and Rev. Dorrian. Ann Turtle Mulholland died aged just 34 on 22 June 1835.

Henry Mulholland, St Claire's father, had a sister, Anne Jane Mulholland, who married a Protestant John Millar a local J.P. and they had both a Catholic marriage service conducted by the Rev P. Denvir P.P. and then in the Protestant church by the Rev. T. Thompson.

When James Cosslett died in 1836 his wife Georgina was left with two children, Charles and Georgina, to raise at Nutgrove. (Nutgrove was recorded in The Down Recorder issue dated 4 February 1837 as being a demesne and flour mill available for letting.) When Mr McCammon took over Nutgrove, ending the era of Cosslett ownership, Georgina looked for a new spouse of a similar social standing. This man was Hugh Mulholland, a very successful businessman who lived at the Quay, Lisburn. He was a sawyer, coal merchant. lighter owner and a member of a very successful extended family.

Georgina was married for a second time at Hollywood, County Down by Father Anthony Cosslett, no doubt a member of the Cosslett family, on 6 June 1838 to Henry Mulholland. They would go on to have another family all raised as Catholics. One of whom St Claire (Sinclair) would become General Sinclair Mulholland.

The family emigrated from Belfast to New York on the ship 'Victory' in 1850. (www.69thpa.co.uk/pages33.html.)

Emigrating to Philadelphia with his parents while a boy, he became interested in the military and was active in the ranks of the militia. At the outbreak of the Civil War he was commissioned Lieutenant-Colonel of the 116th Pennsylvania Volunteers which was attached to Meagher's Irish Brigade, and later was made its colonel.

He was wounded during the famous charge of the Irish Brigade up Marye's Heights, at the battle of Fredericksburg, 13 December 1862. At the battle of Chancellorsville, 3, 4 May 1863, he led his regiment and distinguished himself by saving the guns of the Fifth Maine Battery that had been abandoned to the enemy. For this he was complimented in general orders and received the Medal of Honor from Congress. In this campaign he was given the command of the picket-line by General Hancock and covered the retreat of the Army of the Potomac across the Rappahannock. On the second day of the battle at Gettysburg St Claire witnessed a general absolution, delivered by Fr William Corby to the men of the Irish Brigade about to go into battle. He later wrote, 'that every man, Catholic and non-Catholic, fell on his knees with his head bowed down.' The scene he said, 'was more than impressive. It was awe inspiring. Most of them were in their grave clothes.'

At Gettysburg, when his regiment was decimated in the first day's action, he changed to the 140th Penn. Volunteers and led it into action. He was wounded a second time at the battle of the Wilderness, 5 May 1864, and for this gallant conduct was brevetted brigadier-general. At Po River he was wounded a third time but remained in hospital only ten days, and resuming his command was dangerously wounded again at Tolpotomoy. He recovered rapidly and commanded his brigade in all the actions around Petersburg, particularly distinguishing himself by storming a fort for which he was brevetted major-general 27 October 1864.

After the war he was appointed Chief of Police in Philadelphia in 1868, and was commended for the good order in which he kept both the force and the city. President Cleveland appointed him United States Pension Agent and he continued in this role under Presidents McKinley and Roosevelt. He devoted much of his leisure time to art studies and as a lecturer and writer on the Civil War. He compiled a history of the 116th Regiment of Pennsylvania Volunteers and another of those to whom Congress voted the Medal of Honor. He was active in the Catholic affairs of Philadelphia and a leader among the best known and most respected laymen. He died at Philadelphia, 17 Feb 1910. (Conyhgham, The Irish Brigade and its Campaigns (Boston, 1869); America (New York, 26 Feb., 1910), files; Cath. Standard and Times (Philadelphia, 26 Feb., 1910.)

Sunday 1 December The Catholic parishioners of Lisburn, after divine service, made a collection in the chapel when nearly 20/- was received and presented to the Rev. John McCourt at present officiating in that parish, in testimony of their esteem, for his public and private virtues. (Freeman's Journal 29 December 1839.)

1840

Father Smyth was succeeded by Rev. Bernard Dorrian from Ardkeen, County Down.

Monday 10 August

The Right Rev. Dr Denvir, Bishop of Down and Connor, administered the sacrament of confirmation to upwards of five hundred male and female children in the Catholic Church of Lisburn. Before administering the sacrament, he examined the children on the grounds of the Catholic doctrine;

and, in his usual lucid and eloquent manner, explained and proved from the Holy Scriptures, the origin and nature of the sacraments of the Catholic Church. The discourse of his lordship appeared to make a great impression on those who were present at the interesting proceedings. (The Tablet 22 August 1840)

Rev. John McCourt is listed as Parish Priest. (New Commercial Directory 1840.)
He was in Ahoghill/Portglenone parish 1847-1886 and presided over the building of the church in Cullybackey.
(en.wikipedia.org/wiki/Mass_rock_(Portglenone)).

His sister, Susanna, wife of Henry McCauley, Jr. died in 1865 at her residence at Carlisle St., Philadelphia. She was formerly of Carnlough, County Antrim and sister of Rev. John McCourt, P.P. of Ahoghill. (genforum.genealogy.com.)

December James Duffy (45), a Catholic from Lisburn, was imprisoned in the house of correction in the North Riding at Northallerton in England.
Married with three children he had been a cotton weaver and had kept a beer shop in Sheffield. He had been convicted of conspiracy, sedition and riot and sentenced to three years in prison. The prison inspector reported;

'I have reason to think that from a Club called the Hibernian Society composed of Irishmen, meeting at his Public House in Sheffield, he was thought of importance to be brought over to their views, and was placed in the chair at their meetings on some few occasions. He describes himself as an O'Connellite and Repealer but no Chartist. He is a most besotted Roman Catholic and has been attended frequently by his Priest.' (National Archives on Chartism.)

1841

The last major change to Lisburn church was made in 1841 by Father Brendan Dorrian, brother of Bishop Dr Dorrian, when it was re-roofed, new galleries added and a tower constructed. This information had been added to the marble stone of 1786.
Erected, as Rev. Mark McCashin later wrote, at a time when Catholics were only commencing to raise their heads, it would be a further fifty-five years before the growing Catholic population and relative prosperity in Lisburn meant that it was no longer suitable to meet the needs of Lisburn's

Catholics. It is unclear where Mass was celebrated while this major reconstruction work was underway.

January Daniel O'Connell, the Irish political leader who campaigned for Catholic Emancipation, the right for Catholics to sit in the Westminster Parliament and for the repeal of the Act of Union, accepted an invitation to speak at the Loyal National Repeal Association in Belfast.

Among those who attended this meeting were Rev. Bernard Dorrian P.P. Lisburn, Rev Edward Kelly P.P., Garvagh, Rev. Joseph Canning C.C., Lisburn, Rev. McChrystal, Lisburn. (Morning Post 28 January 1841)

His visit was vociferously opposed by Rev. Henry Cooke who had declared that the repeal was 'just a discreet word for Romish ascendancy and Protestant extermination'. The prospect of O'Connell's presence in Belfast alarmed the government and over two thousand troops were deployed to Belfast to deal with the expected rioting.

Having been advised about the level of animosity towards his presence in Belfast and the prospect of assassination to prevent his appearance he arrived a day earlier than expected.

When he was due to pass through Lisburn on his way to Belfast thousands of loyalists, referred to in the press as the 'True Blues' took to the streets to protest and to prevent any Catholic show of support for him. However he had already managed to slip through incognito stopping off at the 'Derriaghy Inn' (later renamed as 'The Travellers' Rest' and now 'The Village Inn') outside Lisburn for some liquid refreshments. The glasses he and his party used were treasured for many years afterward. (Christ Church Derriaghy - W.N.C. Barr.)

Disappointed to have missed O'Connell the loyalists of Lisburn burned his effigy. (A History of Ulster - Jonathan Bardon). In Belfast all the windows of the Royal Hotel in which he was staying were smashed and only a body of Dragoons prevented a mob from entering the building. Likewise when he was taken under escort to a banquet 'Orangemen broke the windows of the banqueting rooms'. An effigy of O'Connell was tied to the back of a cart and dragged through the streets. It was then hung from a tree by the wayside and upwards of five-hundred bullets were fired through it.

As it was impossible for O'Connell to retrace his journey he was taken under police escort to Donaghadee where he boarded a boat which took him to Portpatrick in Scotland en route to London. (Kirby Papers, Irish College Rome 1854.)

21 January Two days after O'Connell's visit to Belfast two 'Grand Conservative Demonstrations' were held in Belfast bringing together the nobility, clergy and other friends of the British Constitution. It included Lords Downshire, Hertford and the Earl of Hillsborough. The Marquess of Downshire called on Roman Catholic clergymen to 'exclude from the house of God all political feelings'. (The Repealer Repulsed - Google books.)

24 May The Radical Reformers of the united parishes of Blaris and Lisburn held a meeting on the grounds of the Catholic Chapel 'for the purpose of adopting an address to the Queen, praying to her majesty to appeal to the nation by a dissolution of parliament before accepting the resignation of ministers'. Rev. J. McChrystal was present. This and other similar meetings around the country appealed to the Queen to preserve her faithful Irish people from a Tory faction, 'under the domination of Orangemen'.

The consumption of alcohol particularly by the poor and the working class, often to escape the realities of life, was a major problem in Ireland. It became known as 'the curse of the Irish' and led to the stereotypical image of associating the Irish with drunkenness. A number of attempts to reduce or prohibit alcohol consumption had met with little success over the years. In 1829 the Gaelic speaking Presbyterian minister John Edgar, born near Ballynahinch, founded the Ulster Temperance Movement but it was a Capuchin priest Fr. Theobald Mathew from near Cashel who was to meet with the greatest success. In 1838 he formed a Total Abstinence Society and having encouraged 130,000 in Cork to 'take the pledge' he decided to take his crusade through Ireland travelling to almost every parish. He later took his campaign to Scotland, England and America where he met with equal success.

July Fr. Theobald Mathew visited Lisburn and would have preached at the church in Lisburn. He wrote of his visit;

'In coming originally to the North, I had great difficulties to contend with. I was told I would be assassinated in Ulster; but I had confidence in my cause, as I came in the name of the Lord, proclaiming aloud, 'Glory to God in the highest, and peace on earth, to men goodwill.' I knew the people of Ulster were too virtuous to refuse me their aid in this total abstinence movement,

on any sectarian grounds. I had also too much reliance on the honour of Irishmen to suppose the people of this province would arise in their might, and crush one humble individual, who was merely trying to promote public morality. In the words of the poet, slightly altered, I may say, in conclusion blessed for ever the day I relied on Ulster's honour and Ulster's pride.

We had no military, no police, no constables; but, in lieu of them, we had several excellent young gentlemen from Belfast, Lisburn, and other places who kept order.

I could have apprehended nothing save goodwill and kindly feeling from one end of Ulster to the other, and this was amply demonstrated by my visits to Lurgan, Lisburn, Belfast, Downpatrick, Derry, and other places; and the 'Prentice Boys' of Derry showed me the greatest kindness, but it was not to me alone, but to the glorious cause. Thousands of them came out to Moira from Belfast and other places, and actually detained me three days longer than I intended to have stopped; and was not this truly delightful?' (Father Mathew: A biography by John Francis Maguire.)

A female total abstinence society was formed in Belfast. Fifty females, many employed in Durham Street Mill, took the pledge. Within the last three weeks, upwards of 600 new members have joined the Belfast, Lisburn, and Bangor societies. (Northern Whig September 1841.)

1842

Wednesday 17 August Friends and admirers of Rev. James McChrystal entertained him at a public supper in the Harp Tavern, Lisburn, before he left for a curacy in Belfast. Among those present were the Rev. B. Dorrian P.P., Lisburn, Rev. Joseph Canning, Glenavy, Rev. McMullan C.C., Lisburn, Messers H. Mulholland Sen. and Jnr., T. McKeon, John Gillan, McKaveny, Magee, McLoughlin, Hillan, Hagan, &c. When the cloth was removed the Rev. Dorrian, the respected parish priest, was called to the chair, upon which a splendid gold watch was presented to the Rev. Mr. McChrystal, as a testimonial of esteem from his friends in Lisburn. (Freeman's Journal 29 August 1842.)

1843

29 October The solemn ceremony of consecrating the new and much improved Catholic church of Lisburn, took place. The Right Rev. Dr Denvir was the celebrant, assisted by a number of the neighbouring clergy. Rev. McMullan offered up the holy sacrifice of the Mass, after which the Right Rev. prelate preached from Esdras. The collection amounted to £101.15s and, as many have subscribed since, the sum must have been greatly increased. (The Tablet archives, 11 November 1843.)

The Rev. William MacMullan succeeded Father Denvir. He was a native of Clanvaraghan, in the parish of Kilmegan, and a nephew of the late Father MacMullan, P.P., Loughinisland. After completing his preliminary education at the Diocesan Seminary, Belfast, he entered on 27 August 1835, the Logic Class in the College of Maynooth, when, on the completion of his course, he obtained a place on the Dunboyne Establishment and was ordained by Dr Murray, at Pentecost, in 1842.

After about two years as curate in Lisburn he was appointed on the 4 April 1845, P.P. of Hannahstown, from which he was appointed to Dunsford and Ardglass on the 12 February 1848. He died on 16 March 1876, and was interred in Loughinisland, in the tomb which was erected over the remains of the Most Rev. P. MacMullan, Bishop of Down and Connor. (A historical account of the Diocese of Down and Connor, ancient and modern.)

Rev. Dorrian celebrated Mass every Sunday at a house, which he rented for that purpose, in the townland of Magheraliskmisk (Magheragall). As the congregation grew he arranged to erect a little church in that townland to meet the spiritual requirements of the Catholics who were scattered over the extensive civil parishes of Magheramesk and Magheragall. His death in 1847 prevented this plans being implemented and the church, though much required, was not built.

29 July Rev. James Mulholland, A.B., born in Lisburn in 1808 died. He was in the eighth year of his priesthood. (Rev J. O'Laverty - Historical Account of the Diocese of Down and Connor, Ancient and Modern Vol. 1 1878 and Vol. 2 1880.)

1844

Daniel O'Connell's Loyal National Repeal Association warned the Westminster parliament not to take Irish support for granted 'now that war abroad was all but declared,' and said that in England's difficulties lay Ireland's hope.

'The Minister has said that if war comes he looks for help to Ireland. England shall have help, and the Irish, in any danger, will stand as a wall of fire around their Queen. But, has not the Minister, after his insults and excitements and injustices to Ireland, a right to fear her answer? Has he not a right to fear that Ireland may fold her hands and say, Let those who reap the profits of the victory bear the danger of the battle?'

4 September At a meeting contributions to the Association were acknowledged including 1/5s from Lisburn, 'the most Protestant town in Ireland'. (The Tablet archives 7 September 1844.)

THE FAMINE YEARS

Lisburn did not escape the impact of the famine in Ireland which began in 1845. In 1846 the potato crop in the Lisburn Union, which comprised of the town and twenty-six surrounding townlands, failed completely. The Lisburn workhouse, built in 1841, was filled to overflowing following the winter of 1846-47, the distress being made worse by a depression in the linen industry which affected both urban and rural weavers. Relief beyond the workhouse was provided, usually as soup or stirabout to about 1,200 individuals totally dependent on this daily sustenance. By the harvest of 1848 the worst was over for the people of the Lisburn Union but not so for other parts of Ireland.

By 1849 the British government had already spent almost £10 million in helping to relieve distress in this part of the United Kingdom and decided to provide no more financial assistance from the Treasury. It planned to introduce a Rate-in-Aid Act requiring ratepayers in Ireland to meet the cost of relieving the distress in Ireland. This decision placed a question mark over the Act of Union, for if this was a real union then all parts of the United Kingdom which funded the Imperial Treasury should share equal responsibility for helping a part in particular need. The introduction of Rate-in-Aid was vehemently opposed in northeast Ulster as it was seen, not only as an additional tax but as a weakening of the link with Britain. It again brought religion into politics as it was claimed that the industrious, peaceable, hard working (Protestant) portion of Ireland was being required to pay towards the support of the idle and turbulent (Catholic) paupers in the west of Ireland. It was portrayed as the innocent being made pay for the guilty or as Christine Kinealy in her book 'This Great Calamity' states, making poverty support poverty. A plea by the Catholic Church in Ireland for the government to continue to provide support in the most distressed areas was dismissed. The Rate-in-Aid Act was passed in 1849.

1845

A meeting was held in the Market House in May to protest against the increase in the grant to the College of Maynooth and to petition parliament that the bill be rejected on the third reading. After 'sundry imprecations on the Pope, Maynooth and O'Connell' those present joined a 'mob of ragged boys who had been parading the town all day with drums and fifes playing all sorts of party tunes.' It was reported that the 'Catholics merely laughed at their extravaganzas.' (Freeman's Journal 21 May 1845.)

The Belfast Newsletter reported on a great anti-Maynooth demonstration in Lisburn.

Before July 1845 a temporary act prohibiting processions had expired. The Grand Lodge of Ulster resolved not to have a procession at the twelfth of July. The Orangemen of Lisburn adopted a different course as did those in Armagh where there was severe violence when lodges insisted in walking through a Catholic part of the town.

12 July Mr Watson headed the Orange procession in Lisburn and for that action was dismissed from the Commission of the Peace. The procession passed off peaceably with not an act, word, or look of offence between either party. (Freeman's Journal 14 July 1845.)

20 August At Lisburn great preparations were made for an Orange meeting on Wednesday 20 August to consider Mr Watson's dismissal. A dinner to Mr Watson was announced. Hatred to the Government breathed in every word of the announcement. A platform was erected in an enclosed space capable of holding 10,090 persons and the Marquis of Downshire was expected to preside. The agitation and excitement of the Orangemen were at the height. (The Tablet 23 August 1845)

21 August Such was the support for Mr Watson that Orange lodges from Belfast and surrounding districts poured into Lisburn. As the Dublin day mail coach was making its way between Hillsborough and Lisburn it became caught up in a procession. The music caused the horses leading the coach to become unmanageable and they broke free from the coach. The coach was then surrounded by the crowd, many of whom were intoxicated, shouting 'To hell with the Pope' and 'First time we have stopped her Majesty's mail'. The mail later proceeded into Lisburn where it got a new team of horses and later overtook a peaceable procession returning to Belfast. (Freeman's Journal 22 August 1845.)

On Saturday in the Assembly Rooms, gaily decked with Orange banners and flowers, Mr Watson, ex-D.L. and ex-J.P., was entertained by his brother Orangemen. Mr Watson, rejoiced in the honour of his dismissal by a pro Popery Ministry. The Marquis of Downshire and Col. Verner (" Verner and no surrender"), the Marquis of Hertford—(hissing)—the Town and Trade of Lisburn were toasted. Mr Stewart was interrupted in returning thanks for Lisburn by loud dissent from his statement that he had nothing to fear from his Catholic neighbours. (The Tablet 30 August 1845.)

4 October The Marquess of Hertford arrived in Lisburn and was accompanied on his tour by Captain Meynall MP for the borough. An address to be presented to Lord Hertford stated

> ' I have learnt that the noble marquis has sanctioned the grant of a piece of land, in the rear of the Roman Catholic chapel to build a Romish seminary upon! This is an undoubted fact, as already a contractor is advertised for to proceed with the building and this is Protestant Lisburn! I understand Dean Stannus had actually given Priest Dornan the grant before the marquess' arrival. This speaks volumes.'

The proceedings at the meeting at which the address was considered were most stormy. The address was protested against by every gentleman in town and the protests sent instantly to his lordship. (Freeman's Journal 8 October 1845.)

There was of course no plan to build a seminary but ground was to be provided for a cemetery. This statement was simply to raise tensions.

23 October The tensions appear to have been set aside when the marquess entertained his tenants to a sumptuous open-air banquet in Castle Gardens.

While people elsewhere in Ireland were dying of starvation in the famine, the bill of fare included ninety-seven joints of boiled beef, seventy turkeys, seventy-two geese and one hundred and ninety-two meat pies to be washed down with 3,200 pints of strong ale and thirty barrels of beer. The brass band of the Cameronians provided the music. Among the estimated four thousand who attended was Rev. B. Dorrian P.P. (The Ipwich Journal 25 October 1845.)

5 October The Rev. B. Dorrian delivered a most impressive discourse in Hannahstown Chapel on the doctrine of Penance. The house was densely crowded with persons of various denominations, who seemed much edified by the calm persuasive eloquence of the gifted preacher. Immediately after the sermon a collection was made, amounting to 70 shillings, a sum which could scarcely have been expected in a small country chapel. (Belfast Vindicator - The Tablet - The International Catholic News Weekly)

1846

Sunday 6 September A solemn High Mass was celebrated in Lisburn Catholic Chapel. At the conclusion of this service, a sermon was preached by the Rev. Peter Denvir, of Dunsford, and a collection taken up to assist in paying off a balance due to the parochial committee, for recent improvements and for the erection of schools. The collection amounted to £192. (Northern Whig - The Tablet 12 December 1846)

On last Sunday and Monday, Lisburn witnessed a solemn celebration of those devine and beautiful ceremonies which distinguish and adorn the worship of the Catholic Church. On Sunday there were a High Mass and sermon; and on Monday a plot of ground, set as part for a cemetery, was solemnly consecrated. On both occasions, especially on the former, large numbers from the adjoining districts, and from Portadown and Belfast were present. Not a few too of the Liberal Protestant Dissenters of the locality were in attendance. When High Mass sung in a very imposing style by Dr Laphen, Dublin, assisted by the Rev. Messers McGarry and Maguire, as deacon and sub-deacon - the Rev. Dorrian acting as master of ceremonies and the Right Rev. Dr Denvir attending as Pontifex assistens had proceeded as far as the end of the Gospel the Rev. Peter Denvir of Dunsford preached from the words of St Paul to the Hebrews - 'Jesus Christ, yesterday and today and the same for ever' - a truly impressive discourse. Its effect may be estimated from the very large collection nearly £? taken up on the occasion. The collection is to be applied to the liquidation of the debt incurred by the parochial committee in erecting a school-house and making improvements on the chapel. (Freeman's Journal 28 November 1846.)

1847

Rev. Bernard Dorrian had planned to build a church at Magheragall but as a result of caring for victims of the famine in 1847 in the crowded wards of the Lisburn County Infirmary he caught a fever and died. His remains lie in the ancient cemetery of Down cathedral. (Gravestone inscription - I H S, In charity pray for the soul of the Rev Bernard Dorrian, P.P., of Lisburn, who died of fever on the 27th of March 1847 aged 38 years Requiescat in pace)

No further action on church building was taken until 1889.

From the death of Rev. Dorrian until the appointment, on 12 April 1847, of his successor the parish was administered by Rev. Richard Killen.

15 May Daniel O'Connell died in Genoa, aged seventy-one, while on a pilgrimage to Rome. It was said that he bequeathed his soul to God, his body to Ireland and his heart to Rome. It was claimed that is heart was placed in a silver case and contained in a Carrara marble monument in the Irish College in Rome.

The Irish College founded in 1628 to educate students for the priesthood in Ireland was located at the Church of St Agatha dei Goti before moving to its present site on the Via S.S. Quattro. The O'Connell monument was brought to the new site but there was no trace of the silver case or his heart.

His friend Charles Bianconi, the founder of public transportation in Ireland and twice mayor of Clonmel, commissioned the Italian sculptor Benzoni to carve the monument which shows O'Connell refusing to accept the Oath of Allegiance in the House of Commons. (Rev George Hayes, Irish College, Rome.)

23 September Rev. Killen wrote to Mr John Hanna, Ballykinlar, Clough commenting that he had been in Belfast and the bishop had kept close to the house since his return from Dublin. There was nothing new to report from Lisburn other than the potatoes were yielding to the disease and the markets were rising.

He also recorded the inscriptions relative to Lisburn chapel which included;

> *'This stone is sacred to the memory of the Rev'd Hugh Smyth P.P. of Blaris who departed this life 18 Nov 1840 aged 84 years. Of this long life above 30 yrs were spent in the zealous discharge of his sacerdotal duties distinguished by a kind and benevolent disposition which procured for him the sincere respect and esteem of all good men. Requiescat in pace'.*

> *'Underneath are the remains of the Rev'd Jas Mulholland A.B. born in Lisburn on 24 August 1808 and departed this life 29 July 1843 in the 8th of his priesthood. Precious in the sight of the Lord is the death of his saints. Requiescat in pace.'* (Diocesan records)

He also mentioned a chalice made in 1758 for Rev. Theophilis MacCartan, Doctor V. I. Pater of Lochinisland. (Rev. MacCartan was appointed bishop of Down & Connor 10 September 1760 and died 16 December 1778.)

1848

30 January Rev. John McKenna was appointed to Lisburn parish. He was described as a tall thin man of delicate constitution and a very fine preacher. (He died on 29 August 1857 and is buried in the ancient graveyard of Ballykinlar, his native parish, but there is no headstone over his grave.)

27 April Rev. Killen, in a letter from Coleraine about 'the ecclesiastical antiquities of the parish of Lisburn' wrote,

> *'It is known only to few that Bishop Stuart ever lived within a few perches of the present chapel of Hillsborough. I think no priest has lived in the same house since his time.'* (Francis Stuart OFM, bishop from 1740 - died May 1749.)

1849

30 April At the parochial house the parishioners of Lisburn and Hillsborough presented Rev. John McKenna with a horse, jaunting car, harness and a silver mounted whip.

In an address read by William John Magee, on behalf of Daniel

McLernan (Chairman) he said that the gift was presented as a sincere indication of the esteem in which he was held. In his response Rev. Magee said that he accepted the gifts with pride and pleasure especially at a time of national misery - a reference to the Irish famine - and when in addition to paying for the upkeep of the parish £22 had been contributed to the Pope's fund. In a further reference to the famine he said that 'Ireland's prosperity was rocking on artificial barrenness, stripped at the trunk of its native covering, while the slender fibres that were once uptorn and set in a distant soil convey but scanty nutriment. He then quoted 'a lovely air';

"No more let Erin's sons contend,
Nor envy one another,
Afraid of freedom making friend
 Of brother unto brother.

Rights equal-no ascendancy-
To triumph no pretender;
Happy homes and conscience free!
Of honour no surrender!"

Commenting on the late Rev. B. Dorrian he said that while he was his senior in the diocese he was certainly beneath him in merit. (Freeman's Journal 5 May 1849.)

12 July At the Lisburn demonstration at the Brookhill residence of James Watson Rev. Hartley Hodson speaking on the principles of Orangeism said that they maintain no bad feeling with their Roman Catholic brethren, they breathe no spirit of intolerance; but thus they desire that they may be as they are - that they may be led by the good hand of God to throw off the shackles of Rome and walk in the light and liberty wherein Christ makes his people free. (Belfast Newsletter 13 July 1849)

1851

Rev. McKenna is listed as parish priest. (The Tablet archives 1851)

1853

July Rev. John McKenna organised a parish Mission to be conducted by missionaries invited by Bishop Denvir. Admission to High Mass ranged from one shilling to one shilling and sixpence. Similar in many ways to Protestant revival meetings the Mission had an ecumenical favour, with Protestants from the 'more respectable classes' attending to listen to the sermon.

Other Protestants took exception to the Mission and the result was rioting in the town. The 'Northern Whig' blamed Rev. McKenna for the riots on the ground that the Mission had been organised to coincide with the Boyne celebrations. (Down History & Society – Oliver Rafferty S.J.)

The previous year there had been anti-Catholic and anti-Irish riots in Stockport, England stirred up by an anti-Catholic cleric, Rev. Hugh Stowell, who preached a fervent brand of fundamentalist Protestantism denouncing popery. On 15 June 1852 Lord Derby's Tory government as a pre-election vote winner issued a proclamation forbidding Catholics to walk in procession through the streets with the symbols of their religion. On 27 June the Catholics of Stockport held their traditional procession without displaying banners or Catholic emblems. The procession passed off peacefully but the next day an effigy of a priest was paraded by the local Protestant Association and this led to riots which resulted in death and serious injury. Two Catholic churches were desecrated and completely destroyed.

Similar anti-Catholic sentiments were expressed in Lisburn in 1853.

'The Ulsterman' newspaper reported the attacks on the missionaries;

Throughout the whole of this past week considerable apprehension was entertained in Belfast and Lisburn in consequence of an ill-conditioned and fanatical rabble in the latter town who made a most offensive demonstration against the reverend missionaries at present in Lisburn. On the evening of Friday 1 July a crowd of Orangemen of the lowest class assembled in the town and amused themselves by shouting and screaming and politely damning 'to hell' the Pope and the reverend fathers. In consequence of a fear entertained that serious injury might be done to the chapel that night the sexton waited up on watch. Nothing however was done that night and next day passed off quietly too but when evening came, symptoms of disturbance were manifested by a large number of these misguided fools. About three o'clock a dozen blackgard-looking fellows had gathered near the chapel railings, the iron gate being locked. One of the fellows called out to the sexton and began to utter the most gross and offensive language in reference to Fathers Furlong and Vilas. Nothing more serious however occurred.

On Wednesday a body of police under Sub-inspector Hill proceeded to Lisburn and as information had been given by a most respectable Protestant, that there was every likelihood that a combined display would be made that night by some Orange lodges to burn Father Furlong in effigy, Sub-inspector Hill brought an additional force of constabulary from Belfast to Lisburn. The streets were patrolled during the evening, a proceeding which appeared to have somewhat disconcerted the rioters for they contented themselves with shouting the usual refrains of 'To hell with the Pope'; varied sometimes with the chorus of 'To hell with Father Furlong' and throwing an occasional stone at the priests and congregation as they were leaving the chapel. One of the stones hit a young girl on the forehead. Of course we need hardly say that the respectable Protestants of the district discountenanced this disgraceful conduct, for irrespective of their love of peace and order the gentle unpresuming, and truly apostolic character of the respected parish had won for him the regard of all respectable and sensible men of every creed and party. ('The Ulsterman' copied by Freeman's Journal 14 July 1853.)

Bishop Denvir had been informed, in a letter written by the wife of one of the conspirators who feared her husband might be implicated in murder, about a plot hatched by the Orange citizens of Lisburn and Downpatrick etc to murder the two Rosminian fathers.

He stated,

'The Orangemen then determined on the destruction of the church, the Catholic schools and the Pastor's house in that town just as in Stockport and some thousands of them gathered at that place in small bodies armed with daggers and loaded pistols concealed under their clothes. Some came from as far away as Downpatrick. The crowd yelled 'To hell with the Jesuits and to hell with the monks.'

He described how one hundred extra police were brought into the town and when they were incapable of controlling the mobs two companies of armed soldiers were brought from their barracks in Belfast (a twelve minute drive by railway from Belfast). A large number of Catholics went to protect the missionaries but 'were unable to withstand the Orange multitude'. The main problem was getting the priests safely from the parochial house to the church and back.

'The missionaries were attacked with stones and other missiles and received a few punches in a closely covered vehicle between the church and the Pastor's house. At the last hour of the mission a renewed attack was made on the Pastor and one of the missioners, both saved by the speed of their horses.'
(The Kirby Collection Catalogue 1854)

The murder plot did not succeed, but there were widespread sectarian disturbances in the town. It was technically illegal for religious orders to operate in the country, their presence being proscribed by the Emancipation Act 1829. (Catholicism in Ulster 1603-1983 Oliver Rafferty)

18 October   The outcome of a recent election in the town, when an independent Mr Jonathan Joseph Richardson was returned, caused some friction within the Orange Order in Lisburn when it was discovered that some Orangemen had voted for Richardson. The district secretary of the Orange Society commanded those individuals to appear before a meeting of the district to answer certain charges for supporting the Liberal candidate in opposition to a brother Orangeman. In one case an additional charge was that an individual, required to attend, had attended at the Popish chapel and had given countenance to Father Furlong on his recent visit to Lisburn.

The unionist 'Northern Whig' newspaper commented 'If anything could possibly have tended to exhibit in their true colours the Orange faction in Lisburn, this last display of their character must fairly place them before the empire, and hold them up to reprobation of every right-minded individual.' (Northern Whig October 1853)

1854

12 June   Bishop Cornelius Denvir, Belfast, wrote a lengthy letter to the Irish College in Rome covering a number of topics and refuted an inaccurate representation that had apparently been made to the Holy Father about the Diocese of Down and Connor.

Reacting apparently to criticism that he had not provided for the education of ecclesiastical students he explained that in 1833 a Diocesan seminary had been built 'at very heavy expenditure' close to his own house. He also voiced his support for female education and suggested that Religious Institutions would remedy the deficiencies, mentioning the establishment of the Sisters of Mercy convent at Downpatrick.

He went on to deny that he had no solicitudes for the education of the poor and said that he had spared neither time, labour or expenses in procuring sites for schools and chapels. 'Every week for the past 18 years I have been occupied in this very work ... the problem with sites is due to the animosity inspired by the bigotry and Orangeism, the latter being much augmented in strength here since Smith O'Brien's unfortunate émeute in 1848.'

(William Smith O'Brien was an Irish Nationalist, a Member of Parliament and leader of the Young Ireland movement who was convicted of sedition for his part in the Young Irelander Rebellion in 1848.)

In somewhat of a rant he went on about 'the diabolical spirit of antipathy prevailing here against religious orders, I mean the Protestants and Calvinists of the Scotch invaders who in 1641 and subsequently, seized upon the property of the monasteries as well as of the Catholics gentry and they still hold them'.

He commented that the entire Diocese of Down and Connor and Dromore is vested in about twenty individuals who are patrons of the Orange Secret Society.

In a reference to Lisburn he wrote. 'The landlord of this place who is also the landlord of several surrounding parishes has brought an action to recover possession of the church, schools and the Pastor's house, all out of lease. They have instituted a lawsuit to turn us out. We have taken defence of this and a Country Antrim jury must either protect us or have the parish of Lisburn without a Catholic church, without school and a Pastor's house.'

This is probably a reference to the Marquess of Hertford. The various Marquesses of Hertford had, over the years, different attitudes to the Catholic Church. The lawsuit would appear to have been unsuccessful.

Commenting on the fact that the north of Ireland was something of a backwater where the regular clergy were concerned one possible explanation advanced by the bishop was that there was enormous prejudice, at least in northeast Ulster, against religious orders.

1855

April Rev. Patrick Phelan, ordained in Clarendon Street Chapel, Dublin in November 1854 by Dr Whelan, Bishop of Bombay, was appointed first to

Glenavy and in April appointed curate in Lisburn. (Other records state he arrived in Lisburn February 1854.) (Down & Connor Ancient & Modern.)

1857

After the death of Rev. John McKenna the parish was under the spiritual charge of Rev. Patrick Phelan, (eventually parish priest of Saintfield), and of Rev. Felix McKeating, parish priest of Ballykinlar, until 6 January 1859, when Edward Kelly, parish priest, was appointed.

When Roger Johnson Smyth. MP for Lisburn died on 19 September 1853, in a subsequent by-election Jonathan Joseph Richardson had been returned unopposed. The Richardsons were a powerful manufacturing family but not a united one for in 1857 Jonathan's cousin put himself forward as a liberal and Jonathan withdrew with some ill feeling. In that election two candidates fought, perhaps not literally, though in that year 'there was a considerable riot' in which Orangemen and Catholics joined 'in brotherly amity to crack the skulls of victims chosen according to strictly non-sectarian principles.' (The Lisburn By-Elections of 1863 - Stephen A. Royle.)

Twenty tenants of the Marquis of Hertford received notices to quit on account of their votes at the Lisburn election. (The Tablet 4 July 1857.)

'The Banner of Ulster' (March 1857) announced the demise of Mr Henry Mulholland, of Lisburn, which took place at his house in Seymour Street, on the evening of the 12th ult. Mr Mulholland was one of the oldest of Ulster's linen merchants, having begun his career about the summer of 1794, aged 22. Perhaps no man was more deservedly popular with his fellow-townsmen of all shades of opinion.

1859

Lisburn was without a parish priest until Rev. Kelly was appointed in 1859. He was ordained in Dublin by the Most Rev. Dr Murray in February 1844, and was shortly afterwards appointed Professor of Classics and Mathematics in the Diocesan Seminary, the duties of which office he continued to discharge until his promotion to the parish of Lisburn.

7 November Among the duties of Rev. Kelly was that of chaplain to the Workhouse. He wrote to the Board of Guardians setting out his objections to the Catholic inmates being taught by Protestant teachers and said that in future he would undertake the entire religious teaching of the Catholic children in the Workhouse. He requested that a male and female from the inmates should assist him in imparting religious instructions to the children. Advice was sought from the Poor-law Commission Office in Dublin. Their response was that they considered the request to be reasonable. (At that time there were five Catholic children in the Workhouse schools - one boy, four girls).

The Lisburn Board considered this to be ruse, as in their opinion there were no paupers capable of delivering religious instruction and better qualified paid assistants would be requested. The chairman's decision was that the Board decline making or sanctioning such appointment. He said that the Roman Catholic chaplain was paid £30 per annum and he would hardly share his salary with monitors. He was also annoyed that Rev. Kelly had taken the matter up directly with the Commissioners in Dublin. (Belfast News Letter 22 February 1860.)

1860

The 'Belfast News Letter' in an editorial took Rev. Kelly, who they referred to as 'our local celebrity,' to task for having made a direct approach to Dublin regarding the Workhouse matter and called on the Lisburn Guardians to do their duty with equal boldness. (Belfast News Letter 17 February 1860)

1 June Rev. Mooney was appointed as a curate in Lisburn. Educated at the College of the Noble Irish in the University of Salamanca he had an extensive and valuable library which he later left to the Diocesan College of Belfast.

1861

Lisburn Boys' School opened by Rev. Kelly with Mr I. Walsh as headmaster. (It shared old and dilapidated premises with premises on the site of the former St Joseph's Hall with the Girls' School).

(The Male & Female National School House along with RC Chapel and Burial Ground is listed in Griffith valuation 1862.)

Prior to this Catholic children had attended a number of interdenominational schools in Lisburn and the country areas. Up to this time integrated education appeared to be the norm with most of the schools' headmasters and mistresses being of the Protestant faith. An exception was, in 1830s, a school operated in a private house in Castle Street by Edward Law, who was a Catholic. The fee was 5s to 8s 4d per quarter and, as with the other schools, was interdenominational. The Catholic Church, as with other churches, operated separate Sunday Schools.

19 June For several evenings Orange bands with drums and fifes marched through the town offering insults to the Catholics. On 19 June at about nine o'clock about one thousand marched up Bow Street to the market house where they played party tunes. When Head-constable Stafford and one of his men appeared on the scene he was called names and stones thrown at him. He returned to the barracks and called out the ten constables available. When they went to the market square they too were stoned. Sub-constable Naan was hit on the head and had to be escorted back to the barracks. The police then regrouped and the Head-constable gave orders to fix bayonets and they charged at the crowd, successfully dispersing them.

About ten o'clock a man named Megan, a Catholic, left his house to watch the riot and was stabbed in the back. He was attended to by Dr Musgrave and was said to be in a precarious state. The injured policeman was stated not to be in danger. (Freeman's Journal 20 June 1861 & Hansard HC Debate 21 June 1861.)

21 September Dr Denvir wrote to the Irish College, Rome about the effect the Civil War in America was having on the cotton and flax industry in Ulster and mentioned that the potato crop had been a failure. (Irish College Archives 1861-1866)

1862

22 September An appeal was made to the Irish public, by Dr John Gray, through the medium of the Freeman's Journal (which he owned) for funds to raise a national monument in honour of O'Connell. With the sanction of the Most Rev. Paul Cullen, Archbishop of Dublin, collections were taken at the doors of the city churches and the country parishes were expected to follow this precedent. It was arranged that the proceeds would be returned by the respective pastors.

19 November Rev. E. Kelly made what was recorded as a miscellaneous subscription to the fund (amount not listed) on behalf of the Catholics of Lisburn. (Report of the O'Connell Monument Committee - Library of the University of California.)

The foundation stone was laid in Dublin in 1864 and attacks on Catholics returning to Belfast by rail triggered sectarian rioting resulting in attacks on schools and churches. (European Religion in the Age of Great Cities - Hugh McLeod.)

The monument to Daniel O'Connell, in Dublin's Sackville Street, was unveiled to enormous crowds in 1882. The street became known as O'Connell Street and the name was changed in 1924.

THE COTTON FAMINE

In 1862 there was a fine example in Lisburn how the churches worked together in the face of a common enemy - poverty. The Catholic Church in Lisburn was credited with reaching out to help all creeds at a time of crisis for weavers in Lisburn and the surrounding area.

Because of the American Civil War the export of cotton from the plantations in the southern states ceased, not because the cotton fields had been destroyed or left untilled but because of action by the Confederacy to apply economic pressure on Britain to gain recognition as a separate state. The export of cotton, the majority of which went to the British markets, eventually reduced to a stage where the large mills in Lancashire, dependent on the raw cotton, ceased production. This affected the Irish hand-loom operators who worked from home. At the close of 1860 in about a ten mile radius of Belfast there were about 20,000 individuals engaged in weaving and perhaps 80,000 embroidering muslin. It was however Lisburn district that suffered most where, even in good times, weavers were barely able to survive, supporting their families on three shilling a week. The real impact of

the shortage of cotton supplies did not really kick in until 1862. A Relief Committee was established in Lisburn with Rev. Edward Kelly as a member.

1863

Tuesday 10 February At the general meeting of the Relief Committee;

'The Rev. Edward Kelly, P.P., gave some sketch of a visit he had paid to the homes of some of the people in Chapel Hill, Long Stone, and the lanes leading from those streets. He said there was great want of bed-clothing in the houses of many families, and he would suggest that members of the Ladies' Committee should be requested to look after these people. It was well known how much good had arisen from the exertions put forth by that Committee; in fact, it had done work which could hardly be said to be in the way of their other friends doing; and if the matter to which he alluded were placed in the hands of the ladies, he was certain the poor people would have their wants fully attended to.'

[This decrease of employment has been going on for nearly two years, and is now at the lowest point ever reached. In fact, whole families for weeks past have been eking out existence on a class of food which would hardly be given to the lower animals. I shall give a few cases: One poor woman in the neighbourhood of the Maze, and who received relief off the Committee yesterday, has a sickly husband out of work and six small children. She declared that had it not been that a neighbour gave her some turnips which she had boiled and used as food, she and her children might have been lost - these turnips being the entire sustenance they had had from Saturday till Monday. In another instance a family of ten was found not only without food, but on being questioned on the matter, it turned out that not a single shirt or other article of body linen was among the wretched group.

Inquiry having been made on this point in the next cabin that was examined, a poor fellow said that he and his wife had still some remnants of underclothing, but that of such necessaries the children were utterly destitute. Again, there is an almost total want of beds and bedding in the habitations of the cotton weavers. In not a few cases a parcel of damp straw, without either sheet or blanket, forms the sole sleeping place of the father, mother, and two or three mere infants, each resting at night in the ragged garments worn by day. Even in the less destitute abodes of the operatives, the Committee found entire families without a single shred of blanket, an old sheet and quilt constituting the sole amount of bedclothes. One case there was where eight children, from the ages of four to eighteen, slept with the parents in one department.

The wages of the people in work are far below the lowest ever known. Not even in the former history of the labour market in the West of Ireland could sadder examples be found. It is not unusual to find men who must work at the loom fourteen hours a day to earn a net income of 4s per week - some make only 3s, and others again 2s 6d for six days work. In all their privations there has been kept up a spirit of independence, and a disposition to battle as long as possible against the inroads of want that seems almost incredible. It is quite usual to find families existing on a sort of gruel, made of the cheap description of Indian meal, and this only twice a day; others, again, have been living on boiled cabbage, with a little oatmeal shaken over it.

The appeals for support and finance by the Committee were successful, and gifts of food, clothing, services and money were received from home and abroad. The winter was severe and the claims on the relief fund increased, but the aid given to the poor households never exceeded one shillings worth of meal and coal to each member of the family, and this enabled large numbers to be supported.] (The Plight of the Cotton Weavers at Lisburn, Maze and Broomhedge in 1862-1863 by Gilbert Watson.)

The Secretary said that his friend Father Mooney had that morning called his attention to the subject alluded to by the Rev. Mr Kelly; and as that gentleman had special opportunities of forming correct opinions on the matter, he felt assured the Committee would attend to it.

Mr. George Pelan bore testimony to the great exertions made by the Catholic curate. He said Mr Mooney's attention to the poor — not only of his own Church, but of all other creeds—was worthy of his character as a Christian minister. More than one gentleman in town had spoken to him on the subject and he was glad to have the opportunity of alluding to the promptitude and energy displayed by the Rev. Mr Mooney in furthering the objects of the Relief Committee.

Lord Hertford, an absent landlord, who owned an estate of sixty-seven thousand acres encompassing Lisburn was asked to provide financial support to help relieve starvation in the Lisburn district. 'He did not contribute a single shilling.'

Among the appeals made abroad were to Lisburn men who had carved out successful businesses in America. Thomas Richardson, who was educated at Friends' School, Lisburn and part of a family that controlled bleach works, spinning mills, and factories in three countries, and importing and shipping businesses in Liverpool, Philadelphia and New York, sent the barque 'Old Hickory' to Belfast with food to feed the starving weavers.

When Mr J.J. Richardson, Lissue, a member of the Relief Committee, learned that the 'Old Hickory' had arrived in Belfast he suggested that it be chartered to take emigrants on its return journey. (A similar crisis among Lisburn's cotton weavers in 1827 had resulted in a petition to parliament to provide for assisted emigration to North America.)

Many of the families facing starvation did not want to accept charity and it was proposed that some means should be devised to send a number of families to the colonies.

Following negotiations with Captain Meade preparations were made to fit out the ship to carry passengers.

27 May Two hundred and fifty three emigrants, men women and children, gathered at Lisburn railway station at 10:00 a.m. to board a special train provided by the Ulster Railway to take them to Belfast. Among the crowds on the platform was Rev. Kelly P.P.

On arrival in Belfast the women and children along with luggage were taken to the quay on carts. The men walked. At 4:40 that afternoon 'Old Hickory' left for Philadelphia (it would take 45 days to reach its destination). Each head of family was issued with a cash order drawn on Messers T. Richardson, Philadelphia of ten shillings.

Note: On the 10th ult., at Philadelphia, Thomas Richardson, of New York, son of James N. Richardson, of Glenmore, near Lisburn, to Anna C., daughter of Richard Price, of that city. (The Armagh Guardian 8 July 1845.)

The greatest of the Quaker families was the Richardsons, who had already come to hold a leading position in the linen industry in the eighteenth century. James N. Richardson of Glenmore near Lisburn, who died in 1842, had seven sons who controlled bleach works, spinning mills, and factories in three countries, and importing and shipping businesses in Liverpool, Philadelphia and New York. (A History of Friends' School Lisburn by Neville H. Newhouse.)

This was only a partial solution and rations continued to be distributed but because of the expenditure incurred with the emigration scheme the committee instructed that all rations should be reduced by half.

Unexpected relief came from New York when another Lisburn man Alex Turney Stewart, a successful merchant in America wrote to the committee to inform them that a barque, 'Mary Edson' was on its way to Belfast with provisions (Indian corn, barrels of flour and 50 tons of bacon) to the value of £5,000 to help alleviate the sufferings of Lisburn's destitute weavers.

It was agreed that the ship would also take up to one hundred emigrants on its return journey and on 13 July the scenes in May were repeated at the railway station as 137 souls headed for America.

The winter of 1863/64 was severe and much of the remaining funds were expended on clothing but in October 1863 Mr Robert Hart, originally from Lisburn but now Collector of Customs at Hong Kong wrote from Shanghai providing a £100 subscription 'for the relief of unemployed operatives in Lisburn and its vicinity.'

By the summer of 1864 cotton imports resumed and cotton weaving recommenced but some degree of poverty remained into 1865. (The Cotton Famine 1862-63, William Mullan & Son Belfast and London 1881.)

At the end of March 1865, news came of the death of Mr Thomas Richardson, of Philadelphia. Immediately afterwards a meeting of the Committee was held to express their regret at the demise of a gentleman who had been so efficient in collecting funds in his city. The following report of the meeting in the Belfast papers included:

> 'The Rev. Edward Kelly P.P., concurred in all that had been said relative to the late Mr Richardson; and in thus noticing the Christian kindness of that gentleman, the Committee, he was certain, would have the sympathy of all those other contributors who, in the time of suffering and distress, so liberally came forward to add their gifts to the general fund. In a distant land, some three thousand miles from the place of his birth, he had recollected the home of his boyhood; and when he learned that aid was required to keep the helpless from want, he worked with a will among his fellow citizens of Philadelphia to collect money for the old land at home. He (Mr. Kelly) would, therefore, suggest that a letter of condolence should be sent to their late friend's widow, and probably some gentleman present would draw up a resolution to that effect.'

21 February One of the most contentious elections ever was held in Lisburn and was an all-time low in political chicanery and bribery. John Dougherty Barbour, son of mill owner William Barbour was standing as a Radical against Edwin Wingfield Verner a Conservative. Barbour wined and dined twenty individuals, eligible to vote, at his home, Hilden House, for nine days keeping them prisoner and in a state of perpetual intoxication to secure their votes.

It was claimed that those Catholics in Lisburn who were entitled to vote, favoured William Barbour because he had visited Rev. Edward Kelly and paid £25 towards repairs to the 'chapel house' after which Fr Kelly advised his flock to vote liberal and 38 out of 40 voters, including Kelly himself apparently did so.

Barbour won by six votes but was unseated in June 1864 following an appeal.

12 July

Appears to have passed off tranquilly in Ireland, but on 13th there was a row in the North. Early in the day great excitement was caused in Belfast by cart-loads of Orangemen passing through the streets on their way to Lisburn, where a monster meeting of from 14,000 to 15,000 was afterwards held. Large numbers were collected till a late hour but no disturbances took place. An invasion was expected to have been made on the Roman Catholic district, and therefore an army of opposition stood prepared. About eleven o'clock, Mr Lyons, a magistrate, was passing through the disturbed districts for the purpose of clearing the streets when some person thew a large stone which struck him on the back of the head, inflicting a very severe wound. No arrest was made. From a very early hour, the Orangemen continued to pour into Lisburn on cars. (Sydney Morning Herald 29 September 1863.)

September Several hundred Orangemen from country districts paraded through the streets of Lisburn to about eleven o'clock. Windows in shops were broken and individuals attacked. Their anger was directed at those who had voted for William Barbour which of course included many Catholics. (Freeman's Journal 2 September 1863.)

16 September Rev. Joseph Dixon, Armagh wrote to Dr Kirby at the Irish College, Rome suggesting that they ask Dr Denvir 'who is too timid (regarding Orangemen-author) and incapable of organising the Diocese to hand over the reins to his young and vigorous coadjutor Dr Dorrian'. (Irish College Archives 1861-1866.)

1864

23 March 1,000 persons, men, women, and children, marched through Lisburn with drums, fifes, shouting, and firing pistols in relation to an election dispute. Over one hundred police were sent to Lisburn, and they afforded protection to the timid inhabitants of that place. (Hansard HC Deb 14 April 1864 vol. 174 cc 969-7.)

12 July The 'Banner of Ulster' cautioned the Orange Order that the law is directly opposed to all processions, whether of the Protestant or Roman Catholic party, and it is to be presumed that their clergy in many cases exhorted them to avoid such irritating displays so inconsistent with Christian charity and goodwill among men. Yet not only in the enlightened capital of Ulster, but in a number of provincial towns, preparations on a large scale were made for the great Orange festival, and vast numbers of the Orangemen were to turn out in procession. At Lisburn about 20,000 or 30,000 people assembled in some fields. There were upwards of 80 lodges, each represented by flags; and the Orangemen marched in procession through the town. Arches of Orange lilies were stretched across some of the streets. About half-past-4 o'clock an attack was made on the police barracks, and in a few minutes all the panes of glass and windows frames were smashed. About seven o'clock a number of extra constables came up from Belfast, having been telegraphed for by the sub-inspector. Nothing more of any consequence occurred, everything having passed off quietly. (The Tablet 16 July 1864)

8 August

One of the most serious episodes of sectarian rioting in Belfast took place. It was said on a former occasion that the cause of this illegal assemblage and disturbance on the 8th August was the procession in honour of laying the foundation stone of the O'Connell monument in Dublin. Now, that was a very Irish way of accounting for these disturbances; for the procession in Dublin took place at two o'clock in the afternoon, and the intention to burn the effigy on Boyne Bridge was known in Belfast on the Saturday before. On that evening the Sandy Row party, the Orangemen, assembled in their own district with guns, as it was admitted by the police that some shots were fired, and they burnt the effigy of O'Connell on the top of the bridge. The magistrates and police were present during the proceedings.

The trouble spread to Lisburn where 'an Orange mob paraded the town with the usual insignia.' (Hansard HC 13 June 1865)

The election debacle of the previous year ended when after fourteen months, two elections, assaults on persons and property, alleged assassination attempts, kidnapping, bribery and untold corruption the 313 electors got a legitimate Member of Parliament, Edward Winfield Verner. (The Lisburn By-Elections of 1863 - Stephen A. Royle)

October Rev. John Landy was appointed curate in Lisburn.

The Sister of Charity were conducting primary schools in Belfast, Downpatrick and Lisburn. (Catholicism in Ulster 1603-1983 Oliver Rafferty)

1865

19 February Rev. James Francis Mooney died at the home of his brother in Castlewellan.

1866

Mr D. Burns was appointed as principal of St Patrick's National School. He only served one year in this post.

10 July Dr Denvir died.

1867

Mr M. Brown appointed as principal of St Patrick's National School. (Records held by St Aloysius PS claim that Mr T. O'Hagan was appointed and remained until 1872.)

19 January A financial crisis caused by the failure of the banking house of Overend, Gurney & Co. pushed up interest rates and it became difficult for businesses to obtain loans and once again hand-loom weavers were unemployed. At a meeting of the Relief Committee Rev. Edward Kelly said that in the course of his own parochial duties, he had that morning witnessed the extreme of poverty in a great many houses, and he regretted to add in not a few cases where, a short time before, the inhabitants had been in comparative comfort.

29 March In a debate in the House of Commons Sir John Gray referred to an alleged offence against the administration of justice in Ireland and the apparent impartial manner in which courts were dealing with sectarian rioting. Among a number of incidents he mentioned was a case which occurred at Lisburn. The charge was that of having "riotously assembled," and having "stabbed" certain persons at such assembly, the defendants got off with a verdict of acquittal. (HC Deb 29 March 1867 vol. 186 cc 846-87.)

28 May Rev. Kelly wrote to his bishop Rt Rev. D. Dorrian about a requirement to have Mass celebrated every day for the intentions of the Founder (of the church) rescinded. He was making a case that it was not practicable, and indeed inconvenient, to celebrate a daily Mass for the same particular intentions and especially at the same particular altar as he had only two curates in Lisburn at that time and had two parish churches. This may have seemed a fairly minor matter but in the eyes of the Church an ecclesiastical foundation is a contract and stipulated Masses or other works must be fulfilled as a matter of justice and, if not fulfilled, those responsible for the omission sin gravely and are bound to restitution. (Decrees of Urban VIII, "Cum Sæpe" 21 Jan., 1625.) This would be an ongoing matter. (Kirby Papers, Rome 1867.)

THE LAND LEAGUE AND HOME RULE

1868

This was a pivotal year for Lisburn and for Irish history in Ulster politics.

It was a time of change in the social order and in attitudes. The issues of the day, land reform and Home Rule would continue to dominate politics for years to come and increasingly divided the people of Lisburn along sectarian lines.

Despite what had happened in the preceding years Lisburn was a liberal town with evidence of cooperation among the churches and demonstrated by the benevolence of Protestant landlords to the Catholic population in the provision of land for church purposes.

The politics of the landlords were generally shared by their tenants and in Lisburn where the majority of tenants shared the Protestant religion with their landlord they were content with this common bond to defer to their landlord's views. As the larger tenants became more prosperous with the economic growth in Lisburn and Belfast and as they sought social advancement and independence they formed a new social tier. They were however always aware of their vulnerability in tenant-rights and could not afford to cross their landlord. They were mindful that Hertford had increased his rents in Lisburn in 1852 when his tenants had opposed his nominee in an election. Nevertheless tenants began to press for legislation that would give them some security, the ability to own the land they worked and not leave them at the mercy of the landlords.

The need for land reform would lead to the formation of the Irish National Land League in 1879 with Charles Stewart Parnell elected as its president and what was known as the 'Land War'.

The Land League spread rapidly in Ulster and the breakdown in the relationship between tenant and landlord caused the latter great concern. Protestants as well as Catholics were supportive of the League which held out the promise of lower rents and land security. The landlords, including those in the Lisburn district, began to consider how to defeat the Land League's objectives in order to protect their economic, social status and political interests. They needed to undermine Protestant support for the League by portraying it as a Catholic organisation. The simple maxim was divide and conquer and they turned to the Orange Order for support. The landed gentry who had ignored what they regarded as the lower-classes in the Orange Order for decades now took on a leadership role within the loyal orders.

The developing Catholic nationalism and Protestant unionism also provided a new focus for Orangeism in relation to the Home Rule issue.

30 March The Orangemen of Lisburn wrote to Benjamin Disraeli, First Lord of the Treasury, requesting that the Party Processions Act should be repealed. They said that the processions had the effect of strengthening the attachment to the British Constitution and were, for the most part, conducted in peace and order, Roman Catholics witnessing and even joining in them.
(Belfast News Letter 7 April 1868.)

27 April There was a 'Great Protestant Meeting' in Lisburn to protest against Gladstone's proposals for Home Rule which was equated with an attack on Protestantism. The Lisburn Protestant Defence Association was inaugurated 'not in a spirit of aggression but in a spirit of self defence'. Speaker after speaker denounced popery and the 'arrogant and intolerant priesthood of the Church of Rome.'

> *'Where we have Protestantism we have prosperity but where Popery is rampant there is nothing but wretchedness and rags. Dear friends Roman Catholics have been clamoring long enough for concession. I think Protestants should now ask for something and not let Popery get everything. We will let them go no further.'* (Belfast News Letter 27 April 1868)

12 July The Orange anniversary passed off quietly all over the North, except at Lisburn and Dungannon. The attack on the police in the former place, at the close of the meeting held there by Brother Johnston and his friends, was cowardly in the extreme, and it is to be hoped that some of their assailants will be severely punished. (The Tablet 11 July 1868)

20 September Rev. William Close was appointed as curate to Lisburn. He died in the same year aged forty and was buried at Tullyrusk, his native parish. (Extract from 'The Grand Bazaar and Fancy Fare' - New Schools Crumlin, Oct 1914.)

15 November Rev. Wm. Dempsey, born 2 February 1846 in the townland of Coldagh, Ballymoney was appointed as curate in Lisburn and served until October 1870.

Mr T. O'Hagan appointed as principal of St Patrick's National School.

THE ARRIVAL OF THE SISTERS OF THE SACRED HEART OF MARY IN LISBURN

1870

13 November The Sisters of the Sacred Heart of Mary whose mother house was in Beziers in the south of France arrived in Lisburn and established a convent in Castle Street. The principal calling of the Order was teaching.

In the early 1860s the Sacred Heart of Mary community in France counted several Irish sisters, but the climate and culture evoked health problems for some and Fr Gailhac thought that a foundation in Ireland would be beneficial. One of his earliest attempts to found a convent in Callan had to be abandoned due to a conflict between the parish priest Fr O'Keeffe and the Bishop.

Shortly afterwards mother St Thomas Hennessy was chosen to accompany a novice returning home due to ill health. Here she met with Fr Kelly, parish priest of Lisburn, who was very anxious to establish free education for the poor and a paying school for the better off Catholics, and so, on the 13th November 1870, the first community outside Beziers was opened in Lisburn.

(http://www.ferrybankparish.com/sacredheartofmary/shmhistory.htm.)

Rev. D.H. Burke: November 1870 – March 1871
Rev. Michael O'Malley from Towerhill, Cappamore, Limerick was appointed curate in December 1870 – February 1875.
Fr Michael O'Malley who was P.P. of Cushendun was appointed to Glenavy on 1 June 1894. He was born at Towerhill in the parish of Cappamore, Limerick in 1845 and after studies in Thurles and Waterford was ordained by Dr Dorrian in St Malachy's Church, Belfast, on the Sunday within the octave of All Saints, 1870. After his curacies in Lisburn. St Peter's, Belfast, and Whitehouse he moved as P.P. to Cushendun in 1883. Fr O'Malley was a great favourite in Glenavy and was widely known as a preacher and a confessor. Indeed he was called on at times to give retreats in some other parishes. (Glenavy The Church of the Dwarf 1868 - 1968 - Rev. Patrick J. McKavanagh.)

1871

Under the leadership of Mother Superior Saint Thomas Hennessey the group of sisters in the convent opened a primary school for girls. Within months the sisters had opened a poor school and a paying school at the convent, and were teaching religion classes on Sundays to children, young girls and women of all ages.

1872

29 January Rev. Edward Kelly wrote to the vice-rector in The Irish College, Rome expressing gratitude for a statuette of the Blessed Virgin Mary, a replica of the statue in Piazza di Spagna, Rome, to be presented to the Lisburn Bazaar by Pope Pius IX. (Irish College Archives, Rome.)

14 February In a further letter to The Irish College Rev. Kelly arranged for the statuette to be brought to Ireland by Rev. John Walsh, a Carmelite priest based in the church of Santa Maria, in Traspontina, Rome. In the letter he requested the Rector Tobias Kirby to obtain from His Holiness the special favour of the Papal Benediction for the nuns of the Lisburn Convent and for himself. (Irish College Archives, Rome.)

Mr James McDonald appointed as principal of St Patrick's National School on the retirement of T. O'Hagan.

17 March St Patrick's Day had been marked by commemorations of the Manchester Martyrs and demonstrations in support of Fenian prisoners in Cork, Drogheda and Dublin.

(Three Irishmen were convicted of murdering a police sergeant while freeing two leading Fenians, who had been sent to re-organise the Fenian movement in England, from a police van in Manchester. They were publicly hanged on 23 November 1867. The men, the Manchester Martyers, were apparently innocent and victims of a public and police clamour for revenge, something that would be repeated in 1975 following the Birmingham pub bombing by the IRA.)

There were no demonstrations in the north although shamrocks were widely worn.

15 August A number of events in support of Home Rule and the Fenians were announced for Our Lady's Day. Parades were planned in Belfast, Castlewellan, Cookstown, Derry, Dundrum, Gilford, Lurgan, Lisburn, Newcastle, Newry, Portadown, Portglenone and Warrenpoint. Some of these attracted large numbers of supporters, others were only local parades, prior to moving on to a larger demonstration. Editorials in the Northern Whig (14.8.1872) and the News Letter (15.8.1872) noted that the Orangemen had been allowed to hold their demonstrations in July without any interruptions and therefore Protestants should allow Roman Catholics to do likewise. It was further noted that the demand for Home Rule was a constitutional objective and demonstrations in support of such a demand should be allowed.

The Protestant community led by Rev. Hugh Hanna organised a counter-demonstration in Belfast which predictably resulted in violence and rioting in the city which then spread to other areas. In Lisburn, local Orangemen were called out to ensure no demonstration took place. (From Riots to Rights, Nationalist Parades in the north of Ireland - Centre for the study of Conflict, University of Ulster at Coleraine November 1997)

9 October The Sisters from the Sacred Heart Convent planned to hold a fund raising bazaar in Lisburn Town Hall. The event was advertised in the newspapers and posters displayed on walls around the town. Objections, made by members of the Protestant community who stated that they would assemble and wreck the Assembly Room if the Catholics were allowed to hold their bazaar in it, resulted in the venue being changed to the Convent. To ensure that they would not use the Town Hall it was occupied by Orangemen.

'On Tuesday night an Orange mob made its appearance in Lisburn with drums, fifes and flags and having paraded some streets they rushed with frantic yells into the market-house, which is situated near the assembly-rooms and took possession of the building. An extra force of 200 constables was brought into the town. Flags were soon hung from the tower of the market-house and the occupants remaining outside cheering, yelling and drumming until five o'clock yesterday morning. The bazaar and prize drawing opened yesterday in the new convent premises when there was a very large assemblage of the Catholics of the town and neighbourhood. It was continued today and although the weather was most unfavourable there was again a large attendance.'

10 October

That night the Orangemen keep possession of the streets, cheering and yelling and shouting out the most insulting epithets to the Catholic inhabitants. Last night they burned the effigy of Father Kelly, a clergyman who is held in the highest respect not only by Catholics but by all liberal and intelligent Protestants. After they burned an effigy of Rev. Edward Kelly in Market Square they proceeded en masse to the Convent to break up the bazaar. Police action prevented the mob from breaking into the Convent while others protected St Patrick's Church and Rev. Kelly's home.

Today the excitement continued, so great that the authorities drafted in more police into the town and a detachment of the 78th Highlanders were also brought from Belfast.' (The True Witness and Catholic Chronicle 8 November 1872)

Thomas Biggs, Haslem's Lane, Thomas Law, McCartney's Entry, and Thomas Patterson Jame's Street were later charged with rioting and being engaged in the burning of the effigy of Rev. Kelly. (Freeman's Journal 8 November 1872.)

1873

5 February Rev. P. Convery, born in Killelagh, Maghera on 3 September 1846, was appointed curate in Lisburn. He served to August 1874.

March At a meeting of the Council of the Catholic Union held at the Council Rooms in Henrietta Street, Dublin about the Government University Bill the election of new members included Rev. E. Kelly P.P. Lisburn. (Freeman's Journal 12 March 1873.)

May Rev. Kelly, chaplain of Lisburn Workhouse, was charged with tampering with the religion of a Protestant inmate. In a written statement he said that he had visited Mary Kelly on 19 May in hospital and she had declared, in the presence of the mistress of the Workhouse and of the head nurse, her wish to be attended by a Catholic priest and consequently to change her religion. He complained that this request made on 18 May had not been immediately conveyed to the Roman Catholic chaplain. When he attended to her on 19 May he baptised her and admitted her to the communion of the Roman and Catholic Church. This version of events was disputed by Rev. Robert Lindsay the Protestant chaplain who said that he did not admit that the woman was ever a Roman Catholic either in principle or practice. He administered to her until her death a month later. After due consideration by the Board of Guardians the matter was dropped. (Belfast News Letter, 1 May 1973.)

1874

17 March The Convent was attacked by members of the Orange Order on St. Patrick's Day when it was reported that the children were singing 'Irish' songs.

5 May A meeting of the Council of the Catholic Union of Ireland, was held at the Council Rooms, Henrietta Street, Dublin.

(The Catholic Union had been established in 1872 by the Catholic Church to protect Catholic interests that may be affected by legislation. The secretary of the Union was Bartholomew Teeling, a relation of the Lisburn Teelings.)

Among those attending was Rev. E. Kelly P.P. Lisburn. The following resolution was unanimously adopted: 'That the Central Council of the Catholic Union of Ireland has learned with sincere pleasure of the establishment of a Diocesan branch in Belfast; and offers to the Down and Connor members of the Union its warm congratulations on the success of their zealous efforts to further the movement.' (The Tablet archives 16 May 1874.)

1 August Rev. Thomas Jones was appointed as curate in Lisburn. He had previously served in Glenavy parish. (Extract from 'The Grand Bazaar and Fancy Fare' - New Schools Crumlin, Oct 1914)

13 November Rev. Kelly wrote to Rev. Dr Tobias Kirby thanking him for his prompt letter of 6th ult. which stated that the request to reduce the number of daily Masses was forwarded to the Holy Father who had granted his request. Kirby had already written to Dr Dorrian on this matter and that he should consider the dispensation satisfactorily granted. (Kirby Papers, Rome.)

1875

5 April An article appeared in the Freeman's Journal advertising a boarding school and a day school for young ladies at the convent of Sacre Coeur in Lisburn.

5 November Rev. Kelly wrote to Rev. Dr Tobias Kirby in response to a letter dated 21 October to ask His Holiness for a commutation of the Foundation Mass. It would appear that Rev. Kelly wished to be assured that the dispensation already granted was permanent. It may seem a little strange today for a parish priest communicate directly with the Pope. (Kirby Papers, Rome.)

1876

February Rev. David B. Mulcahy was appointed curate in Lisburn. He had been in Portglenone prior to this and went to Ballynafeigh on 24 November 1878. He had an extensive knowledge of the Irish language and history.

A missal, Missale Romanum, dated 1876 is in the parish archives.

12 July At the demonstration at the field at Laurel Hill on the outskirts of Lisburn Dr. George St George addressed the Orange brethren.

When he urged union among all Protestants, counseling them not to make too much of minor difficulties but holding as they did the grand fundamentals of Christianity, they should seek to present a united front to the common foe Popery, his speech was greeted with cheers.

The Rev. S. Campbell said that they were not opposing Roman Catholics - but the system.

Dr St George would later play an important role in local and regional politics and would return to his theme of unity forty-five years later when he advocated that loyalists in Northern Ireland should link together to form one group. Then it would be to exclude Catholics in Lisburn from employment opportunities.

Religious disturbances in Belfast spread to Lisburn.

'There has also been great excitement in Lisburn, which ended in rioting. Four public-houses belonging to Roman Catholics had their windows smashed. The stones were thrown in showers at the police, about twenty-four of whom were injured. The Riot Act was read and a number of arrests were made. The riot continued for several days.' (Nelson Evening Mail 17 October 1876)

Commenting on Sir Thomas Chamber's motion against convents and those M.Ps who supported the motion, a letter to the Tablet mentioned that Sir R. Wallace showed his gratitude for the support of the Catholics of Lisburne (sic) by voting for the suppression of convents. I have thus called attention to the votes of those members in whose constituencies, as far as I know, there is a Catholic element. (The Tablet 6 May 1876)

18 October Rev. John McConnell, from Lisburn parish died aged 49. He was parish priest of Portglenone. (Freeman's Journal 1876.)

1877

Rt Rev. C.H. Borghi, late Bishop of Detroit, describing his journey to Rome in 1877 wrote; .....

> *'We paid a hurried visit to Lisburn, which, among the several cities along the railroad between Dublin and Belfast, looks the most prosperous. The manufacture of the finest linen is not the least of its trade, here you see the system of bleaching the linen in perfection. There is but one Catholic church in the town and the public spirit is sufficiently unkind to prove that there is a remnant of the Huguenot poison left.*
>
> *Arriving at Belfast we engaged a cab to take us to the 'Royal Hotel' to which we had been recommended on account of the religion of the landlady, she being a good Catholic. ....'*

17 March A party dispute in Barbour's Row, a village situated about a mile and a half from Lisburn and principally occupied by Catholics resulted in the death of William Dunne. About a quarter to eleven a party of person passed through the village singing 'Rule Britannia'. Party expressions were then used and disturbances followed. A crowd of about thirty persons, principally females, gathered. Peter McKnight (18) was seen running into a house and returning with a file in his hand. It was claimed that he struck Dunne in the side of the neck. Edward Green (16) was also charged with murdering Dunne (30). (Freeman's Journal 10 April 1877.)

Rev. D. B. Mulcahy of Lisburn who attended the Council of the Society for the Preservation of the Irish Language stated 'We have distributed five dozen of the First Irish Book to young and old in Lisburn and have got three dozen more for distribution.' (Freeman's Journal 21 November 1877.)

25 November Rev. Patrick McGee, born in Ballyorgan, Kilclief on 21 February 1848, was appointed to Lisburn as curate.

1878

Rev. P. Magee: March 1878 – January 1879
Rev. M. Hamill: May 1878 – June 1885

The Rev. Patrick McCambridge's time in Lisburn is commemorated in an engraving on a silver chalice in St Patrick's. The inscription reads 'Rev. Patrick McCambridge 1878'. (There is a Rev. Patrick McCambridge listed in St John the Baptist Drumaroad, Castlewellan/Ballynahinch 1898-1906 and St Joseph's Killough 1906-1925.)

1881

Sir Richard Wallace, M.P., distributed this Christmas to the tenants on his Lisburn estate, through the clergy of the several denominations, various grants of money. He gave also to the poorhouse Christmas dinner, and through the ladies' charitable societies about 400 flannel petticoats to poor women. (The Tablet archives, 28 December 1881.)

1882

February Rev. Bernard McCartan, born in Tyconnett, Loughinisland was appointed curate in Lisburn from February 1882 to May 1886. In 1889, fifteen years after his ordination he was appointed as parish priest of Hannahstown. He served there for twelve years. The parochial houses at Hannahstown and the Rock which he built at the renovation of the parochial churches were memorials to his life-work. He died in the Mater Infirmorum Hospital on 19 November (year n/k).

March Robert Fitzsimmons, Treasurer and Michael O'Shea, Hon. Sec. forwarded a bank order for £53 15s as deposit for 225 shares including 10 shares fully paid to The National Exhibition 'following a meeting convened by our patriotic parish priest Rev. E. Kelly and encouraged by his no less patriotic curates.' The National Exhibition was a display of Irish art and industry held in Dublin that year. (Freeman's Journal 20 March 1882.)

May Rev. John McAlister, born 1 May 1850, educated in the College of Namur, Belgium and the University of Louvain, was ordained by Dr Dorrian on 6 November 1881 and after spending some time at Saintfield was appointed to Lisburn in May 1882 – August 1885.

1884

The appointment of Mr Thomas Barbour to Her Majesty's Commission of the Peace was marked on his first appearance on the Lisburn Magisterial Bench by the presentation of 'very handsome donations' to the Railway Street Presbyterian Church £50, to Lisburn Cathedral £25 and a further sum of £25 placed at the disposal of Rev. E. Kelly, parish priest of Lisburn for the benefit of the Roman Catholic church in the town. (Under the heading Unsectarian Philanthropy - The Lisburn Standard 13 September 1884.)

Questions were raised in parliament about Saturday night drumming parties outside the Catholic church on Chapel Hill which disturbed evening confessions. (Lisburn - The Town and its People, 1873-1973 Brian Mackey, Blackstaff Press, Belfast.)

THE GAELIC ATHLETIC ASSOCIATION

1 November At a meeting in the Hayes' Commercial and Family hotel in Thurles, North Tipperary Michael Cusack stated that it was absurd that Irish sport was organised by Englishmen and the result had been a decline in native pastimes. He called for a body to draft rules to aid their revival and to open athletics to the poor.

That was the first step in the founding of the Gaelic Athletic Association. Among those asked to be patrons was Archbishop Croke. The Association grew rapidly and caused something of a social revolution in rural Ireland. Because of the Home Rule issue it was difficult to keep politics out of what quickly became a nationwide organisation and a divide appeared between those who favoured peaceful political methods and those who sided with the Irish Republican Brotherhood who favoured physical force. Archbishop

Croke who had distanced himself from the IRB faction brought the two sides together by forming a committee equally representing both sides. The GAA would however be viewed by northern Protestants with suspicion.

Football and hurling matches went unreported by the nationalist press in Belfast for a considerable period but games played in Lisburn at Blaris would later come to national and international attention. (The GAA Library and Archive)

1885

August Rev. G. Crolly, born in Ballyrolly, County Down in August 1860 was appointed curate in Lisburn in August 1885 – October 1890.

Among the first Gaelic Athletic Association clubs founded in Co. Antrim was 'Lisburn Red Hands' club. There was also the 'Teelings' football team. (antrim.gaa.ie/history)

1886

8 March Thomas Goodman was among a number of distinguished amateurs from Lisburn who performed at a concert in Ballymacrickett schoolrooms organised by the choir of St Joseph's, Glenavy. A singer, impersonator and comedian he appeared along with Messers. Crossan, Herbert and Mulholland, all from Lisburn. (Lisburn Standard 13 March 1886.)

1 May Rev. Robert James Murphy born in Erinagh, Parish of Bright on 22 April 1856, was appointed curate in Lisburn and served to October 1890.

On Easter Monday a demonstration took place at the Maze, a popular race course not far from Lisburn. Lord Arthur Hill was in the chair and this at once tells us the character of the proceedings. Mr. Johnston, Mr. de Cobain, Colonel Waring, the Rev. Dr Kane, and other conspicuous Orangemen were present. In his opening speech Lord Arthur rang the changes on 'Mr. Parnell and his gang;' he assured the meeting that were the Government once handed over to the Irish party he and his friends would be hunted out of the land.

The Rev. Dr Kane seconded the following resolution:

'That if this measure of the Prime Minister should be forced upon us, and that we are handed over to the government of those who have been our bitterest enemies and the foes of the crown and constitution, and whose first efforts will be directed against our religious and Ulster commercial interests, we hereby solemnly and calmly declare that we shall not acknowledge that Government; that we shall protest against taxation by an Irish Parliament, and will refuse to pay taxes imposed by it; and, farther, that we shall resist to the uttermost all attempts to enforce such payment, and we call upon the men of England, Scotland, and the colonies who are with us in this great crisis in our history, to support our protest now, as well as hereafter, should we be compelled to take a more determined stand for the maintenance of the civil and religious liberties which our forefathers' arms obtained for us.' (The Tablet archives 1 May 1886)

A procession of some twenty or thirty-thousand with banners and drums and colours marched the seven or nine miles from Belfast to Lisburn. With drink circulating freely a number of them had got beyond the bounds of sobriety. There was an old man, one of those half-daft, harmless old creatures that everyone pities and is kind to, living in Lisburn. He was a Roman Catholic. Some way he got into the crowd and some of the Orangemen began hustling him about and insisting on his calling out 'To hell with the Pope' which he would not. Anyway it ended in their knocking him down and kicking his brains out, and evidence told of the white brains scattered on the roadway.

Following subsequent arrests and trial the two men charged were acquitted. An Orange procession was waiting at the courthouse door with two saddled horses on which the men were mounted and the procession escorted them to Lisburn where with flags flying and drums beating they marched round and round the place where the poor old man's brains had been battered out. (New Zealand Tablet 8 July 1898 - An 'Ulster Presbyterian' recalling an incident a dozen or more years previously.)

15 August Catholic houses in Lisburn were wrecked by what were described as Orange rowdies on Sunday. The attacks were renewed on Monday when the windows of the Catholic Reading Room and the Irish National Foresters were smashed, along with shots being fired into the home of a Catholic shopkeeper. (Freeman's Journal 16 August 1886.)

1887

Rev J. Boylan, a curate in the parish, founded the Shamrock Football Club. (Lisburn, The town and its people 1873-1973, Brian Mackey). In 1905 Rev. Joseph Boylan was listed as RC Chaplain for the Belfast workhouse, later to become Belfast City Hospital. In 1914 he was a curate in St. Malachy's, Belfast

1889

Rev. Edward Kelly, assisted by Revs. R. J. Murphy and G. Crolly undertook to provide the inhabitants of Magheragall with a church. To raise funds for this, new schools and a new hall in Lisburn a Bazaar was held in Lisburn in 1889.

Work on the construction of St Joseph's Hall started at the end of May.

1890

17 February The Boys' and Girls' School had been relocated to Sudbourne Hall, situated in an entry in Castle Street opposite the Convent, while St Joseph's Hall was being built and returned to new premises at St Joseph's Hall. Boys occupied the upper floor-the big room-with girls on the ground floor. (Sudbourne Hall was the name of Sir Richard Wallace's (1818-1890) country house near Orford, Suffolk. Wallace, Conservative and Unionist MP for Lisburn (1873-1885), was famous for his generosity to the people of Paris during the Siege of Paris (1870/71) and the provision of drinking fountains).

17 March St Patrick's Day was observed in Lisburn in the usual way. All the local public works were off; the thoroughfares were thronged all the day and many pedestrians wore in their breasts and hats the favourite sprig. The day was ushered in by the Conservative Flute Band. Nothing occurred during the entire day to call for the interference of the local authorities, and no extra police were drafted into the town. (Irish News March 1890)

July Rev. Kelly died and was buried in Milltown Cemetery, Belfast.

1 October Rev. Mark McCashin was appointed as parish priest by Most Rev. Dr McAlister to succeed Rev. Kelly who had died in that year. Rev McCashin had been ordained on 22 September 1867. (Irish News January 1908.)

Curates:

Rev. Jas. Greene: October 1890 – July 1893

Rev. J. Lennon: October 1890 – July 1893

Rev. C. McDonnell: October 1890 – May 1892

When Fr McCashin, was transferred to Lisburn from Glenravel, County Antrim, Henry Duffin, the parish caretaker in Glenravel and his wife Rose (nee O'Rawe) from the Craigsdunloof area of Glenravel, were persuaded by Rev. McCashin to move to Lisburn.

(Several years later the family moved again, this time to Belfast, eventually settling at 64 Clonard Gardens. Henry and Rose had seven children. Sadly their eldest son died as the result of an accident at the age of eleven. Tragedy was to strike again a few years later when their only daughter Mary died of meningitis. She too was only eleven years old. Rose passed away in 1918, leaving behind her husband Henry with the five remaining sons, John, Dan, Pat, Jim and Charlie. Further tragedy was to visit the family on the evening of 23 April 1921 when brothers Pat and Dan were murdered in their home, 64 Clonard Gardens by members of the Royal Irish Constabulary led by District Inspector Ferris. Both brothers were members of the Irish Republican Army.) (http://first-thoughts.org/on/Parish+Priest/)

ST JOSEPH'S CHURCH MAGHERAGALL

22 November Rev. Mark McCashin placed an advert in the 'Lisburn Standard' appealing for subscriptions towards the cost of the new church at Magheragall and towards the fitting out of the church and the new hall under construction in Lisburn. The total debt of the parish was £900. A special train had been organised from Belfast stopping at all stations and terminating at Brookmount, (which, per the advert, is a short distance from the Church. It was about three-quarters of a mile from Brookmount railway station).

23 November The new church at Magheragall, dedicated to St Joseph, opened and was blessed and dedicated to Divine Service by Most Rev. Dr. McAlister with Very Rev. A. McMullan P.P. V.G., Ballymena delivering the sermon.

On Sunday, at Magheragall, the Most Rev. Dr McAlister, Bishop of Down and Connor, dedicated the new church. For over 30 years the great want of adequate church accommodation in the locality has been a source of much anxiety. The late parish priest of Lisburn, the Rev. Father Kelly, had warmly espoused the project and gave very considerable assistance. He died recently, not having lived to see the happy fulfillment of his cherished and holy ambition. The present pastor, the Rev. M. McCashin, however, pressed forward the work, aided by the Bishop, and the sacred edifice having been at length completed was solemnly consecrated on Sunday. The High Mass, coram pontifice, was begun at 12 o'clock, and the solemn ceremony of dedication was performed previously by the Bishop. A special train from Belfast to Brookmount conveyed great numbers from that city, and Lisburn, and intermediate stations. The Very Rev. Alexander M'Mullen, P.P., V.G., preached the sermon. The sacred edifice was thronged throughout the ceremonies, many persons, unable to gain admission, waiting outside. The weather was very bad, and had a most deterrent effect on persons who would have liked to be present. The new parish church will accommodate about 300 persons. The architect was Mr. Byrne of Belfast and Messrs. Connolly of Lisburn, the eminent firm of builders and contractors, carried out the architect's design most successfully. The entire work is one that all who had to do with it may well regard with peculiar pride and satisfaction. The amount outstanding as a debt on the building was much reduced by the generous contributions of those present at the service as well as by many well-wishers. A new hall and schools had lately been erected in Magheragall. A bazaar of a most successful character had been held in Lisburn, the proceeds of which was devoted to defray the cost of the building of the hall and schools, but there still remained a debt of £350 for the providing of suitable furniture. This being added to the cost, unpaid, of the building of the church left the parish in debt to the extent of £900. Of this the collection made at the dedication on Sunday of the church met a portion. It is to be hoped that the residue will be soon subscribed, and the load removed off the minds of the good Bishop and priests. (The Tablet 29 November 1890)

Assisting in the dedication ceremony were Rev. Lennon C.C., Rev. Greene C.C., Rev. McDonnell C.C.. Admission to the dedication ceremony was 5/- for the reserved area and 2/6 for the unreserved area. The collection was taken up by a number of people including Joseph Rice, William McIlroy, W.H. Connolly, M. O'Shea, M. Savage Jun. and John Magee, all from

Lisburn. The sum of £350 was taken at the collection.

Members of the congregation who had travelled some distance were entertained to lunch at the home of Mr. Heaney. (Lisburn Standard 29 November 1890.)

The newly created Gaelic Athletic Association used a field at Blaris for football, linking the Catholic population of Lisburn with this area. In the second Ulster football final, played at Blaris in 1890, Armagh Harps beat Owen Roe O'Neill's of Cookstown (Tír Eoghain). (The Story of Gaelic Games in Ulster - Cardinal Tomás Ó Fiaich.)

The agent of the Wallace estate, E.L. Capron visited Lisburn at the request of the tenants to discuss the purchase of their holdings. An entertainment was held at Ballymacarrick night school consisting of songs, recitations and readings. Father Macauley, the respected parish priest (title as parish priest incorrect - author) addressed the audience and directed his attention chiefly to the boys attending the evening classes, by urging on them the necessity of regularly attending to study in the winter period of the year. (Irish News December 1890.)

1891

February Rev. M. McCashin was informed by the Town Commissioners, Railway Street, Lisburn that the Chapel Hill cemetery, behind the church, had to close under the Public Health Act.

June Rev. Mark McCashin was presented with a new missal by his sincere friend Very Rev. P. O'Neill, Downpatrick. (Parish archives)

Michael Hussey, an Irish speaker from Kerry, was appointed as principal of St Patrick's National School.

July

The Nuns of the Sacred Heart.—Last week the Convent of this Order at Lisburn was thronged by guests, the occasion being the annual pupils' day preparatory to their leaving for their homes. In the unavoidable absence of the Most Rev. Dr McAlister, Bishop of the Diocese of Down and Connor, the Very Rev. Mark McCashin, P.P., the spiritual guide to the convent, presided.

After some musical exercises of an instrumental character had been given by the pupils, the prizes were distributed to those successful by the Rev. Father McCashin who expressed himself to his young hearers as much pleased with their progress during the year—mentally, morally and physically. The Rev. gentleman's observations were received with much enthusiasm by the young ladies. Several pupils of this college have obtained certificates from the London College of Music. (The Tablet 1 August 1891.)

1892

7 March The funeral of Patrick Gallery (46), who had died at his brother's home on the Dublin Road, took place at St Patrick's. He had been employed for a number of years at Barbour's Mill and had spent several years as book-keeper and confidential clerk at the Barbour Flax Spinning Company in Paterson, New Jersey in the United States. The cortege described as numerous, respectable and representative included mourners from across the business community in Lisburn. Rev. Lennon and Rev. Crolly officiated at the funeral service. (Lisburn Standard 12 March 1892.)

A new school for Magheragall was erected close to the church and opened in 1892. A house for the teacher was attached to the school. The cost of the church, school and teacher's residence, stable and front wall cost the Parish of Lisburn about £1,100. (Lisburn Bazaar Book 1906)

18 July With the sanction of his Lordship, the Most Very Rev. Dr McAllister, a Retreat conducted by Very Rev. John Naughton S.J. was given in the Convent of the Sacred Heart of Mary in Lisburn. (Freeman's Journal 24 June 1892.)

1893

Rev. C. Malone: July 1893-March 1896
Rev. J. O'Boyle: July 1893-November 1895
Rev. J. O'Boyle (future Canon): July 1893 – December 1895 (headstone)

June

In the middle of broad daylight, at the hour of one o'clock on Sunday an attempt was made on the life of the Rev. Mother of the Lisburn Convent. One could scarcely conceive that such a dastardly outrage would be committed in Darkest Africa. The facts of the case are as follows. The parlour window of the convent (which looks out onto the street) was raised half up for ventilation purposes. The Rev. Mother was engaged in the parlour at the hour of one o'clock. Suddenly there was thrown through the window a large butcher's hook with three prongs, weighing a pound and a half. It fell on the floor without doing any harm. It was evidently aimed at the nun but fortunately missed its mark, owing to its being impeded in its passage by the window curtains. Whoever threw the missile at once scampered off. Whether the hook itself may lead to the detection of the dastardly scoundrel who threw it remains to be seen. (Irish News June 1893.)

1 July Wellington Young, Solicitor, 25 Chichester Street, Belfast wrote to Rev. McCashin to advise him that complaints had been made to Lisburn Town Commissioners regarding interments taking place in the cemetery at the rear of the church. Because of overcrowding corpses were not being buried at the correct depth. He said that the courts had instructed him that they must object to any further interments there. Reference was made to ground granted to the Church by Lady Wallace for a new cemetery.

August Dr Samuel Musgrave, Drumglass House, Belfast bequeathed £100 to the parish priest in Lisburn and similar sums of money to a number of other churches in Lisburn. (Belfast News Letter 10 August 1893) Dr S. Musgrave Sn had been a doctor in Lisburn (see reference 1861). His son also Samuel (1819-1893) was born in Lisburn.

September Jas. Jefferson, Medical Officer of Health, recommended that a field at the rear of the parochial house which had been identified by Rev. McCashin as the new Catholic cemetery should not be used for that purpose as it was too close to dwelling houses.

1894

A Sunday School was held in the home of Mrs Mulholland of Edenhill (Magheramesk). From an initial group of four or five individuals in addition to Mrs Mulholland's family the numbers grew and Mrs Mulholland's parlour could not contain the people who came for informal devotions.
    Encouraged by the number of people attending Rev. McCashin decided

to build a school for the Catholic children in the district. In the absence of a central location he bought a plot of land from Mr D. Mulholland and the school, which included accommodation for a teacher was built for £400. There was also a stable. Mass was celebrated in the school on the first Friday of the month.

12 July Clarke & McCartan, Solicitors, Ulster Building, Waring Street, Belfast provided authorisation to proceed with the new cemetery at the rear of the parochial house.

23 July With the sanction of his Lordship, the Most Very Rev. Dr McAlister, a Retreat for Ladies, conducted by Very Rev. J.A. Cullen S.J., was given in the Convent of the Sacred Heart of Mary in Lisburn. (Freeman's Journal 21 July 1894.)

September Rev. McCashin held a short service at the home of Mr John Smith J.P., 3 Maryville, Southwell Road, Bangor before his remains were removed for interment in Milltown cemetery, Belfast. Mr Smith had embraced the Catholic religion a short time before his death. Rev. McCashin had met Mr Smith when he visited his niece in Lisburn convent where he was secretly paying for her support. (Belfast News Letter 24 September 1894 & 14 January 1898.)

21 December A storm, the worst since 1839, struck Lisburn demolishing factory chimneys including that of Messers Barbour & Sons the largest chimney in Ireland. The boarders and nuns at the Sacred Heart of Mary convent escaped injury when a huge tree fell on the building knocking in a gable wall. (Freeman's Journal 24 December 1894.)

December Rev. McCashin along with Bishop Most Rev. Dr McAlister and other clergy were present at a meeting held in St Mary's Hall, Bank Street, Belfast for the purpose of furthering the erection of the new Mater Infirmorum Hospital. (The Mater Infirmorum (Mother of the Sick) Hospital had been serving the people of Belfast since it admitted its first patients on 1 November 1883, in premises on the Crumlin Road in Belfast, known as Bedeque House. It was initially founded by the Sisters of Mercy but has always treated patients without regard to class or creed. The new hospital opened in 1900). A total of £5,000 was received at this meeting, £2,500 from Bishop McAlister. (Irish News, 28 December 1894.)

In 1894 there were 2,657 Catholics in Lisburn, 21.7 % of the population of the town. (Hansard HC Debate 4 Jan/8 January 1894)

1895

3 October Bishop Henry wrote to Rev. McCashin granting permission to conduct religious services in the school near Moira. This was the recently built school at Magheramesk. (Diocesan records)

22 November The silver jubilee of the founding of the Convent of the Sacred Heart of Mary, Lisburn was celebrated by the community and the pupils. His Lordship Most Rev. Dr Henry, Lord Bishop of Down and Connor presided at the ceremony held in the chapel attached to the convent. Rev. Professor O'Loan preached. (Freeman's Journal 23 November 1895.)

Rev. M. Leahy: November 1895 – August 1898

PLANS FOR A NEW CATHOLIC CHURCH IN LISBURN

1896

1 March This was a time of renaissance in church building in Ireland and there was a degree of pressure to keep in line with other churches in the diocese. The existing church in Lisburn could not accommodate the numbers attending Sunday Mass. It was estimated that there were about 4,000 Catholics in Lisburn at that time. (An overestimate). The estimated cost of a new church was £14,000 and this sum would have to be raised by voluntary subscription.

At six o'clock on the evening of Sunday 1 March a meeting was held under the chairmanship of Rev. McCashin to organise the building of a new parish church. He detailed the accounts for the parish over the preceding six years taking into account new buildings elsewhere in the parish and was £580 in debt. He was confident that this amount would be cleared with the receipt of coppers at the church doors, etc. He reminded those present that it was the pennies of the poor that ensured the success in a movement in which they were engaging.

A subscription list was formerly opened with Fr McCashin subscribing £100. Mr J.R. Mulholland also subscribed £100 and Mr McIlroy £50. A total of £658.10s was pledged at the meeting. It was agreed that the parish priest would organise a fortnightly collection through the town and suburbs. Messrs E. & J. Byrne, 4 Waring Street, Belfast were appointed as architects and the contract was awarded to Messrs H. Laverty & Sons, Cambridge Street, Belfast. (Lisburn Bazaar Book 1906.)

It always had been the intention of the architects to cap the tower of the new church with a spire 'rising to 170 ft.' but because of cost restraints the addition of the spire was postponed to a later date.

(Byrne E&J - B 78, 16 Jun 1900, 594; IB 42, 1 Jul 1900, 403; C.E.B. Brett, D. Dunleath, Historic Buildings…in the borough of Lisburn (UAHS, 1969), 7 (no. 7.)

Rev. John Rooney: August 1896 – February 1899
Rev. P. Mullan: August 1896 – July 1898

1897

11 March Bishop Henry wrote to Rev. McCashin detailing the order of fund raising events informing him that the first bazaar after the Mater Hospital Bazaar was for the Good Shepherd nuns to help build new accommodation.

Speaking at the annual distribution of prizes at the Convent of the Sacred Heart of Mary, Lisburn, the Most Rev. Dr Henry, Bishop of Down and Connor, said:

'The most important element in the education of the young is not to be found in proficiency in the accomplishments of the world, or in the knowledge of art, literature, and science, but in the knowledge and practice of religion. This element is, as it were, the very soul of Christian education. The highest authority has laid down the highest principle of all education when He said, 'Seek first the Kingdom of God and His justice and all these things shall be added unto you.' According to this principle Christians must be trained even from their earliest days to regard everything in this world as subordinate to the attainment of their immortal destiny. Hence the Church the mother and mistress of all men, can never sanction any system of education—primary,

intermediate, or university—which would exclude the teaching and practice of religion from its curriculum. Religion must enter into the daily life of every Christian, whether at home or at school, and be the motive of his thoughts and acts. Some who profess Christianity would confine the teaching and practice of religion to the home and the church, and shut it out of school or college. Logically this is to train up a generation that will consider religion good for the home and the church, but not for the practical business of life. Take away religion from the practical business of life and morality will soon follow. When the morality of a people is gone even their physical condition will before long degenerate, while their intellectual attainments will only serve to guide them to deeper depths of vice and ruin.' (The Tablet archives 24 July 1897)

1898

January Rev. McCashin was in court when the brother of the late John Smith, a Belfast pawnbroker and jeweller, alleged that his brother was of unsound mind when he made his will which included a £300 legacy to Rev. McCashin and £1,000 for Masses to be said for the repose of his soul. This was strongly disputed by the solicitors who drew up the will. (Belfast Newsletter 14 January 1898)

Rev. John McLaverty: July 1898 – August 1899

The old church on Chapel Hill built by Rev. Magee in 1786 was demolished in 1898. It had stood as a landmark in Lisburn for 112 years. While excavating for the foundations for the new church a pike head was found and was presented to the parish priest Rev. McCashin as a memento of the rising in 1798. (Irish News, June 1898)

27 July The National Bank, Belfast wrote to Rev. McCashin approving, at the rate of 4%, an advance for the building of the new church to replace the existing church and construction work began. A temporary wooden structure at the parochial house was used as a place of worship while the new church was being built.

Speaking at the annual distribution of prizes at the Convent of the Sacred Heart of Mary, the Most Rev. Dr Henry, Bishop of Down and Connor, said that without religion development of character is an impossibility.

'Education is essentially religious. Without religion there may be instruction, but such instruction is not education for a Christian.' (The Tablet archives 23 July 1898.)

1899

Sunday 23 April For the first time since the Reformation Mass was celebrated in the school for the Catholics of Maghaberry. Mass continued to be celebrated there on Sundays and Holy Days.

1 August Rev. Daniel McEvoy (January 1899-August 1899) was transferred from Lisburn to Glenavy parish.

Rev A. J. Neeson: August 1899-September 1900.

Drumbo had a temporary church from 20 September 1896 to 16 April 1899. It was erected on the grounds of the Belfast Water Commissioners at Carryduff for Catholic navvies working at the Knockbracken reservoir at that location. Built as a temporary school for the workers' children it was recognised as such by the Commissioners of National Education and the teacher Miss Agnes Smith was provided with the usual class salary. Mass was later celebrated at a branch of the Belfast Asylum at Purdysburn and Dr Graham, the Medical Superintendent of the Asylum, gave permission for the Catholic servants in the district to attend Mass. The first Mass at Purdysburn was celebrated by Father A. J. Neeson on 24 June 1900.

He was later parish priest of Kircubbin from November 1913 to the time of his death on 9 December 1943. (History - St. Mary Star of the Sea, Killyleagh.)

20th Century

1900

8 June The relationship between Rev. McCashin and his bishop was frosty at best. Two days before the formal opening of the new church in Lisburn Bishop Dr Henry wrote to Rev. McCashin to say that John Rooney was going through Belfast collecting funds for the church in Lisburn and he regarded McCashin's action as highly reprehensible in view of recent events in this city. To emphasise his displeasure he wrote,'I hereby prohibit you to appoint him as a collector on Sunday next.' (Diocesan records)

The bishop was of the opinion that collections in Belfast should not be diverted from support for the Mater Hospital.

10 June The new Lisburn parish church, St Patrick's, built at a cost of £13,000 by Messers H. Laverty and Sons, was formally opened on a beautiful sunny Sunday. The church was blessed by Dr Henry and the sermon was preached by Dr Healy, Bishop of Clonfert and later Archbishop of Tuam. Work on the new building had started in spring of 1898 under the direction of Rev. Mark McCashin.

The description of the finished church was described in the 'Irish News' of 11 June 1900.

'The church is built of white Scrabo stone and Scotch red stone with the inside lining of 9 inches of brick and cement. The church is 140 feet long by 64 feet wide which is divided into nave and aisles by a colonnade of Scotch stone with Aberdeen granite introduced, the chancel being defined by a rich grouping of polished granite, mixed in colour by Cork red and Galway green, from caps of which the chancel arch springs. The height from floor to ceiling is 50 feet, the roof over being treated in 'groining.' The entire floor of the body of the church is laid with white and black mosaic work. Other reports stated that the aisle, nave and sanctuary was in terrodzo (terrazzo - author) in warm tints. The seating, Communion rails and organ gallery are made in polished pitch pine.'

The Ulster Architectural Society commented;

'1900; on site of earlier church of 1794. The exterior rather disconcerting: the striped spire (later) grey stone with paler dressings, but below roof-level, grey stone with red sandstone dressings; an uncomfortable change of gear. The interior much better, lofty and dignified simplified Romanesque with very robust capital carvings; good high altar and reredos; painted circular lunettes of saints, with full-lengths of Saints Malachy and Columbanus flanking East Window.

The ornate artwork on the walls were later painted over during the renovation of the church by Rev. Sean Rogan in the 1990s. The intricate tapestries of Saints Malachy and Columbanus were rescued from a rubbish skip by a parishioner and preserved. (Pat McHugh)

The lower, rather plain, main windows in the church were later replaced during Canon O'Boyle time as parish priest. The stained glass windows were designed and installed by the world famous Franz Mayer company of Munich and London. A number of windows were dedicated to the memory of the parents or relatives of parishioners. Very Rev. James Canon O'Boyle had a window dedicated to the memory of his parents, Peter and Sara O'Boyle; evidence that the present windows are not the originals.

A large number of people from Belfast attended the dedication ceremony and a special train had been organised leaving the Great Northern Railway station at 11:20 a.m.. The church was crowded as High Mass was celebrated. In his homily Most Rev. Dr Healy, addressing the congregation from the pulpit paid tribute to 'the substantial help that many persons of different creeds have given to the parish priest to build this church.' Making an oblique reference to the political situation he said, ' We seek no favour, ask no privilege. We demand only fair play, and we are perfectly willing to carry out the great maxim of the gospel to do to others, as we would have others to do us. But there must be no ascendancy, no dictation, no special privileges to one church or creed. There is no meaning in crying 'No surrender' when there is nothing left to surrender; no meaning in crying 'No Popery' when popery holds its own in spite of you. Ascendancy is dead and any attempts to galvanize it into existence will neither be pleasant or profitable.' He saw the donations from people from different churches as a good omen for the future.

St Joseph's Choir under the direction of Mr T.H. Picton participated in the ceremony.

The collection in the church amounted to £2,260.

Among the many priest who attended were the local clergy:
Very Rev. Mark McCashin PP, Rev. F. Digney CC, Rev. A. Neeson CC and
Rev. H.J Murray.

Rev H. Murray: March 1900-August 1903
Rev C. McFaul September 1900-September 1901

1901

The Census of Ireland shows that on the night of Sunday 31 March 1901
Rev. McCashin (57) and curates Rev. Arthur Neeson (41), Henry Murray
(26) and Charles Edward McFaul (27) were resident at the parochial house,
48 Longstone Street, Also resident were housekeepers Mary Duggan (30)
and Elizabeth Campbell (40).

In 1901 there was a spate of church robberies throughout Ireland. St
Patrick's Chapel was visited by thieves, who effected an entrance to the
sacristy, and proceeded to ransack the place, bursting open a press, from
which they took coppers to the amount of about 2s. l0d. The contents of a
cash-box the amount is not known were also abstracted, the box apparently
having been opened with a skeleton key. Burnt matches and a piece of
candle were found on the floor. The visitors made good their escape before
daylight, and up to the present their whereabouts has not been discovered.
(Priests & People - Michael J. F. McCauley 1902.)

A framed certificate from Bishop Henry - Henricus to the Ecclesia Sancti
Patricii dated 5 Julii 1901 to Marcus McCashin is held in the parish archives.

June Mr Trew was preaching in Market Square when he made derogatory
remarks about Roman Catholics. Mr McGrogan, 'a respectable looking
Catholic,' objected to the comments being made and was arrested, for his
own safety, and charged with being drunk and disorderly. In court Mr
Young, the town solicitor, asked why Trew was not summoned for using
incentive language and said that he should be and that he would conduct
the prosecution. The case against Mr McGrogan was dismissed. (Northants
Evening Telegraph 14 June 1901.)

Rev C. O'Loan: September 1901-September 1905.
Rev D. McWilliams: September 1901-February 1904.

1902

8 February The relationship between Rev. McCashin and the bishop had not improved when the bishop, in response to a letter from Rev. McCashin, wrote from Chichester Park stating that he could not say when it would be convenient to give permission to make another public appeal for funds to reduce the debt in Lisburn parish.

25 February Rev. McCashin wrote to the Bishop Rev. Dr. Henry to advise him that the Catholic population of the Parish of Blaris was 3,720.

All the school buildings were given over to the Boys' School on Chapel Hill and the girls relocated to the Convent School in Castle Street, which was named Castle Street Female National School. The school, grant aided by the National Board of Education, was built to accommodate 224 girls and around the turn of the century there were 24 nuns in the convent. (Priests & People - Michael J. F. McCauley 1902)

It was replaced by St Joseph's Primary School in the 1960s and later became co-educational.

The Ulster Architectural Society commented:

Opened as Convent 1902, but partly earlier; stucco buildings of 1870s in style of William Batt; and incorporating an earlier house. Chapel, 1967; McLean & Forte. A strikingly original and wholly successful design. Due to shortage of space, the chapel is perched in mid-air on angled concrete columns, at second-storey level, overlooking the Castle Gardens and the wooded valley. The ground floor contains school accommodation; above it there is a paved first-floor play-space, with a geometrically coffered ceiling, amidst the columns; on top, as naturally as could be, rests the chapel. The design makes superb use of a steeply-sloping and difficult site, and while entirely contemporary harmonises admirably with the early 19th century frontage buildings.

Inside, the chapel is equally successful: there is admirable abstract blue-and-clear stained glass: the altar is indirectly lit by a red glass window: there is an excellent geometrical ceiling: the walls are plainest white, with simple

Stations of the Cross in pale carved wood: the overall effect is of a rich simplicity, stopping short of Puritanism.

Mass was celebrated every day at the Convent.

An article appeared under the heading 'Irish Nuns for America'.

> Ireland may be poor and Ireland may be unfortunate, but Ireland still continues to send out into all the world missionaries of the Catholic faith. The Waterford News of recent date contained the following: "On Saturday last twelve Irish nuns of the order of the Sacred Heart left the Ferrybank, Waterford convent, for America, in various portions of which they will pursue their sacred calling. Amongst the devout ladies who have thus gone forth in the cause of holy religion was Sister Elenora, sister of Mr. Thomas Shiel, Edenderry, King's County; four of the nuns hail from Waterford, three from Lisburn, and four or five from Seaforth, Liverpool, where the good Sister Elenora has been for the past fifteen years, as well as in Lisburn and the motherhouse of the order in France. We wish these devoted Christian missionaries Godspeed." (The Sacred Heart Review 1 February 1902 Boston College)

Sunday 3 August A train carrying women and girls, members of the Sacred Heart Society of Lisburn, when returning from an excursion to Warrenpoint, through Portadown came under attack from stone throwers. (Hansard HC Deb 08 August 1902)

> A young Irish Franciscan lay brother, Fra Diego from Lisburn, volunteered for the Province of Holy Land, and was sent to Port Said. Burning with zeal this good Brother set to work with a will. He first attacked the abuses in the hospital, stopped the distribution of tracts and attempted proselytism by appealing to the good faith of the matron and doctors. He went aboard the King's ships in his humble Franciscan habit, and sandalled feet. Naturally the men were a little shy at first, and some there were to laugh and jeer; but the officers treated him invariably with respect. The men he soon won by his zeal and unfailing tact. The result is the little church of St Eugenie is crowded on Sunday mornings with Bluejackets, who inspire respect into the whole population by their fine manly bearing. (The Tablet 30 August 1902.)

7 September Among the thousands who attended the Newcastle Feis (in a field now occupied by East Down Institute) was Rev. H. Murray. He recalled travelling from Lisburn to Newcastle in 'a brave-open topped horse cart'. Born 12 October 1874 Rev. Murray was later parish priest at Killough

1925-1933 and then became Canon Murray PP, Newcastle until 1955. (downgaa.net/archive & Murrays from Slievenisky))

1903

12 February Bishop Henry again wrote to Rev. McCashin informing him, 'I cannot see my way to give my permission for an appeal so soon after the opening of your church.' (Diocesan records.)

Reilly's Trench Church was refurbished c.1903 when a new altar was installed. New windows, a new floor and seats were provided and a small gallery built for the choir. The school and the teacher's residence were refurbished in 1903. (Lisburn Bazaar Book 1906.)

1904

12 February St Joseph's Hall, Lisburn was crowded, the assemblage being a record one. The attraction was a dramatic and musical entertainment by the Children of Mary. (Catholic Northwest Progress 1 April 1904)

21 March Michael Hussey, (38) principal of St Patrick's National School died. He had been boarding with widow Margaret Armstrong at 24 Railway Street, Lisburn (Irish Census 1901). He was a native of Cahirciveen, County Kerry and had been principal at Glenravel, where he had met Rev. McCashin, the parish priest at Glenravel. He later asked Mr. Hussey to take on the role as principal of St Patrick's National School in Lisburn.

Mr John Fitzpatrick was appointed as principal to replace Mr. Hussey.

17 April Sixty extra police had to be drafted into Lisburn to prevent violence by objectors to a hurling match being played at Blaris. Charles Craig M.P. for Antrim South raised the matter in the House of Commons on 20 April stating that Blaris is the centre of a Protestant district and the playing of hurley matches on Sunday offends the religious feelings of the inhabitants. (Hansard 20 April 1904.)

The Orange ruffians of Lisburn made murderous attacks on the Peter O'Neill Crowley Hurling team of Belfast and on the Lisburn Teeling team when playing on a field at Blaris. An enormous crowd of Orangemen assembled at the field, but despite their threatening attitude, the game was played in face of strong opposition and interference to the finish. When the teams were returning to the town, under escort, they and the police were subjected to a fierce fusillade of stones and in the scuffle and the numerous baton charges many persons were injured. Several of the police sustained ugly wounds and altogether the riot was described by the police as the worst they had been in. A great amount of malicious injury was done to property. Hay ricks and hedges were set ablaze, gates were pulled down to make weapons with which to attack the hurlers and during the most wicked part of the riot shots were fired by the mob. A solicitor, who by request, was assisting the police to turn the mob was badly injured by a policeman's baton. (Freeman's Journal 18 April 1904.)

It was reported that fighting took place during the game and about a dozen policemen and one Belfast detective were seriously injured. The County Inspector of Police was struck with a stone and a large number of civilians received ugly wounds during baton charges. A neighbouring house was converted into a temporary hospital where the wounded were treated. Those seriously injured were taken to County Antrim Infirmary. Several times during the game the crowd endeavored to encroach upon the field and stop the game from proceeding, and on one occasion when the ball got among the spectators, a fight ensued before the players obtained possession of it. (The Teesdale Mercury 20 April 1904.)

18 April What was described as an organised Orange mob assembled in Lisburn and attacked the Catholic presbytery and smashed the windows of Catholic traders in the town. (Hansard 19 April 1904.)

19 April A drumming party, followed by a considerable crowd marched into Lisburn from the Maze district. Only a few police were stationed in the town and they were powerless to interfere with the crowd which began a brisk stone throwing attack in Chapel Hill, smashing the windows in the Catholic chapel, parochial house, occupied by Father Mark McCashin and St Joseph's Hall. The windows of three Catholic publicans in the locality were also broken. No arrests were made. (Freeman's Journal 20 April 1904.)

21 April There was a renewal of Orange rioting in Lisburn. A drumming party, carrying a Union Jack paraded the Roman Catholic part of the town and after a stoning party numbering a hundred youths rushed through the

Longstone, smashing windows in the priest's house, St Joseph's Hall and the Catholic church. The dwellings of Catholic residents were also smashed. The police do not appear to have made even an effort to arrest these ignorant and bigoted Orangemen and law breakers. (Catholic Northwest Progress, May 20 1904.)

1905

Sister M.L. Dempsey was the Superioress at Lisburn Convent.

1906

1 January A bazaar was held in St Joseph's Hall to raise funds to help clear a debt of £9,000 incurred in the erection of St Patrick's Church, parochial house, several schools and teachers' residences. 'Lisburn Bazaar Book 1906' was produced and besides providing details of the various stalls and the people manning them contains some of the historical information listed in this book. The bazaar raised £4,884.00 and a few thousands more were added by donations, charity sermons and parish collections. (Catholic Year Book 1934.)
Mr J.R.T. Mulholland J.P. declared the bazaar open. (Freeman's Journal 20 November 1906.)

Curates: Rev. Jas. McGrath C.C., Rev. J.F. Fullen C.C., Rev. John Macaulay C.C.

The side chapel of St Anthony in St Patrick's was the gift of William McIlroy Esq. Hilden Cottage. (This chapel was located in the small vestibule which is now the side entrance to the church. It has since been removed and there is no trace that the altar ever existed.)

In 1906 it was considered that a church and graveyard would be necessary to meet the needs of the Catholic community in Maghaberry in the not very distant future.

Miss Maggie Downey was the teacher at Reilly's Trench National School in 1906.

An important decision was given by Mr. Justice Madden in the Nisi Prius Court in a Probate suit, McCashin and another v. Hamilton. It was a suit brought by the executors of the late John Hamilton, flesher and cattle dealer, 6, Longstone Street, Lisburn, who died on October 1, 1905. The executors were the Very Rev. Mark McCashin, P.P., Lisburn, and the Rev. Father Neeson, P.P. (sic). The will was disputed by Mr. Wm. Hamilton, of Lisburn, on the usual statutory grounds, and alleged undue influence on the part of the Very Rev. Mark McCashin. By the will the testator appointed as executors the Very Rev. Mark McCashin, P.P., Lisburn, and the Rev. A. Neeson, C.C., Braid. He bequeathed Father McCashin too for the celebration of Masses for the repose of his soul, a sum of £50 for the celebration of Masses for the repose of the souls of deceased's relatives, and £50 for the celebration of Masses for the repose of the souls of his wife's relatives. He bequeathed to Father McCashin, or to the parish priest for the time being of Lisburn, £100 for the celebration of Masses for his wife's soul, to be said immediately after her death. He bequeathed £10 to his brother William, and £100 to his executor, the Rev. A. Neeson.

The will proceeded to say:

'I direct that, as soon as convenient after my death, the entire of my assets shall be realised, and the proceeds invested in such securities as my executors shall think proper, the income thereof to be paid to my wife; or, in case she should predecease me, I hereby bequeath the entire of my residuary estate to the said Very Rev. Mark McCashin, same to be applied by him in the erection of a spire on St. Patrick's Church, Lisburn, or in building a high altar in said chapel. I empower my said executor, the Very Rev. Mark McCashin, if he thinks proper, to apply the said residuary estate for such other charitable purpose or purposes in the diocese of Down and Connor as he shall in his uncontrolled discretion select or appoint. In case any of the legacies or bequests herein contained should lapse by the operation of law, I hereby, in such event, bequeath the amount of such legacy or bequest to the Very Rev. Mark McCashin for his own use absolutely.'

After the hearing of the case the jury came into court with the finding that the testator knew and approved of the contents of the will, with the exception of the last clause, namely, that which provided that in the event of any of the legacies for Masses failing, the residue would become the property of the Rev. McCashin. The jury found that the testator did not understand the meaning of that clause. Mr. Justice Madden said he would decree probate of the will with the exception of that clause. (The Tablet 26 May 1906.)

6 March Mr Joseph Devlin M.P. addressed a large and representative meeting in St Joseph's Hall, Lisburn under the auspices of the Lisburn Catholic Club. Very Rev. McCashin P.P. presided. (Freeman's Journal 6 March 1906.)

23 November Their excellences the Lord Lieutenant and Countess Aberdeen arrived in Lisburn having motored from Antrim. The object of the visit was to inspect the Nicholson memorial tablet in the Cathedral. The countess, as a child, had lived in a house now occupied by the site of the convent and after being greeted by Rev. Pounden at the Cathedral they called at the Convent of the Sacred Heart of Mary. (Freeman's Journal 23 November 1906.)

1907

23 January Bishop Henry wrote to Rev. McCashin approving the establishment in his parish of a branch of the Association of the Ladies of Charity of St Vincent de Paul and reminded him of the necessity to have this branch affiliated with the Central Council in Paris. (Diocesan records)

21 April Rev. F. Louis Butler, a well known preacher formerly of Dominick Street, Dublin, opened a Mission in the parish church, Lisburn. The parish of Lisburn is one of the largest in Ireland and is about sixteen miles in length and is six, and in some places seven miles, in breath. During the mission a number of priests from Belfast and the surrounding parishes were busily engaged hearing confessions. Father Mark McCashin said that the Mission was one of the most successful he had ever witnessed. (Freeman's Journal 2 May 1907.)

July A somewhat remarkable meeting was held recently at Lisburn in furtherance of the cause of primary education. The meeting complained of the inadequacy of treatment received by Ireland from Government in the matter of education as compared with England or Scotland. It stated that the salaries of all grades of teachers should be increased by a least 50 per cent, such increment being annual and automatic and that pensions equal two-thirds salary should be given on 35 years' service for men; 30 years for women. These demands are not so remarkable in themselves as is the fact that they were advocated by a thoroughly mixed platform. The resolutions were proposed by Captain Craig M.P., an Ulster Orange member and seconded by the Rev. Father McCashin P.P.

For once in this matter Orange and Green sank their differences to promote a common cause. (Irish News, July 1907.)

24 September When Annie Smith entered the Convent of the Sacred Heart she disposed of what ever money she had. She cashed in shares in the Great Northern Railway giving her sister £50 and the remainder to Mother Loyola, superioress of the convent (Diocesan records.)

1909

March Susan O'Hagan, at the grand age of 106 years passed away at her home at Smithfield, Lisburn.

In 1811, when only nine years of age, she entered the service of the Hall family at Hilltown, County Down and remained with them through an unbroken period of 97 years. A devout Catholic, she frequented the Sacraments and in her last moments was assiduously attended by Very Rev. Mark McCashin P.P. V.F. She possessed a retentive memory and recalled the reception accorded to the soldiers returning from the battle of Waterloo. (Irish News 4 March 1909.)

24 May At a very largely attended meeting of Division 405 of the A.O.H. Lisburn a resolution was unanimously passed that they gave their entire support to the United Irish League and the Irish Parliamentary Party, under the guidance of Mr. Redmond. (Freeman's Journal 28 May 1909.)

November At a meeting of Lisburn Board of Guardians in December the matter of the religion of a child was raised. Patrick Smith of Belfast Workhouse had stated that a little girl Lillie Dunbar, the illegitimate daughter of his deceased wife, who had died in Lisburn Workhouse, had been transferred to the custody of the Lisburn Board of Guardians. He said that the child had been baptised by a Catholic priest in Lurgan and his wife's last words to him before she died were that he should look after the child and when he found himself unable to support her he should hand her over to Rev. Mark McCashin, parish priest to be brought up in the faith in which she had been baptised. The matter was referred to a committee to investigate and report. (Freeman's Journal 1 December 1909.)

1910

10 January The entire Fegan family perished in a fire which gutted their two-storey house at 54 Bridge Street, Lisburn. Lamplighter David Fegan (49), his wife Sarah Ann Fegan (37) and four children, Patrick (8), David (6), James Edward (4) and Mary Jane (2) all lost their lives. Three men also lodged in the house but they made their escape through a back window virtually untouched by the flames that engulfed the house. After a funeral mass at St Patrick's the family were buried in a single grave in Holy Trinity cemetery. (Ulster Star.)

14 August The church at Magheramesk opened. Before that Mass had been celebrated in the schoolhouse.

Miss Agnew was the teacher at Magheramesk National School in 1910. (Ros Davies' Co. Down, Northern Ireland Family History Research Site.)

December The houses of Lisburn Catholics were attacked during the East Down elections in December 1910. (Freeman's Journal 5 July 1912.)

John McManus, 31 Chapel Hill, was sexton of St Patrick's Church. The curates were Revs. Fullen and Monaghan. (Ulster Towns Directory 1910.)

1911

8 February Rev. Michael O'Malley who had served as a curate in Lisburn died at Randalstown where he had been parish priest. (Freeman's Journal 8 February 1911.)

April The Census of Ireland shows that on the night of Sunday 2 April Rev. Mark McCashin (67) and housekeeper Elizabeth Campbell (50) were resident at 48 Longstone Street. In the previous census all residents in the parochial house were listed on a single return but in 1911 separate returns were completed for Patrick Rafferty (34) curate and housekeeper Catherine Ward (29), originally from County Carlow and for James B. Murray (28) curate and for Michael P. Hayes (33) originally from County Limerick.

The real condition of things, political and religious, in Ulster, reports 'The Freeman's Journal,' was explained at a nationalist meeting in Edinburgh by Mr. Valentine Gill, a Protestant belonging to County Antrim, who marvelled at sensible men in Britain or anywhere else paying the smallest attention to the claptrap emanating from certain unionists in the North of Ireland. He belonged, he said, to near Lisburn—a regular hotbed of Toryism—and could guarantee that a Catholic would not be allowed in an Orange Lodge or at an Orange meeting there as he had been received by the members of the United Irish League. That in itself showed the intolerance of the Orange body on the one hand, and the toleration of the nationalists on the other. He was brought up in a parish where there were three Orange Lodges, and they could well understand it was not a healthy place for a Home Rule plant. Ulstermen were not, he assured them, what the unionist party represented them to be; but he admitted there was a section or clique who would not let the native Irish have a say in their country's affairs if they could help it. They would appoint to public positions anybody before they would have a Catholic. There was no possibility of anyone getting a post of any consequence n Belfast except he was a Freemason or an Orangeman. (The Tablet 22 April 1911)

1912

Tuesday 25 June Two 'motor brakes' set out from the Sacred Heart Convent to take a group of eighty girls aged between five to thirteen-years-old to the seaside at Ballyhornan in County Down. They were accompanied by three nuns. When the vehicles reached Young Street they came under a fusillade of stones from loyalists in the area.

An ambush was organised for their return journey at the Ballynahinch Road in Lisburn and the children again were cursed at and stoned. Despite the crowd having gathered and that there were about 40 police in the town only one policeman was on duty in the area. The children and the nuns came under a sustained attack from Young Street to the Union Bridge. Not satisfied with the sectarian attack on innocent children the crowd formed an improvised band and marched to the convent where they sang loyalist songs. Although a police barracks was only 200 yards away the police did not intervene. (Irish News June 1912.) The incident went unreported by the local unionist newspaper, the 'Lisburn Standard'.

29 June In contrast when, on 29 June at Castledawson in County Londonderry, where an Ancient Order of Hibernians parade attacked a parade of Presbyterian school children the unionist press devoted headlines and many column inches to the incident.

In a failure by police to anticipate the potential for violence when a parade of Hibernians returning from a Home Rule demonstration in Maghera would meet head-on with a Protestant Sunday School parade in Castledawson there was a violent clash.

Whitehouse Presbyterian church had organised its annual excursion to Castledawson and after assembling in a field about five hundred, mainly women and children, led by Tyrone Flute Band and carrying a union flag marched to the railway station. It was claimed that one of the Hibernians grabbed the union flag and this started a riot, which was joined by local Protestants. (Lisburn Standard 6 July 1912.)

Catholic school children were attacked in Lisburn the day after. (Orange parades: The Politics of Ritual, Tradition and Control - Dominic Bryan, Pluto Press.)

Protestant workers in Belfast's shipyards expelled 2,500 Catholic workers in retaliation for the attack on the Sunday School parade. (Attacks on Catholics continued for four weeks, the Castledawson incident being used as a pretext for anti-Home Rule rioting.) (Hansard 31 July 1912.)

The number of pupils at Lisburn Boys' School topped the 200 mark. (St. Aloysius Silver Jubilee booklet.)

6 July Rev. McCashin enclosed a cheque in a letter to Mr Devlin for the Parliamentary Fund adding

> ' I see you are passing through a strenuous fight. I hope we are nearing the end of the struggle. It is consoling and encouraging to see how well the people in every part of the country are standing to their guns and backing up the representatives. With kindest regards - I am sincerely yours M. McCashin. (Freeman's Journal 15 July 1912.)

1913

The telephone number of the parochial house was Lisburn 59.

2 July In a House of Commons debate unionist M.P. Peter Kerr-Smiley asked the Chief Secretary the names of the Roman Catholic female and infant national schools in the County of Antrim which are now in the charge of nuns, and from which graded national teachers were dismissed to make way for the nuns.....

Mr Birrell replied;

> *'The Commissioners of National Education inform me that the only schools in the County of Antrim which are now in charge of nuns are St Mary's Convent National School, Larne, and Lisburn Convent National School. There were three lay teachers in the former school and one in the latter, all of whom received appointments in other national schools. Both these schools are paid by capitation grants, and the teachers are not, therefore, required to possess the qualifications laid down in the Commissioners' Rules. The nuns of St Mary's Convent have, however, procured certificates from the English Education Department. There are no lay assistant teachers employed in these schools, and the Commissioners are not aware that there are any schools of the kind referred to in the last paragraph of the question.'* (HC Deb 02 July 1913 vol. 54 cc1885-6W.)

Under the heading 'Religious Liberty as Understood in Darkest Ulster' the 'Sacred Heart Review' wrote:

The idea of religious liberty that prevails wherever Orangeism is strong is well set forth in an incident which recently occurred in Lisburn, Ireland. A priest intending to visit a dying woman who had been one of his flock, and who he had no reason to believe had changed her faith since he had last seen her, was prevented by militant Protestant neighbors from approaching the sick woman. 'When I arrived on the scene,' writes the priest (the Rev. M. P. Hayes) 'and when it was discovered I was a priest, I was ordered to leave the house at once. I was then informed for the first time that she was a Protestant, and that within the past few days she was visited by a local parson, notwithstanding the fact that, at her own request, I have been attending her for her religious duties for the past three years. I remonstrated with the threatening bystanders on the cruelty and injustice of depriving the poor woman of the ministrations of the clergyman to whom she belonged, especially now in her dying condition. My remonstration was of no avail. I was ordered again to leave the house, or if not I would be put out by force. As a last resort I appealed to the testimony of a neighbor who lived opposite, and who saw me call many a time, that I was in attendance on her for years. The fact was denied, and my allusion to the house opposite very nearly brought a male inhabitant to strike me. I, judging in the circumstances that discretion was the better part of valor, returned to Lisburn. I requisitioned there the services of three policemen to guard me in this the discharge of my duty. Their services were cheerfully and quickly offered. In company with them I returned to the house again, and, with their needful assistance, I was enabled to proceed to give the last rites of the Church to the dying woman, amidst the shrieks, maledictions and other unmentionable language of an infuriated mob. Upon taking our departure a cry was raised that they would have their revenge on me some Sunday morn when I would pass that way to an outside church of the parish. For the present I desire to make no comment on this most scandalous affair. I merely ask you to publish the facts that the public may judge of the condition of affairs in this region of so called religious liberty and equality.'

Occasionally we read in non-Catholic papers of Protestant missionaries who are hindered in their religious work by 'benighted Catholics' in Mexico and other Catholic countries. But we are quite sure there will be no comment by our Protestant contemporaries on such an occurrence as this in that part of Ireland where the exponents of the 'pure Gospel' hold undisputed sway. (The Sacred Heart Review 30 August 1913, Boston College.)

1914

The following curates were serving in Lisburn in 1914; Rev. M.P. Hayes, Rev. J. Walsh and Rev J. B. Murray. (Extract from 'The Grand Bazaar and Fancy Fare' - New Schools Crumlin, Oct 1914.)

1915

After 1915 the official title of the Convent School became Lisburn Convent/National/public Elementary/Primary School. (Public Record Office of Northern Ireland, Belfast.)

17 March On St Patrick's Day the annual social and reunion of the parish of Lisburn was held and the occasion was used to pay tribute to the esteem and respect in which the distinguished pastor of Lisburn, the Very Rev. Mark McCashin P.P., was held by his parishioners and to signal their gratitude at his recovery from a severe illness. The tribute took the form of a beautiful illuminated album address and a splendid Enfield Coupe 10 h.p. two-seater car. Mr. Michael O'Shea presided.

A special guest was Mr Joseph Devlin M.P. who as part of his speech commented on Rev. McCashin's work for national progress and Catholic advancement and said that he hoped Fr McCashin would live to see an Irish Parliament in College Green and live for many years afterwards in a newer, brighter and happier era for the country he loves so well.

Rev. Joseph Boylan, an old Lisnagarvey man, said he was delighted to be present to do honour to their great and good old parish priest.

Rev. McCashin in his reply said that while he had been in hospital he had been on the brink of the grave. (Freeman's Journal 19 March 1915.)

21 May The following article was published in the 'Lisburn Standard'.

'No. 8 Platoon of the 11th. R.I. Rifles (South Antrim Volunteers) from Clandeboye, accompanied by the band, arrived in town in Monday afternoon for a week's recruiting in Lisburn and district. Quite a large crowd accompanied the band in its march round the town. As a result of two days' recruiting in Lisburn a very satisfactory number of recruits were sent on to Clandeboye on Tuesday evening. Broomhedge was visited on Wednesday, Aghalee and Ballinderry yesterday; to-day (Friday) the soldiers are at Brookhill, and they will finish up tomorrow in the vicinity of Ballymacash. The recruiting all over has been satisfactory, some particularly fine raw material having been unearthed in the country districts. Close on 200 recruits were secured for all branches of the service, the majority going to the Ulster Division. A goodly number of nationalists enlisted in the Irish Brigade, and on Wednesday evening the local company of the Irish National Volunteers had a farewell route march. The company numbering 120 strong, carrying rifles, marched out from St Joseph's Hall via the Longstone, away round by Halftowns, Blaris and home by the Dublin Road.'

11 June About six hundred men of the 11th Battalion of the Royal Irish Rifles who had been making a farewell parade in Lisburn, ending with tea in the cathedral schoolhouse, invited the Connaught Rangers (who were, coincidentally, receiving tea in St Joseph's Hall with new recruits) to join them for entertainment in Castle Gardens. The warmth of the occasion led the 'Lisburn Standard' to rejoice that 'at long last Lisburn stood united as one man in a common cause.' (Lisburn - The Town and its People, 1873-1973 Brian Mackey, Blackstaff Press, Belfast.)

At the end of the year the 'Lisburn Standard' published a 'Lisburn Churches Roll of Honour', listing the names of men from the town who were serving. Some 212, nearly one quarter of the total, were parishioners from Lisburn Roman Catholic Church. (Pat Geary's Great War Database, Lisburn and district.) This was a significant representation of Catholics in the armed forces as at that time as Catholics made up approximately ten per cent of the population of Lisburn.

Later the names of 266 Lisburn men who were killed during the war would be listed on the war memorial in Castle Street, Lisburn.

1916

19 October

Mr James Rice. J.P., died at his residence, Bow Street, Lisburn. Sorrow will be shared by the people of Lisburn of all creeds and classes, and will be keenly felt in commercial circles throughout the province.

In early life he entered the firm of Messrs. Wm. Barbour and Sons, Hilden, and eventually became head of the flax department, both there and at Courtrai, Belgium. A good many years ago he severed his connection with the concern, embarking in business for himself as flax merchant, his headquarters being in Hill Street, Belfast, where he carried on an extensive trade, and was well known in all the leading flax markets. Some years ago he was appointed a magistrate for the County Antrim, and while health permitted, sat at Lisburn, his adjudications being always characterised by impartiality, fairness and consideration. The late Mr Rice, who was unmarried, belonged to an old local family, being the son of the late Mr James Rice. He was a devout member of the congregation of St Patrick's Catholic Church, to which, as well as other organisations, he was a generous contributor. A most sympathetic, kind-hearted man, he was always ready to do a good turn for 'a friend in need,' and by many he will be greatly missed.

The funeral took place to Holy Trinity Cemetery, Lisburn, on Saturday at 2 o'clock. (Lisburn Standard 20 October 1916)

All sections of Lisburn's business community made up the large cortege which made its way from St Patrick's to Holy Trinity Cemetery where Rev. McCashin and Rev. Magowan officiated at the graveside. James' brother was Moses Rice and his nephews James, Edward, Fred and Thomas were present. James would later have his uncle remembered in a stained glass window in St Patrick's.

25 December On Christmas night over 300 attended the annual Lisburn Catholic Club dance in St Joseph's Hall. Music was provided by St Joseph's Orchestra which had been formed nine months earlier by Mr P. L. McManus. 'Plants, evergreens, tastefully arranged, and shaded lamps added charm to the scene.' Joseph Devenney, P. J. Fitzsimmons, John McLarnon and W. Gilmore officiated as M.C's. There was a break for tea at 11:00 p.m., provided by the ladies of the Dance Committee. Miss E. McMahon, Mr O'Hanlon, James Dornan and Mr P. Dickey, among others, provided 'a capital musical programme'. The dance continued 'to an advanced hour'. (Lisburn Standard 5 January 1917.)

1917

The increasing toll on the men from Lisburn who had gone off to fight in the Great War was listed as the Roll of Honour in the Lisburn Standard. The casualties of war were listed under Lisburn and district churches. Under the heading Lisburn Roman Catholic Church, Parish Priest Rev. Mark McCashin 35 Fallen, 8 Missing and 18 Prisoners of War were listed. (Lisburn Standard 28 December 1917.)

Among the war dead in Holy Trinity cemetery is W. J. Kelly, a Private (3091) in the Royal Irish Regiment who died on 25 July 1917.

1918

21 April By 1918 the Irish bishops had become so disillusioned with British intentions in Ireland that they ruthlessly opposed the introduction of conscription. Following a meeting in Maynooth the bishops under the presidency of Cardinal Logue ordered a national novena in honour of Our Lady of Lourdes and a special Mass to be said on 21 April in all churches and chapels in the country 'against conscription'.

The Irish Conscription Act, passed on 16 April 1918 was abandoned following a general strike on 23 April which brought government administration in the country to a standstill. (Catholicism in Ulster 1603-1983: An Interpretive History - Oliver Rafferty.)

14 October

The death took place on Monday of Mr Edward Donaghy, sen., Beechmount, Lisburn.

Mr Donaghy was the pioneer of the industrial concern of Messrs. E. Donaghy & Sons, a firm well known in Ireland and across the Channel. The factory in Graham Gardens, one of the largest in the country, is equipped with the most modern machinery. One of the branches is in North Street, Belfast, which is carried on by Mr Henry Donaghy, whose younger brother (Mr E. Donaghy, Jun., J.P.) is a managing director of the firm, and personally superintends the work at the manufactory. The eldest son (Mr Patrick Donaghy) is prominently known in commercial circles.

Just over two years ago Mr Donaghy had a very serious illness, and was confined to bed for a long period. His splendid constitution, however, stood him in good stead, and many people who then expected to be at his funeral in the course of a few days had instead the pleasure at meeting him at a social function in his honour, in connection with the firm of which he was the veteran founder and head. The social was held on Friday evening, 7 October 1916.

Mr. Daniel Mooney, to whom the toast was entrusted, during the course of an interesting speech said that he had been closely intimate with Mr Donaghy for a quarter of a century, and had at all times found him a thorough old gentleman. Everyone who knew him had got to respect him, not only for his social and other sterling qualities, but for his great commercial abilities as well.

He founded the business, and fought his way to the forefront of Irish manufacture, and was (at that time) the boot manufacturer in Ireland who held a War Office contract. Edward Donaghy stuck it through thick and thin, through good times and bad, and by determined striving and honest value had built up a business second to none. They in Lisburn were exceedingly proud of their grand old man.

Mr Donaghy replied in a characteristically humorous speech.

Taking to his bed some weeks ago, there was little hope, at his advanced age of nearly ninety years, of him making a second almost miraculous recovery, and the end came peacefully and not unexpectedly on Monday morning.

There was no more highly-respected citizen in Lisburn than the late Mr Donaghy. He was selected and nominated as an urban councillor, but could not see his way to accept the honour. He, however, accepted the position of poor-law guardian for the urban district, and displayed much wisdom and intelligence in the business transacted at the Board, which he regularly attended while health permitted. He was an affable, good-natured man, possessing a rich fund, of humour. In religion he was a devout Catholic. He abstained from taking any active part in politics, and was much respected for his broadminded and tolerant views. His wife predeceased him some years ago. He leaves three sons and five daughters, who, with one exception, are all married.

The funeral took place on Wednesday to Holy Trinity Cemetery, Lisburn, the large cortege, bearing testimony to the high esteem and regard in which the late Mr Donaghy was held. There were a number of beautiful wreaths, including one from the employees of the firm.

The chief mourners were — Patrick Donaghy, Henry Donaghy, and E. Donaghy, J.P. (sons); Patrick Slowey, J.P., and Wm. Crossin. (sons-in-law); Edward M'Cann; Rev. E. J. Crossin, St Malachy's College, Belfast; Hugh P. Crossin, M.P.S.I.; Gerald Slowey, Patrick Slowey, Michael M'Entee (grandsons); Dr J. J. Clarke, Daniel Mooney, Ed. Mooney, Daniel Mooney, jun.; Michael Lavery, solicitor; John Lavery, and Bernard M'Cartan.

The ceremony at the graveside was performed by Rev. H. M'Guiggun, C.C., Hannahstown, and Rev. E. J. Crossin, St Malachy's.

The funeral arrangements were carried out by the firm of Wm Ramsey, under the personal supervision of Mr Robert Ramsey. (Lisburn Standard, 18 October 1918.)

1919

15 August In the evening a number of charabancs were returning to Belfast having attended a Fifteenth of August demonstration in Blackrock, County Louth. They came under attack at various points along the route home. When they reached the Belfast Road in Lisburn a bugle was sounded and a crowd who appeared to have been making arrangements for the 'Peace Day' the following day congregated and with shouts of 'Murder the bloody Fenians' stoned the passing vehicles. Eight of the passengers received injuries and several had to receive medical treatment when the windscreens of the charabancs were shattered.

It was incorrectly reported in the unionist press that there had been hand to hand fighting.

16 August 'Peace Day' was celebrated in Lisburn. The streets were bedecked with union flags and bands led a procession through the streets of Lisburn, the route lined by one hundred soldiers with fixed bayonets.

Wreaths were laid at a specially constructed wooden cenotaph which had been erected in Market Square. As soldiers marched past Sir W. Hacket Pain took the salute. (Lisburn Standard 22 August 1919.) Hacket Pain who had organised the importation and distribution of arms for the UVF would return to Lisburn the following year in different circumstances.

The Catholic population of Lisburn was excluded from the festivities.

THE BURNINGS

1920

24 July Sectarian rioting by loyalists took place in Lisburn following the murder of Col. Gerald Ferguson Smyth by the IRA in Cork. He had been murdered because of a speech he had made to Royal Irish Constabulary officers in Listowel announcing what amounted to a 'shoot to kill' policy being introduced by the British government to deal with the increasing threat from the IRA. There had been rioting in Banbridge, his parent's hometown, after his funeral there. Rioting spread to Dromore and then to Lisburn. The Convent of the Sacred Heart of Mary on Castle Street occupied by a community of 28 nuns was among the buildings that came under attack and 27 of the windows facing on to the street were smashed. The windows of many Catholic-owned shops and public houses were also smashed.

3 August Rev. Mark McCashin died at the parochial house. A native of Downpatrick he was ordained in 1867 and is buried in Holy Trinity cemetery. (Freeman's Journal 4 August 1920.)

(His brother Rev. Daniel McCashin had been the first parish priest of St Malachy's in Belfast. Appointed in 1889 he served as parish priest until his death in 1919. Born in 1846 in County Down and ordained in 1871 he served for thirty years in this church, becoming the first parish priest of St Malachy's in 1909. During this time he was prominent in the affairs of the Church in Down and Connor, being especially close to Bishop Patrick McAllister (1886-1895) and earlier to Bishop Patrick Dorrian (1865-1885). He was very much loved by the people of St Malachy's for his love of the poor and devotion to his priestly tasks. Fr Daniel McCashin is buried in Milltown Cemetery.) (The parish of St. Malachy.)

Rev. James O'Boyle was appointed as his successor and when he arrived at Lisburn railway station from Ballymoney he was met by police who were to escort him to the parochial house. He informed the police that he did not wish to have an escort and if they insisted he would get back on the train. He made his way without the escort. His official appointment date was 15 September but he had taken up the post earlier.

During his tenure as parish priest Rev. McCashin had:

Furnished Magheragall new church with ceiling, communion rail, gallery, seats, vestry press and harmonium.

- Provided seating in St Joseph's Hall and erected a stage.
- Built new schools, a teacher's residence and wall at Magheragall and erected a stable there.
- Rebuilt the parochial house and offices.
- Built Magheramesk school-chapel, school, teacher's residence, stable and offices.
- Rebuilt Reilly's Trench School, teacher's residence and stable and renovated the church as new.
- Rebuilt Teeling Terrace which was parochial property.
- Bought out head rents of the parochial property.
- Bought out a townpark field to enlarge the present cemetery and
- Built the new St Patrick's church.

15 August On the evening of 15 August a party of men in a car stopped another car between Lurgan and Lisburn and questioned the occupants if they were 'rebels.' When a negative reply was given a lady and her companions were asked if they were Catholics. When they confirmed that they were a young girl was severely beaten, the chauffeur was badly mauled and the motor car was practically wrecked. The assailants who were believed to be under the influence of drink drove off in the direction of Lisburn. (Freeman's Journal 16 August 1920.)

Sunday 22 August Sectarian rioting by loyalists following the murder of RIC District Inspector Swanzy by the IRA, outside the Northern Bank in Railway Street, Lisburn, resulted in Catholic-owned business premises in Lisburn being burned and Catholics evicted from their homes. Furniture and personal belongings were burned in the street and where burning of the house would not affect neighbouring Protestant-owned houses it was set on fire.

The IRA believed that D.I. Swanzy was involved in the murder of Tomás Mac Curtain, who was the lord mayor of Cork and a leading member of the IRA in Cork.

Both St Patrick's Church and St Joseph's Hall had to be protected by a strong force of the military, as was the large Sacred Heart of Mary Convent on Castle Street at the other side of the town. There the soldiers were having difficulty in keeping the mob outside the convent at bay as stones and other missiles were fired over their heads at the convent windows. The officer in charge advised the nuns sheltering from the fusillade of stones that they should evacuate the premises as it was impossible to guarantee their safety. Arrangements were quickly made for transportation and while the military held back the mob at the front of the building the nuns made their escape through the garden at the back of the convent. Waiting cars brought the nuns to the tranquil Glens of Antrim where they sought sanctuary. Eight nuns found refuge in Cushendall where the parish priest Fr McCartan, who had known the community well when he had been parish priest in Aghagallon, made available a house for them. Four others found shelter at accommodation provided by Fr George Clenaghan in Glenariffe. The remainder crossed to Liverpool to take refuge in the Sacred Heart Convent at Bootle, Liverpool.

After a few weeks some of the nuns ventured back to the convent to help secure the premises as most of the windows facing Castle Street had been broken. When news of their return became known a crowd assembled outside the convent to finish the work that they had started earlier. Fr James O'Boyle, the newly appointed parish priest, who had previously served in Ballymoney appeared at the doorway of the convent and berated the crowd for their disgraceful behaviour. He said that they were not true Orangemen and compared them with the principled Orangemen he had known in Ballymoney. He threatened to summon the Orangemen of Ballymoney to stop the intimidation of the defenceless nuns. The crowd eventually backed off. It would be six months before the entire religious community of twenty-eight returned to Lisburn. (Survey of a Century 1870 1970 Rev Ambrose Macaulay)

23 August Following the burning of Bow Street the mob progressed towards Chapel Hill. An attempt was made to attack the church but the military presence prevented the attack succeeding. The fury of the mob was then focused on the Catholic parochial house. This large residence set back from Longstone Street and fronted by trees and an impressive circular driveway was at the corner of Priest's Lane (now Tonagh Avenue) and Longstone Street. The house was unoccupied as the priests, whose home it was, had earlier left under the cover of darkness for their own safety. Such was the urgency to escape that they were unable to remove parish records of births, deaths, marriages etc or personal books and possessions. The mob, taking a circuitous route to avoid any military on Longstone Street to protect the parochial house, broke into the building and looted the contents. Books and parish records were stripped from their shelves and piled up in the rooms. Paraffin oil was then poured over the books and set on fire. It was reported that the rioters danced around in priest's vestments as the building went up in flames.

The funeral of Rev. Mark McCashin who had died on 3 August and who had been Lisburn's parish priest for 30 years had taken place a few weeks earlier. Table linen, dinner plates and cutlery hired from the Albert Hotel in Belfast for a meal following the funeral service were still in the house and were looted and distributed among the crowd. Local folklore suggests that the rioters toyed with the idea of going to the cemetery behind the parochial house and digging up the coffin of Rev. McCashin.

With flames reaching high into the night sky and lighting up the surrounding area the mob, unimpeded by police or the military, continued with the orgy of destruction. With the fire brigade being prevented access the building was completely gutted. Later the white walls, all that remained of the building, were covered with graffiti which included 'No Pope or Prists (sic) Here, (priests being an addition to a familiar slogan), 'No Home Rule', 'Site for New Orange Hall.' 'God Save the King', 'To Hell with the Pope,' and 'Hertford Orange Hall.' Crowds of men, women and children were happy to pose as photographs were later taken of the gutted building. In one photograph a woman held a union jack flag in one hand and a hammer in the other. A young man struck a pose holding a rifle. One young woman who had danced around the burning building wearing priest's vestments was later said to have given birth to a deformed child. This was, in local folklore, seen by one side of the community as retribution and on the other side as a curse placed by the clergy.

Sunday 29 August Practically all the Catholics left Lisburn fearing for their lives. Only nine brave souls attended Sunday Mass. It was estimated that about 1,300 Catholics, approximately ten per cent of the entire population of Lisburn, left the town.

Among those who left were the Devenneys who had owned a butchers shop in Bow Street. The shop had been completely gutted by fire as was the adjoining clothes shop owned by the Miss Reids who were stepsisters of the Devenneys. Not only were the shops destroyed but the living quarters above the shops. Joe Devenny later returned and resumed business. James and his son Daniel (11) left for the comparative safety of Belfast.

The Antrim Road home of John Fitzpatrick, headmaster of the Boys' School, Chapel Hill, was attacked by a sectarian mob, the furniture and personal belongings taken from the house and burned in the front garden. Mr Fitzpatrick was headmaster for almost 37 years until his retirement in 1940. His son Brendan succeeded him in 1951 replacing Mr P.J. Fitzsimons. When the Boys' School reopened the numbers attending had fallen from over 200 to 120.

September There was a further attack on the convent resulting in both external and internal damage. A permanent military post was established outside the convent to prevent further attacks. As the attacks tailed off the Catholics of Lisburn began to drift back to their homes and to return to their former jobs. When the mill workers returned to Stewart's Flax mill on Antrim Street and Barbour Threads Mill in Hilden they were confronted by Protestant colleagues demanding that they sign a document: 'I hereby declare I am not a Sinn Feiner nor have any sympathy with Sinn Fein and do declare that I am loyal to king and country.' If they refused to sign they were made to leave by people they had worked with weeks earlier. Management of these and other businesses abdicated responsibility and acquiesced in this intimidation. Many refused to sign and left Lisburn to seek work in England or in towns across the border. Others who had no such option and had to work to survive signed the document. ('The Burnings 1920' - Pearse Lawlor, Mercier Press, Cork.)

Among the premises burned in August was that of Edward Donaghy & Sons boot & shoe factory in Graham Gardens and shop in Market Square. This Catholic-owned factory was the largest boot factory in Ireland and among its contracts was one to supply boots for the Russian army.

The Donaghy family lived at 'Beechmount' Pond Park, surrounded by thirty acres of farmland and with a magnificent view over the Lagan valley. When the rioting started Mrs Donaghy took refuge in the home of the Ritchie family, friendly Protestant neighbours, carrying her three-months-old daughter Monica in a clothes basket. Donaghy's house was protected by the army for some time after and one of their memories was the crunch of the soldiers' feet on the gravel as they patrolled around the house at night. Edward Donaghy re-established his factory in Drogheda and left Lisburn in 1932.

Among the visitors to Lisburn at this time was the Canadian Bishop Michael Francis Fallon (1867-1931). An intellectual he had forecast the first world war twenty years before it started. A supporter of Home Rule he visited Lisburn, while on a trip to Ireland, to see at first hand the destruction following the sectarian rioting. (The Canadian Catholic Historical Association Vol. 74 - "An Imperialist Irishman".)

In September the Belfast Davitt's and St Gall's Gaelic Athletic Clubs were transformed into hostels to accommodate Lisburn refugees. (Freeman's Journal 22 September 1920.)

Robert Dornan, a Catholic who had been employed as a foreman of a shed at Messers Wm. Barbour and Sons Ltd., Hilden, was named in a letter sent to the company on 24 August 1920. The letter read;

> *'Dear Sir, If you are retaining Robert Dornan, foreman of the store in your employment after this week we will burn the mill. So beware - Yours truly - The Red Hand.'*

On the night of 29 September 1920 a large shed at the mill was destroyed by fire and another one damaged, The cost was estimated at £70,000. By the time a claim for compensation was lodged by the company in July 1921 Mr Dornan, a long-term employee of the firm, had died. At the court case it was revealed that 200 Catholic employees had been forced to leave the company. The claim for compensation was dismissed in October 1921 by Judge Wilson at Belfast Recorder's Court who stated that it might have been done maliciously but it might have been done accidentally. (Freeman's Journal 14 October 1921.)

In October posters were placed on walls in Lisburn stating 'A fair warning to Sinn Fein and Sinn Fein Sympathisers - Lisburn will claim, not an eye for an eye, but three or more lives for either the murder of or injury to any local member of the RIC or auxiliary force. So beware.' (Freeman's Journal 12 October 1920.)

In 1920 the curates in St Patrick's were Rev. E. P. Smyth, Rev. M. McLoughlin and Rev. J. Gillen. Rev. McCashin had previously been chaplain to Lisburn Workhouse. Mother Mary Irenaeus was Superioress of the Sacred Heart of Mary Convent which had thirty-two in the community. There was a total of 176 priests in the 60 parishes that comprised the Diocese of Down and Connor (Irish Catholic Directory 1920 p163).

There can be little doubt that the violence which started in Banbridge in July and spread to Lisburn was orchestrated by the UVF. The assassination of Col. Smyth in July which triggered the violence has to be placed in context of the success of Sinn Féin in the 1918 elections as the largest party in Ireland and the inability of the British government to curtail the activities of the IRA as attacks became increasingly common in the northern counties.

The Smyth family in Banbridge were related, through marriage, to the Murland family at Annsborough near Castlewellan, also engaged in the linen-manufacturing industry. Charlie Murland was responsible for organising the UVF in south County Down and Warren Murland was involved in the importation of arms and ammunition for the UVF. The murder of Col. Smyth, who in his lifetime had spent very little time in Banbridge, provided the excuse for loyalist attacks on the Catholic community who in their view were synonymous with Sinn Féin and the IRA.

Likewise the murder of D.I. Swanzy in August was used to whip up anti-Catholic emotions in Lisburn. Today Swanzy's grave lies derelict and forgotten in Mount Jerome Cemetery, Dublin.

It is important to note that while the violence in Lisburn was widespread a number of Protestants placed their own lives at risk to protect their Catholic neighbours. The Cairns, Murray and Dougan families in Hill Street were protected from having their homes burned when a lone Protestant neighbour stood in the middle of the street armed with a shotgun facing a mob and threatened to shoot the first

St Patrick's Church
Chapel Hill, Lisburn
pre 1900

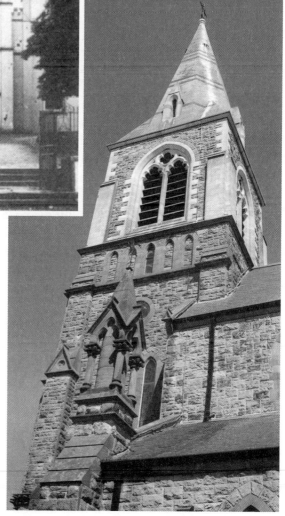

Present St Patrick's Church
Lisburn

Interior of the pre 1900 Church

Altar in the old St Patrick's Church

Interior of the present St Patrick's Church - 1900

Interior of St Patrick's Church - c. 1930s

Interior of St Patrick's Church - 2013

St Colman's Church, Reilly's Trench - 1906

St Colman's Church, Reilly's Trench, Moira Road, Hillsborough - 2013

St Joseph's Church, Magheragall, Kilcorig Road, Lisburn - 2013

Church of Blessed Virgin Mary and St Brigid, Magheramesk,
Maghaberry Road, Moira - 2013

Church of Blessed Virgin Mary and St Brigid, Magheramesk,
Maghaberry Road, Moira - 2013

St Patrick's Parochial House, Priest's Lane,
(now Tonagh Avenue) Lisburn - 1906

St Patrick's Parochial House - August 1920

Parochial House, Chapel Hill, Lisburn - Prior to demolition

Present Parochial House and parish office, Chapel Hill, Lisburn

St Joseph's Hall,
Chapel Hill,
Lisburn
c. 1990

St Patrick's Pastoral Centre, Chapel Hill, Lisburn - 2010

Convent of the Sacred Heart of Mary, Castle Street, Lisburn - c. 1900

Convent Primary School, Castle Street, Lisburn

St Joseph's Primary School Staff 1960s

Mrs Creaney - Miss McDevitt - Sr Tarcisius - Sr Malachy - Sr Austin

Sr Norbet - Sr Vincent - Mrs O'Boyle - Mrs Rowan - Miss Anita Canavan

Apostolic Class at Lisburn Convent
Late 1940s/early 1950s

St Joseph's Primary School Band - 1951

Isabel McArdle aged 94 welcomes Bishop Walsh and Rev. Sean Rogan to
the refurbished St Patrick's Church in 2000.

Brendan Fitzpatrick (centre) - Principal
with fellow teachers and school team

School Football Team
1952/53

Show Time at St Joseph's Hall

St Joseph's Billiards Team Season Winners 1930/31

Jim Gorman   Dan Mooney   Pat McArdle
Joe Duffy   M J Green   John Keegan

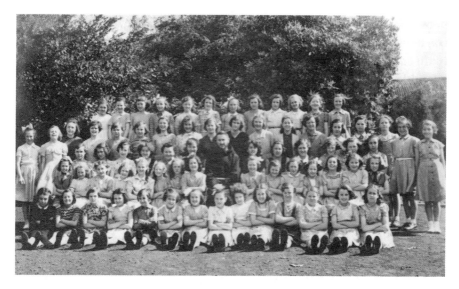

Fr. Joachim with Convent School pupils - 1950s

Parishioners join Fr Joachim on his Ordination Day - 24 May 1953

person who tried to get past him. The McConnell family from Barnsley's Row was protected by Protestant neighbours when they realised that the family had been hiding and sleeping among the brambles alongside the River Lagan every night as they feared being burned alive in their home.

The descendants of these families over ninety-years later still recalled the kindness shown by their 'good Protestant neighbours'.

1921

March Six months after the riots had left Lisburn in ruins, a meeting was organised in the Temperance Institute in Railway Street to start a local branch of the Ulster Ex-Servicemen's Association. In Britain Ex-Servicemen's Associations had been formed throughout the country to provide practical support to enable former soldiers find work and reintegrate into society.

Dr George St George, chairman of Lisburn Urban Council, chaired the meeting. In a theme he had espoused back in 1876 he explained that the role of the association was to link loyalists in Ulster to form one united group of former soldiers and its primary task was to help men to find employment. Ignoring the sacrifices made by the mainly nationalist 16th Division which had fought and died alongside the loyalist 36th Division he made it clear that it did not matter to him that Catholics had fought and died for their country. Robert Boyd at the meeting said,

> 'We not only bar Sinn Féiners (for that read Catholics), but we bar Red Flagers, Bolshevists and all extreme socialists...' He went on to say, 'You have a battalion here 800 strong with Dr St George at your head; there is no person in Lisburn who will refuse you anything.'

The figure of 800 coincided with the number of B Specials in the Lisburn area. Pressure was placed on employers in Lisburn to employ only Protestant workers. Employers who did not comply would be faced with crowds, supported by Orange Order bands protesting outside their factories or business premises. ('The Burnings 1920' - Pearse Lawlor, Mercier Press)

It was the normal practice at the time for employers to indicate in job advertisements that vacancies were open only to Catholics or Protestants.

It would not be until August 1969 that the Governments of the United Kingdom and Northern Ireland issued a joint statement of policy in relation to Northern Ireland. This statement (known as The Downing Street Declaration) re-affirmed the principle that 'every citizen of Northern Ireland is entitled to the same equality of treatment and freedom from discrimination as obtains in the rest of the United Kingdom, irrespective of political views or religion.'

It would not be until the introduction of the Fair Employment Act in 1976 which prohibited religious and political discrimination in Northern Ireland that the practice ceased. Further legislation was later introduced to bring an end to 'word of mouth' recruitment and the display of flags and emblems in workplaces.

Dr George St George, a prominent Orangeman and the first Worshipful Master of the St George Masonic Lodge No. 267, was probably the only Protestant in Lisburn to have a full size Irish Tricolour in his possession at this time.

It was however a rather special Tricolour, the one captured by British troops at the General Post Office (GPO) in Dublin at the time of the 1916 Rising. The flag had been captured by Sergeant Thomas Davis, Royal Dublin Fusiliers, originally from Lisburn and he presented it to Dr St George as a gift.

The flag passed on his death in 1922 to his daughter Ethelreda and from there to her husband Captain Samuel Waring who later gave it to a neighbour in Kells, County Meath, the son of John Sweetman (1844-1936), a renowned Irish nationalist and one of the founders of Sinn Féin.

The flag had gone full circle from Dr St George who was a prominent member of the UVF to a family with links to Sinn Féin. Tommy Davis who had captured the flag later worked as a gateman at Island Mills, Lisburn. (Bloomsburyauctions.com detail/Ny042/26.0.) Had he been alive today he would be astonished to learn that the flag he had stuffed in his knapsack is now insured for $1 million. (The flag on loan to the American Irish Historical Society will be a focal point for the American commemorations of the Centenary of the Rising in 2016, in which the AIHS plays an important role.)

23 March At a meeting of the Lisburn Board of Guardians it was proposed that the vacancy existing in the office of the Roman Catholic chaplain should not be filled.

At a subsequent meeting it was explained that there were at the time twenty Roman Catholic inmates and the Local Government Board considered that the withholding from the inmates the right to receive religious administrations was not reasonable. In line with legislation an order appointing Rev. James O'Boyle P.P. V.F., to the office was made. Following sectarian remarks by some board members there was an attempt to reduce the salary from £30 to £15 but the clerk ruled that it was not possible. (Freeman's Journal March 1921.)

April The priests of the parish, Rev. James O'Boyle P.P. V.F., Rev. John Gillen C.C., Rev. John Murphy B.A. C.C. and Rev. Wm. Walsh B.A. C.C. launched a major appeal to fund the building of a new parochial house. Most Rev. Dr MacCrory presented a motor car or its value, £500, as a ballot prize. Ballot tickets were posted to individuals throughout Ireland with a covering letter carrying a photograph of the ruins of the parochial house. The priests had to live in temporary accommodation while funds of about £5,000 were raised to build a new parochial house. (Freeman's Journal 16 April 1921.)

25 May Paul Kearney a Sinn Féin election agent was set upon and beaten by a gang of men in Lisburn. When he recovered consciousness he asked for a drink of water and was told he would get a drink of his own blood. (Freeman's Journal 9 November 1921.)

30 May The 'Red Hand of Ulster' warned the 'Irish News', 'if any damage is done to Lisburn loyalists up goes the chapel and the convent.' (The Catholic church and the foundation of the Northern Ireland state.)

The new parochial house was designed by Belfast architects Messrs. McDonnell, Lamont and McDonnell and built next to the church at Chapel Hill. A description of the house in 1923 referred to it as a 'simple and dignified domestic Gothic Style' building with 77 feet frontage and a depth of 70 feet.

Along with building a new parochial house Rev. O'Boyle renovated the church and installed stained glass windows and, as his own gift, provided a new organ. (Irish News report of Canon O'Boyle's funeral.)

The present reredos (ornamental screen behind the altar) would appear to have been installed about this time and the original windows replaced with the present stained glass windows. The polished pine altar rails were replaced with marble rails and the altar area extended. Because of this the ornate wooden pulpit which had been located at the second pillar from the altar was moved to the third pillar. The statues of the Sacred Heart and the Blessed Virgin Mary which flanked the altar were moved and placed in front of the pillars in the altar area. (The statue of the Sacred Heart still survives, relegated to the back of the church but the statue of the Blessed Virgin has not survived.) A photograph taken by Lisburn photographer John Lannigan of the interior of the new Catholic Church, Lisburn shortly after it was built, when compared with a photograph taken in 1934 demonstrates the changes that took place around this time.

The memorial windows donated by parishioners are;

Left hand side:

In memory of my sister Brigid and my niece Jane Convery. Erected by Lucy McFaull.

[In 1901 Lucy McFall (32) was living with her mother Mary, a retired spirit merchant and her sisters Brigid and Rose along with her brother Daniel. They owned a public house at 86 Bridge Street. Also living in the same household were Peter (26), a spirit merchant and Jane (24) Convery who were her mother's grandchildren. Convery & McFall operated a funeral undertaking business and also hired out cabs, hansoms, rubber tyred broughams, carriages, cars and busses. They also operated Brakes and Wagonettes, etc. from addresses at 24 Longstone Street and 86 Bridge Street. (Lisburn Bazaar book 1906.) Their public house was destroyed by fire during the sectarian riots in Lisburn in 1920.]

Erected to the memory of the late Edward Savage McIlroy, Hilden Cottage by his brother and sisters.

[Edward Savage McIlroy was a brother of William McIlroy a major benefactor of St Patrick's. In 1901 aged 24 he lived along with his sisters Elizabeth and Annie and brother William with their widowed mother Anna in the 15 room 'Hilden Cottage', situated on the Low Road, Lisburn (since demolished). All siblings were unmarried.]

Erected by James McGrogan in memory of his mother and father.

Right hand side:

In memory of my uncle James Rice. Erected by James Rice Esq.

[Mr. Rice, who was unmarried, belonged to an old local family, being the son of the late Mr. James Rice. He had been employed by Messrs. Wm. Barbour and Sons, Hilden, and eventually became head of the flax department, both there and at Courtrai, Belgium. He later severed his connection with the concern, embarking in business for himself as flax merchant, his headquarters being in Hill Street, Belfast, where he carried on an extensive trade, and was well known in all the leading flax markets.
He was a devout member of the congregation of St Patrick's Catholic Church to which he was a generous contributor, as well as other organisations. He may have been linked with James Rice, single (33) who in 1901 was a flour buyer and was living with his unmarried uncle James (54) who was a flour merchant with premises in Bow Street, Lisburn.]

In memory of my parents Peter & Sara O'Boyle. Erected by Very Rev. James O'Boyle, P.P.

Pray for the donor James McGrogan Lisburn 1935.
[This would seem to indicate that this was a replacement window following an attack on the church in 1931]

Front left behind High Altar:

Pray for Thomas and Mary Dornan.

Left of High Altar:

Pray for Patrick Doyle.

[In 1901 Patrick Doyle (69), single, was living with his brother-in-law Robert Fitzsimons in the Temperance Hotel 3 Market Square, Lisburn. In 1920 R. Fitzsimon's name was still on the building but it was now a confectionery shop owned by Isabella Gilmore. It was attacked during riots in July 1920 and in August Mrs Gilmore had to flee for her life as a mob attacked her shop and threw every piece of her furniture into the street where it was set on fire. ('The Burnings 1920' Pearse Lawlor, Mercier Press.)]

Right of High Altar:

Pray for Patrick Doyle, Lisburn.

[As above]

Front Left:

In Memory John & Anna McIlroy, Father & Mother. Erected by William McIlroy Esq. J.P.

[See above]

Front Right:

In memory of my brother James and sister Sara McIlroy. Erected by William McIlroy Esq. J.P.

[See above]

Back of church:

Left:

Pray for the repose of the souls of the late Thomas and Mary Dorran.

Right;

Pray for the repose of the soul of the late Edward Geehan of Lisburn.
[In 1901 Edward Geehan (38) single, a clerk to a wine and spirit and iron merchants was living with his widowed mother at 88a Longstone Street, Lisburn.]

A Plaque states - *This altar the gift of Robert Fitzsimons Lisburn 1901.*

[See above.]

Above side altars - *Erected by James Rice J.P. To the memory of his father and mother and other relatives who are interred Tullyrusk. On whose souls sweet Jesus have mercy.*

[See above.]

The famous painter Sir John Lavery who painted 'The Madonna of the Lakes' which was donated to St Patrick's Church, Donegall St. Belfast where it is on display, followed with a sequence of clerical portraits, starting with the exceptional Cardinal Logue, 1921 (Ulster Museum, Belfast) and a project to paint a crucifixion for the Sisterhood of Mary Convent in Lisburn. It is not known if this project was ever completed. (www.gorrygallery.ie)

4 September When Michael Collins, elected as Sinn Féin MP for Armagh in the 1921 general election, went to Armagh to make a speech a number of Lisburn Catholics joined a special train from Belfast to Armagh. The 'Freeman's Journal' records that at intermediate stations, such as Lisburn and Lurgan, numbers of people joined the train.

The train from Belfast was guarded by armed troops 'fearing interference by Orange mobs,' but things went peacefully until its arrival back in Belfast.

Shots were fired on the return to Belfast of the train from Armagh. Police and army (Seaforth Highlanders) awaited the arrival at Great Victoria Street about nine o'clock, but the shots apparently were not aimed at targets, more 'in a spirit of bravado' as the 'News Letter' put it. Another version has it that an Orange mob gathered outside the station and surged towards the train, recognising several Sinn Féin passengers. The shots were fired in the air in self-defence. (Michael Collins in Armagh - Des Fitzgerald.)

A Belfast businessman, in the wine trade, visiting a public house in Lisburn on business was recognised as a Catholic and was ordered out. When he called at another public house he was threatened by five or six men who had followed him and when he made his way to the railway station he was assaulted outside the station and was badly bruised after receiving a kicking. (Freeman's Journal 23 September 1921.)

October A further blow was delivered to Lisburn's Catholic business community whose property had been destroyed in 1920. The local magistrates refused to renew the licences of W. H. and J. Connolly, John G. Ferguson, Owen Trainor, Daniel Mooney and Rose and Lucy McFall, all publicans. Mr McElroy ruled that a spirt licence cannot exist where there was no licensed house. Mr P.J. Magee, a solicitor representing one of the applicants said that the Lisburn magistrates were the only bench of magistrates in Ireland who had come to that decision. In every other circumstance the magistrates had exercised their discretion and granted a renewal of the certificates. (Freeman's Journal 15 October 1921.)

It has been suggested that the growth of Catholic-owned businesses in Lisburn, not only in the licensed trade but across a wide range of professions and trades, created unease among the Protestant community that they were losing control of the town centre and was a contributory factor in the riots of 1920. At that time Protestant shop owners identified their property by flying a union flag to ensure that their premises were not attacked.

1922

IRA attacks in Belfast and throughout the newly formed state of Northern Ireland resulted in the introduction, by Richard Dawson Bates, of the Civil Authorities (Special Powers) Act (Northern Ireland) in 1922. This Act came into force on 25 May and imposed a curfew from 11:00 p.m. to 5:00 a.m.. On 4 November 1922 the curfew was changed to 11:30 p.m. to 5:00 a.m.. Anyone not holding a permit was required to remain indoors during these times.

This caused a problem for the Catholic Church on Christmas Eve when the traditional midnight Mass was celebrated. When Cardinal Logue requested Dawson Bates to relax the regulations to enable midnight Mass to be celebrated in Armagh cathedral, and by inference other churches in Northern Ireland, he was informed that if the service went ahead he would place a cordon of police at the cathedral gate; the congregation would be held in the church until 5:00 a.m. and then arrested.

The celebration of the birth of Christ at midnight Mass was therefore cancelled in Armagh and other churches including Lisburn.

While the Catholic population of Lisburn was subject to the curfew, on Christmas night a party was in full swing in the Flowerhill Orange Lodge outside Lisburn. A patrol of B Specials called at the hall, not to enforce the curfew but to join the festivities. This may have passed unnoticed but for a tragic incident. Constable Patterson had unloaded his rifle before entering the hall but had left a bullet in the breech. As he made his way into the crowded hall the rifle discharged. James Haire was killed and the bullet went on to injure James Jones and William Lockhart. The resulting enquiry exposed the double standards being operated in Lisburn. ('The Outrages 1920-1922' - Pearse Lawlor, Mercier Press.)

144

1923

March Sister Mary Alban (Armstrong), sister of Miss Annie Armstrong, Railway Hotel, Lisburn, celebrated her golden jubilee as a nun in the Sisters of Charity at the Hospice for the Dying, Harold's Cross, Dublin. (Freeman's Journal 14 March 1923.)

1925

Our Lady of Lourdes Grotto - A thanksgiving offering from William McIlroy Esq. J.P. Hilden 1925. (This was located in the first niche on the left-hand side of the church. It was later removed during the renovation of the church by Rev. Sean Rogan in late 1990s. The plaster figures and plaster rocks were not stored properly and were destroyed due to rain damage).

6 May When Margaret Sands, 7 Benson Street, Lisburn died among the beneficiaries in her will were Rev. Walsh C.C., Rev. Watson C.C., Rev. Bradley C.C. and Very Rev. James O'Boyle all of Lisburn who each received £5 for Masses to be said for the repose of her soul and that of her deceased brother Daniel. (Belfast Gazette 7 August 1925.)

1927

Rev. H. Bradley a curate in St Patrick's was a fluent Gaelic speaker and played an influential part in the Gaelic League movement in the north of Ireland. He was a member of the Ulster Council of the Gaelic League in 1930 and promoted the learning of Irish in Catholic primary schools. He organised visits by young people from the parish to the Gaeltacht area of Rann na Feirste in County Donegal. His fellow curate Rev. T. Toal also took a keen interest in the Gaelic language revival at this time. He was a member of the Down and Connor Historical Society until it ended in 1938.

Terence Toal and Hugh Bradley may have attended Queen's University Belfast together in 1911. (www.smo.uhi.ac.uk).

22 October Patrick McComiskey (75) who was going to Mass at Lisburn, dropped dead within a few yards of the church gate. (The Tablet 29 October 1927)

1929

Two additional classrooms that had been built onto the rear of the Boys' school at Chapel Hill were accidentally burned down in 1929 and rebuilt as three classrooms in 1930.

Rev. Donaghy is listed as a member of the Lisburn Branch of The Apostolic Work in their record book. (Parish archives.)

1930

St Joseph's Billiard Team Season Winners 1930/31 were Jim Gorman, Dan Mooney, Pat McArdle, Joe Duffy, M. J. Green and John Keegan.

1931

3 July Lisburn Catholic Club celebrated a remarkable series of victories when St Joseph's billiards team won all four cups in the Lisburn and Belfast Catholic Billiards League the previous week. Rev. J. Conalty C.C. vice-president of the Billiards Club presided at a social and concert in St Joseph's Hall. (Lisburn Standard 3 July 1931.)

July Bella O'Donnell, a pupil from Lisburn convent, was awarded first prize for conversation in Irish and for story-telling in the literary competitions at the Feis of the Glens of Antrim in Ballymena Parochial Hall. (Feis Na nGleann: A Centuary of Gaelic Culture in the Glens of Antrim, Padraic O' Cleireachain)

15 August Sectarian rioting broke out in Lisburn on Saturday in a well planned attack on the Catholic community by loyalists.

(Tension had been high following the derailment of a train at Richill carrying AOH members to a demonstration in Armagh. This was in reprisal for the blowing up of a railway bridge by the Cavan Brigade IRA in County Cavan on 12 August to prevent members of the Royal Black Preceptory reaching their demonstration at Cootehill.)
At around 10:30 p.m. a large crowd alighted from a Belfast train at Lisburn railway station and began to curse the Pope. Marching in military formation

they were joined by hundreds as they made their way up Railway Street to the town centre. They went immediately to the Ancient Order of Hibernians Hall on Linenhall Street, near Smithfield and sang 'Dolly's Brae' and 'Derry's Walls'. They then set about breaking the windows in the Hall and attempted to set the building on fire. The usual weekly Saturday night dance was just ending at 11:00 p.m. and men and women who had earlier enjoyed the dance were attacked, kicked and beaten as they streamed from the Hall. The Belfast based dance band had to be escorted by the police to the railway station and a number were assaulted as they made their way along Railway Street.

The police, who were few in number because many of their colleagues had been drafted into Armagh and Portadown to deal with similar disturbances earlier in the day, baton-charged and dispersed the crowd. The crowd moved to Smithfield police station on hearing rumours that someone had been arrested. The police baton-charged the crowd again but a downpour of rain proved just as effective in clearing the street.

They however regrouped and, what was now a mob, moved to Bow Street where windows in Catholic-owned and other premises were smashed and shops looted. Particular attention was paid to Catholic-owned public houses of J. McKenny, Antrim Street, Thos Browne, Market Square, and Miss McKinney which came under attack. Premises belonging to Peter Fusco, Bridge Street, John Maguire, Chapel Hill, and Francesco Ginesi were also attacked. Other shops including Woolworth in Bow Street were attacked.

The mob moved up Chapel Hill attacking Daniel Mooney's public house, smashing the windows before launching a vicious onslaught on St Patrick's Church, the parochial house and St Joseph's Hall. Six large windows in St Joseph's Hall were smashed and a window some twenty feet above the entrance to St Patrick's Church was smashed. A large stained glass window in the church was severely damaged. A fusillade of stones was launched at the parochial house and later twenty stones, some quite large, were found littering the floor of the sitting room.

Towards midnight the convent came under attack and the windows facing Seymour Street were smashed. As it was school holidays there were not many nuns present and the boarders had gone home for the holidays. In Seymour Street Mrs Dornan's grocery and confectionary shop was looted and a car was stopped and petrol stolen from it was used to set fire to the shop. Rev. Edward Whittaker from the nearby Methodist Church along with neighbours prevented the flames from destroying the living quarters above the shop which was completely gutted.

The violence continued overnight in what appeared to be a rerun of the sectarian violence of 1920 and at 10:00 a.m. on Sunday the town was crowded with people. (Lisburn Standard 21 August 1931 & Irish News 17 August 1931.)

Lisburn was generally quiet on Sunday but on Monday night a large crowd gathered in Market Square seemingly to renew the violence. Mr E. S. Clarke J.P., District Master of the Lisburn District Orange Lodge intervened along with some older members of the Orange Order and persuaded some to return to their homes, not however before the windows of Messers Donaghy's premises in Graham Gardens were broken. Extra police had been brought in from Belfast in three lorries and as the violence continued on Monday night the RUC made repeated baton charges to clear and regain the streets of Lisburn. A crowd lingered in Antrim Street and were baton-charged and finally dispersed by the police. Windows in Catholic-owned homes in the Low Road were shattered as a mob made their way along the street from the town centre. (Irish News 19 August 1931.)

Sectarian violence continued in Lisburn and William Lappin of 12 Millview was arrested on 29 August and charged with riotous and disorderly behaviour in Market Square when an armoured police vehicle brought up from Newry to help patrol the town came under attack. (Ulster Standard 4 September 1931.)

Claims for malicious damage and injury amounting to over £1,600 were later made in respect of the disturbances. (Irish News 22 & 24 August 1931.)

25 November A Sale of Work was held in St Joseph's Hall to raise funds to pay for the completion of the spire at St Patrick's. Most Rev. Dr. Mageean, Bishop of Down and Connor who opened the Sale of Work used the occasion to condemn the recent anti-Catholic riots in Lisburn. He stated that, 'the individuals or bodies who countenanced or encouraged such conduct are not animated with the spirit of Christianity and the recent scenes in Lisburn is a disgrace to the Government that professes to rule the Six Counties'. He congratulated two of the most prominent citizens and biggest employers in Lisburn who told the mob bluntly that if there was a recurrence of such conduct they would close their works against those who took part. He also praised the non-Catholics of Lisburn for their contributions and gifts to the Sale of Work. He hoped that the spire would be in place the following year. (Irish Press 26 November 1931 & Diocesan records.)

1932

A framed coloured drawing dated 1932 of St Patrick's with the added spire and plan of the choir area and belfry by architect Gerard I. O'Gorman, Lisburn is in the parish archives.

26 June The 31st International Eucharistic Congress, the premier international Catholic event celebrating the Holy Eucharist, was held in Dublin 21-26 June 1932. Trains and buses carrying Catholics from various parts of Northern Ireland to the Congress were attacked with stones and other missiles going to and from Dublin.

Among the many incidents trains were subject to attacks by stone throwers at Knockmore outside Lisburn resulting in at least one woman receiving serious facial injuries. (Irish News 6 October 1932.)

The stone-throwing at trains were not the only attacks. Portadown, Seagoe, Lisburn, Coleraine and Belfast itself were scenes of disturbance, to the intense disgust and resentment of decent Protestants in thousands. (The Tablet 2 July 1932.)

When the Catholic Donaghy family, whose factory and shop had been destroyed in the 1920 riots, were preparing to leave Lisburn to move to their new home in Drogheda they were informed that, as a parting gift, the family grave in Holy Trinity cemetery had been desecrated on the previous night. One of the memories Monica Donaghy took with her was that when at the school when the convent bell was rung all the children had to go to the basement before the windows were stoned. (Donaghy family.)

1933

St Patrick's Church was finally completed with the erection of a bell tower and a spire. The bell, cast by the Sheridan Eagle foundry in Dublin and dated 1869, had for years rested on wooden props at the rear of the church, awaiting the construction of the spire. The spire, one hundred and fifty-five feet, has three strata of Yorkshire stone representing the Trinity. The cross at the apex is mounted in a five hundredweight solid stone. Many of the parishioners gathered to touch the nine feet, six inch cross before it was placed on top of the spire.

In a magazine published in 1933 by the Convent of the Sacred Heart of Mary the achievement by Canon O'Boyle in completing the tower and spire is praised along with a comment that St Patrick's has now its crowning glory, which adds not alone to the church but the entire town. (These Hallowed Grounds Vol. 1, Lisburn Branch of the North of Ireland Family History Society.)

1934

21 January The choir of the Convent of the Sacred Heart of Mary, Lisburn, which won five first prizes for Plain Chant within the last 18 months, will broadcast from Dublin tomorrow at 8:40 p.m. (Irish Press 20 January 1934.)

12 April The remains of Mr J.F. Walsh, whose premises were burned in Lisburn in August 1920, were removed from his residence 44 Lower Baggot Street, Dublin to Lisburn for burial. (Irish Press 13 April 1934.)

1935

St Patrick's in Lisburn produced 'The Catholic Year Book and Blotter-Calendar.' It was funded by advertisements from local businesses across the religious divide.

The priests in Lisburn were:

Very Rev James Canon O'Boyle, P.P.,V.F., B.A
Rev. James Smith, B.A. C.C.
Rev J. Ivory, B.A. C.C.
Rev. F. Conalty, C.C.

Sunday Masses were at 8:30 and 11:00 a.m. with Sunday school before the 11:00 Mass. Evening Devotions were at 6:30 p.m.. Fee for admission to the Masses was twopence and for Devotions one penny. Children and poor people were admitted free.

Weekday Masses were 8:00 and 9:00 a.m. and Stations of the Cross and Benediction of the Blessed Sacrament every Friday evening at 7:30 p.m..

Confessions were heard on Fridays at 7:00 p.m. and on Saturdays at 6:30 p.m.. Servants unable to attend at those times could have their confessions heard in the Sacristy before 8:30 a.m. Mass on Sundays and 9:00 a.m. Mass on Holy Days.

The parish library in St Joseph's Hall was opened every Sunday after 11:00 a.m. Mass.

Confraternities and Sodalities met on the first Sunday of every month.

The parish of Blaris (Lisburn) in 1934 extended from Moira, Trummery and Killultagh in Antrim to Comber district in Down and circled round the parishes of Magheralin, Dromore, Dromara, Ballynahinch, Saintfield and Newtownards. It bordered on the Holy Rosary, St Brigid's and St Teresa's in Belfast and touched Derriaghy and Glenavy at Stoneyford and Magheragall while separated from Aghagallon at Ballinderry and Soldierstown. (The Catholic Yearbook, St. Patrick's, Lisburn 1934.)

13 August At a meeting of Lisburn Board of Guardians Mr D. Hall said a good many children came to the Six-Counties from the Free State and wondered if anything could be done to stop the practice. Mrs Beattie J.P. said that it was a shame that those children should come there and become the voters of the country in later years. (Irish Press 14 August 1935.)

1936

June

Mrs Christina Armstrong, The Railway Hotel, Lisburn, widow of the late Mr Michael P. Armstrong, Goremount, Glenavy passed away after a long illness. She was a daughter of the late Mr William O'Hara, Aghagallon and was very highly respected. A lady of many attainments and accomplishments, during her residence in the Glenavy district she was noted for her charitableness and kindness, her generosity being extended to all creeds. Of a graceful and pleasant disposition, she had many admirers in all walks of life.

After Requiem Mass at St Patrick's, Lisburn, celebrated by her favourite relative, Rev. Father Celeus, CP, Mount Argus, Dublin, the remains were removed on Tuesday for interment in the family burying ground at Glenavy. The large funeral cortege was thoroughly representative of all creeds and classes and was of a private nature; had it been public it would surely have been the largest seen leaving the Catholic Church here for some years.

The chief mourners were: William P Armstrong (son), Basil Gallivan and Lawrence Robinson (grandsons), Daniel McLarnon and J.D. Robinson (sons in law), William P. O'Hare Bangor (nephew), Rev. Peter Madden C.C., Rev. Fred Burns P.P., Rev. D. Davey C.C., Richard McIlroy Dublin (Father Celeus' father), William Graham JP, P. Madden, C. Mooney, Wm O'Hara, Dr G Giles Belfast, Dr J. Connor The Mount Belfast, J. McLaverty, Peter McCurry MRCVS, C. McCurry, D. O'Hara, P. O'Hara and Dan O'Hara, Masters Cahal McManus and Sheamus Callaghan (relatives).

The clergy present included: Very Rev. Canon O'Boyle P.P., VF Lisburn, Rev. F. Small P.P., Rev. D. McEvoy P.P. Glenavy, Rev. Fr McNamara, P.P. Ligoneil, Rev. John Clenaghan OM Dublin, Rev. J. Clenaghan P.P. Belfast, Rev. Geo. Clenaghan Belfast, Rev. Vincent Davey P.P. Antrim, Rev. J. Armstrong C.C. Holy Rosary Belfast, Rev. Malachy McSorley C.C., Rev. Fr Ivory C.C. Lisburn, Rev. John McSparran, Adm Belfast and Rev. M. O'Hare.

The friends of the deceased present at the funeral were - Mr William McIlroy JP, Hilden, Dr Hunter Crumlin, Captain Robinson, Messrs J McSorley, T. Travers, Wm Clenaghan, T. Clenaghan, Patrick O'Boyle, William Fleming, Michael McAlister, Dr William Robinson, Dr Neil Robinson, D. Robinson, James Robinson MPS, John McAlister, C. O'Boyle, John Morgan, H. Creeney, D. Gallivan Dublin LDS, B. Gallivan, Andy O'Connor and P. McLornan, Dr McSorley, Dr Fred McSorley, Maurice McGrath LDS, Dr McHugh, Dr Smyth, Dr Bell, J. Mulholland, J. Creaney and J. Wilson. (Lisburn Star 26 June 1936.) (The Railway Hotel had reopened in June 1929 by Mrs Armstrong.)

27 April Canon O'Boyle commenting in the 'Catholic Herald' about the revolution in Spain which brought to power an extreme left wing anti-clerical government wrote;

'You have my support in making known the object of the Red campaign against Christianity.—Canon O'Boyle, Lisburn'.

(The murder of 37 priests, brothers and seminarians by leftists in Asturias marks what some see as the beginning of the Red Terror in October 1934. In an ensuring civil war it is estimated that in the course of the Red Terror, 6,832 members of the Catholic clergy, 20% percent of the nation's clergy, were killed. (http://en.wikipedia.org/wiki/Red_Terror_(Spain)

Mr E. Donaghy advertised his new factory as E. Donaghy & Sons, Boyne Shoe Works, Westgate, Drogheda (late Lisburn). (Irish Press 5 June 1936.)

1937

26 August Rev. Patrick Mullan, educated in St Malachy's College, Belfast and Maynooth was ordained on 24 June 1889. He had served as a curate in Lisburn but retired due to ill health and died 26 August.

1939

26 January Sir William McIlroy, K.C.S.G was created a Knight of St Gregory by Pope Pius XI. This was among the last acts of the pontiff who died on 10 February 1939. The document conferring this honour was signed by Cardinal Pacelli who was destined to become the next pope, Pope Pius XII on 2 March 1939. ('Ulster Standard' 24 February 1939).

4 February 'The Irish News' published a lengthy article written by Canon O'Boyle under the heading 'Democracies and Dictatorships - The Catholic position outlined.' Writing about holding firmly to your beliefs he wrote,

> *'The Catholic Church, under no circumstances, can she deviate from the principles which are the bed-rock of her authority.' Commenting on other forms of Christianity he said, '..whose leaders are free to expound and expand the moral code from private interpretation of the Scriptures are not unlike a ship anchored on a sandy bottom. When the wind blows high and the waves lash furiously on her sides she shifts her moorings and at length rudderless she is wrecked on the rocky shore.'*

17 February A variety concert, presented by the children of Lisburn Public Elementary School, was held in St Joseph's Hall. The entertainment included a boxing exhibition and an operetta performed by girls. Mary Genessi was mentioned as a very young dancer and Sean Ferris sang 'The

Low Backed Car'. Canon O'Boyle paid tribute to all for the successful concert. (Irish News 18 February 1939.)

In 1939 there were 180 pupils and four teachers, Mr. John B. Fitzpatrick, Mr. P.J. Fitzsimons, Miss Jean O'Boyle and Mr Edward McCavana, at the Boys' School.

The choir of the Sacred Heart Convent, Lisburn were winners of the Columban Cup at the Belfast Feis. (Irish News with photo 1 June 1939.)

July William John Goodman, who played a prominent role in the affairs of St Patrick's Church died aged seventy-six.

He lived at 3 Grand Street, Lisburn and had been employed for sixty-four years by Wm. Barbour & Sons, Hilden and the Linen Thread Company. For thirty-two years he had been works manager for their firm in Hamburg, Germany. At the outbreak of war in 1914 he was interned in Ruhleben camp, west of Berlin and remained there until the end of the war in 1918 when he returned to Lisburn. He had worked up to ten months before his death. His son William was the chief mourner and Rev. Lynn officiated at the funeral service. (Ulster Standard 28 July 1939.)

October Miss Eta Fitzpatrick, daughter of J. Fitzpatrick, principal of St Patrick's Boys' School was appointed principal of the newly established Girls' Commercial School in Downpatrick. (Ulster Standard 6 October 1939.)

December St Colman's new hall at Reilly's Trench was personally funded by and opened by Canon O'Boyle. It was built in four months under the supervision of builder John McDonald and architect Gerald O'Gorman with voluntary work provided by parishioners. Previously Reilly's Trench school had been used for concerts and dances but could only hold about forty people with the school desks removed.

At a speech at the opening of the hall Canon O'Boyle reminded the audience that 300 years previously the district had been all Catholic and belonged to the Magennis family but had been seized by the Hill family. He said that Reilly's Trench is a historic Catholic spot and the old graveyard is the most ancient in the diocese.

In handing over the hall to a committee he laid down a number of rules;

that the hall would be under the control of the parish priest, it was not to be kept open after 1:00 am and no gambling or intoxicating drink was permitted on the premises. (Canon O'Boyle papers.)

1940

Mr P.J. Fitzsimons, who was on the teaching staff for 33 years, was appointed as principal of St Patrick's National School on Mr John Fitzpatrick's retirement.

1941

The C.Y.M.S. of Belfast gave a concert devoted to the life-work of Carl Hardebeck, collector, editor and composer of Irish music. The Bishop of Down and Connor presided, and spoke at the beginning of a broadcast made, via Athlone, from Belfast to all Ireland. That noted orator of the North, Rev. Dr A. H. Ryan, spoke on Hardebeck's work, and Padraic Gregory, the poet, read an ode in Hardebeck's honour. Harpers came from a great convent school in Lisburn. (Catholic Herald 14 March 1941.)

April Daniel Devenney, who had left Lisburn aged eleven as a refugee when the family owned butchers shop in Bow Street was burned in 1920, was now an accountant and commercial manger of John Halliday & Sons Ltd., footwear manufacturers in Dundalk. At the start of the war he had been asked to set up a fire fighting unit at the factory as a precaution in the event of a bombing or an incendiary attack.

When Belfast came under attack by the Luftwaffe's bombers on Easter Tuesday, 15-16 April 1941 R.D. Harrison, City Commissioner of the Royal Ulster Constabulary send an urgent request to the War Room at Stormont that fire engines from Eire should be requested. Sir Basil Brooke agreed to the request 'as a matter of expediency'. Within two hours the Taoiseach, Eamon de Valera advised Stormont that fire engines would be dispatched from Dublin, Dundalk, Drogheda and Dun Laoghaire.

Dan Devenney left by hired car for Belfast to take charge of the Halliday Auxiliary Fire Engine which was towed by Dundalk Urban Fire Brigade to Belfast. (Petrol was extremely scarce in Eire during the war years.) He passed through Bow Street where twenty-one years earlier he had been burned out of his home.

After working all day in the Oldpark Road area of Belfast Dan Devenney and his men, still wearing their uniforms, went to the Eglington Hotel for a meal as they had not eaten all day but were refused service and ordered out. It was not clear if it was because of their disheveled appearance after a day of fire fighting or because of their southern accents. They planned to return home that night and as they made their way through Lisburn they decided to stop at Tom Brown's pub in Market Square which 'stocked very good Guinness and even better ham sandwiches'.

Dan said that the experience of seeing the bodies of dead children being carried from the rubble of their former homes caused him sleepless nights. He said that the unkindest cut of all was when Basil Brooke the prime minister of Northern Ireland when asked to express his thanks to the Eire government for sending the fire brigades to Belfast said that it was a matter for the minister of Home Affairs. (Dan Devenney's War) and (The Blitz - Belfast in the War Years, Brian Barton.)

Following the attacks by the Luftwaffe in April and again on 4-5 May thousands fled from Belfast to the countryside or to rest centres and billets in nearby towns including Lisburn. Many, described as like crowds at a football match, walked each evening to the hills that surround Belfast and spent the night in ditches to escape the next expected air raid. It was estimated that at least one-third of the population of Belfast was sleeping outside its boundaries.

The Northern Ireland government was ill prepared for these raids from a military point of view and was overwhelmed in trying to deal with the aftermath of the raids. The result was chaos. It was often left to church groups and volunteers to cope with the mass of evacuees estimated at 70,000. It is estimated that about 1,000 individuals sought refuge in Lisburn and St Joseph's Hall was among the rest centres established in the town. Lisburn was regarded by the Ministry of Home affairs as one of the most efficiently organised reception areas in the North but even there it was over two weeks before the rest centers were cleared and billets found for those who had taken shelter in them. A number of refugees abused the hospitality offered to them, begging for clothes which were then pawned. The mass evacuation lifted the lid on the extent of poverty in Belfast with many evacuees being described as 'filthy and verminous with inhuman habits'. The unionist government had perpetuated the myth that the people of Northern Ireland had much better living standards that those living south of the border.

9 May Andrew Matchett, an evacuee from 14 Hartwell Street, Belfast was summonsed for riotous and disorderly behaviour in Lisburn. He had travelled across town at night from a rest centre to see a girl who was in St Joseph's Hall. A lady helper in the Hall who saw that the girl was still up ordered her to go to bed. Matchett caught this lady by the throat and only the intervention of Rev. Kelly saved her from serious injury. Matchett then used filthy and abusive language to the priest which was witnessed by those in the Hall. Head Constable Chesnutt confirmed in court that the man was not drunk. A fine of 20s was imposed. (Lisburn Standard 16 May 1941.)

Among those subscribing to the Air Raid Distress Fund in Lisburn was D. Mooney on behalf of the Catholic Club. (Lisburn Standard 2 May 1941.)

6 June The evacuees still had not been cleared from Lisburn's schools and Rev. Kelly requested that the children at Hilden rest centre (presumably Hilden School) be transferred to St Joseph's Hall and that Hilden rest centre be closed. (Lisburn Standard 6 June 1941.)

15 June Despite the plight of the refugees in Lisburn the Sacred Heart of Mary Convent held a concert on Sunday. The guest artist was Miss Elizabeth Sheridan, a soprano and a former pupil of the school. She had studied in London and was now a leading operatic soprano. Canon O'Boyle speaking at the event paid tribute to Miss Sheridan's singing and to the teachers and pupils of the convent. (Lisburn Standard 20 June 1941.)

1942

27 July Very Rev. James Canon O'Boyle died, aged 80 and after Solemn Office and Requiem Mass in St Patrick's Church his remains were interred at the entrance to Reilly's Trench Church.

He had been born on 5 May 1862 at Duneane, near Randalstown. He was interested in international and local history and while at Lisburn wrote a history of the Plantation of the Lisburn area. Known as 'The O'Boyle

Papers' they were retained by Marjorie Furey, a parishioner and a family relation. A copy is now held in the parish archives. He had also written 'From Washington to Roosevelt', 'Life of George Washington', 'Life of St Malachy' and 'The Irish Colleges on the Continent.' He left behind a huge collection of notes, historic and biographic of diocesan interest but they do not appeared to have survived. He was a regular contributer to the columns of the 'Irish News'.

He knew his parish from end to end and used to boast that he knew everyone in his charge. He travelled abroad and it was on a visit to the Holy Land with his brother Rev. Gerard O'Boyle that their car was involved in an accident and he was injured. On a painful journey home he had to spend quite some time in a London hospital before he was fit to return to Lisburn. He never fully recovered from the injuries and his health broke down completely in the spring of 1942. (Irish News July 1942.)

October Rev. Thomas Blacker was appointed as parish priest.

During the war years St Patrick's Church assisted in the war effort by donating the iron railings and gates outside the church towards the national drive to provide scrap metal. Part of the original railings embedded in the wall outside the church are still visible today.

It has since been discovered that this was primarily a propaganda exercise and that little, if any, of the thousands of tons of scrap metal collected was used for its intended purpose and much of it was secretly dumped at sea.

1943

The funeral took place on Tuesday to St Patrick's churchyard, Lisburn, of Mrs Arthur Shields sister-in-law of Mr Barry Fitzgerald, the famous Hollywood actor.

Mrs Shields, who lived at Sandymount Avenue, Dublin, was a daughter of the late Mr John Magee of Lisburn. Known as 'Mac' she had worked as a chauffeur in the British army before meeting Arthur.

Rev. J. Blacker, P.P., Lisburn, officiated at the graveside.

Arthur Shields and his better known older brother, William (the Hollywood actor Barry Fitzgerald) were born into a Dublin Protestant middle-class family. A Protestant nationalist, he had fought in the Easter Rising 1916 and was later interned in Frongoch, North Wales.

Arthur, along with his brother William, were involved with the Abbey Theatre in Dublin before becoming successful Hollywood actors.

He appeared in numerous films including, alongside his brother Barry Fitzgerald, 'The Quiet Man' (1952).

He was married three times, his first wife being Maisie Magee of Lisburn. (Irish News 29 October 1943.)

1944

Teachers in the Convent primary school included Madames St John, Brendan, Evangalis and Miss Murray. The school had four rooms with two classes in each room. A former pupil recalled that there was a room upstairs.

Those who contributed to the Apostolic Work fund in 1944 included: Rev. P. Madden, Rev. Mother Superior, Dr McHugh, Sir William McIlroy, Miss McIlroy, Miss Armstrong, the Adair family, Miss Lucinda Courtney, Mr & Mrs P. Elmore, Miss Sarah & Lydia Fleming, Mr P. Gorman Jnr, Mrs Gilmore, Miss Mary Johnston, Mrs McLaren, Mrs McDonnell, Mrs J. Robinson and Mrs White. (Parish Archives.)

SIR WILLIAM MCILROY

1945

5 May Sir William McIlroy, K.C.S.G., who retired as Flax Manager with Barbour's Lisburn Linen Thread Company in 1933 died on 5 May. He had attended the funeral of Miss Anna McIlroy, his only surviving sister who had died just a few weeks previously. His two brothers James and Edward and his other sister Elizabeth had all predeceased him.

William McIlroy, whose family originally came from the Falls Road, Belfast and whose father was in the flax trade, had lived in Courtrai, Belgium until his father's death in 1875 when the family returned home. Educated at St Malachy's College, Belfast he served his apprenticeship in the flax department of Barbour's Mill at Hilden. His natural ability coupled with his fluency in French and other languages led to his appointment as flax buyer for the company. He later became flax manager and as part of his work travelled to many parts of the world. Highly regarded he was appointed a Justice of the Peace and also was a member of the County Antrim Infirmary. He never married and as a philanthropic funded many good causes including new x-ray equipment at the Mater Hospital. (www.hidden-gems.eu)

The McIlroys employed Joseph Mulholland as a chauffeur and his son Adrian, a staunch member of St Patrick's parish, remembers his father's green uniform and cap and the McIlroy's green Riley car. The McIlroy family home, since demolished, was at Low Road, Hilden beside the home of Milne Barbour. That house, with an interesting link to Thomas Andrews who designed the 'Titanic', is now the home of Seamus and Ann Scullion of the Hilden Brewery.

A devout Catholic he had been most generous in supporting the church. Among his charitable works he had funded the construction of a Calvary grotto in a space to the left of the front of St Patrick's Church (since removed following repeated vandalism in later years). He donated St Anthony's statue, a Lourdes altar, St Anne's statue and a Little Flower statue to St Patrick's. He also funded the annual summer excursions to the seaside for Lisburn Boys' School.

In recognition of his good works, which included building the church of St Mary of the Angels at Clanvaraghan, County Down, he was created a Knight of St Gregory by Pope Pius XI. The Order of St Gregory the Great is bestowed on persons who distinguish themselves for conspicuous virtue and notable accomplishment on behalf of the church and society, regardless of their religious belief. During his funeral service in St Patrick's on Monday 7 May 1945, (Most Rev. Dr. Mageean, Bishop of Down and Connor presided and the celebrant was Rev. P. Madden C.C.) his Knight's bicornered hat with plume and court sword reposed on the coffin. School children from Lisburn Boys' School marched in front of the hearse to the cemetery. He was buried in the family grave at Holy Trinity Cemetery. Rev. T. Blacker officiated at the graveside. Sir Milne Barbour and Mr. J.D. Barbour attended the funeral service. (Irish News 8 May 1945.)

Sunday 13 May was observed in St Patrick's Church, as in all Catholic churches, as a day of thanksgiving to mark the end of the war in Europe.

1946

1 March Very Rev. Thomas Hugh McAuley was appointed as parish priest on the death of Rev. Blacker. Rev. McAuley was a traditionalist and made it known to parishioners that he would not administer Holy Communion to any woman wearing bright red lipstick which was then fashionable. He was known to comment to women waiting to receive Holy Communion, 'I see you have the war-paint on today.'

Lisburn Feis was held in St Joseph's Hall. (The Patricia Mulholland Papers, National Dance Archive of Ireland, University of Limerick)

1947

1& 2 November The convent held a Fun and Fancy Fair in the Convent Hall. The Saturday opening ceremony was by Lady Antrim and on Sunday by Rev. T. McAuley. There were half-hour dances, side shows and refreshments. Admission 1/6, children 1/- . (Irish Press 25 October 1947.)

Lisburn Convent School was producing excellent results and Mother Saint Clement acquired Rathmore (Dunmurry) with a view to opening a grammar school there. Rathmore was a stately house built by Belfast businessman Victor Coates and like many similar properties whose upkeep was no longer economically viable it was placed on the market. Bishop Mageean bought it on behalf of the Sacred Heart of Mary Sisters. The Ministry of Education did not immediately approve the proposal and, instead, in 1949 the Sisters opened a preparatory school for girls and boys in Rathmore House which became known as the Convent as it accommodated the Sisters as well as the pupils.

In the 1940s boy boarders attending Lisburn Convent slept at Knockmore House (near the junction of Moira Road and Causeway End Road) and walked from there to the Convent each day. This was parish property and was later let to an Italian family who operated a market garden business within the grounds. The house was eventually demolished.

(Note: Knockmore House was formerly occupied by the Boomer family. William Boomer made available a field at Knockmore for Orange demonstrations and in April 1934 was host to 10,000 Junior Orange Order members, families and friends.

Lieut. W. C. Boomer, Royal Irish Rifles, the only son of Mr. Richard Boomer, Knockmore House, Lisburn, took a keen and active interest in the Ulster Volunteer Force, and was a company officer of the 1st Lisburn Battalion South Antrim Regiment of that body, from which the 11th Battalion Royal Irish Rifles (South Antrim Volunteers) was almost entirely recruited. Lieut. Boomer joined the South Antrims as a private shortly after the formation of the battalion, and was promoted to commissioned rank on the 2nd July 1915. He went to the front with the Ulster Division in October of that year, saw much fighting and was wounded three times.)

Rev. P. Madden and Rev. B. McCann were curates in Lisburn at this time.

1948

St Joseph's Billiard Team, Brian McMahon, Paddy McKernan, Pat Lavery, Sammy McShane, T. McDowell, Gerald McGrath and Pat McArdle were 'B' Team winners 1948/49. (Ita McArdle)

Rev. T. Breen was a curate in Lisburn at this time. (Parish archives)

1949

February Outside Lisburn stones were thrown at buses returning on Sunday with supporters of the Ulster team which was beaten by Leinster in the Railway Cup senior final at Clones. Windows in one of the buses were smashed but no injuries to passengers were reported. (Irish Press 22 February 1949)

October Rev. A.H. Scott B.A. C.C. was transferred from Duneane to take up a new post as curate in Lisburn parish. (Irish News 28 November 1949)

Despite incidents such as the attack on the buses the ten-year period after the war was perhaps the 'golden years' for inter-community relationships in Lisburn. While the Catholic and Protestant communities continued to live separate lives they did so in relative harmony. These were the good old days when Catholics would watch the spectacle of kilted pipers at colourful parades on the 12 July.

The war had affected everyone, rationing was still in force and working class Protestants and Catholics faced similar problems. While the IRA campaign in England and Belfast during the war grabbed the newspaper headlines it was of little concern to the people of Lisburn. Equally the IRA's ineffective border campaign in the 1950s did not upset relationships but was used by unionist politicians to maintain a fear factor and exacerbate sectarian tension.

As the decade progressed in 1956 a young preacher Ian Paisley brought religious differences to fore in the conversion of Maura Lyons, an immature teenage Catholic to Free Presbyterianism. Allegations of abduction occupied nationalist politicians, the RUC and eventually the courts before the child returned to her home and her Catholic faith. The publicity raised the profile of Rev. Paisley as he built a career on division promoting hatred of the Catholic religion incorporated with a hatred of Irish nationalism. He preached that Rome was hand-in-hand with the Dublin government in a plot to overthrow Northern Ireland and the Protestant religion. Pandering to the insecurities of the mainly working class Protestant population many were willing to accept this as true.

In 1964 he brought thousands of his followers on to the streets in protest against the display of a tricolour in the window of a republican candidate's office in Divis Street Belfast, forcing the RUC to remove the flag and leading to two days of sectarian rioting.

When Terence O'Neill became prime minister of Northern Ireland and in 1965 met with Seán Lemass, An Taoiseach of Ireland, he was denounced by Paisley as a traitor. The anniversary of the 1916 Rising in 1966 was used to promote fear in the Protestant population as unionists talked about 30,000 IRA men from the Irish Republic set to invade Northern Ireland. Such talk was sufficient for the formation of the paramilitary Ulster Protestant Volunteers (UPV). There was of course no plan for an invasion and in any event the IRA was a spent force. The UPV's mirror image the UVF was involved in 1966 in the sectarian murder of Catholics in Belfast. The UPV would, in March and April 1969, bomb a number of electricity stations and place the blame on the IRA.

The emergence of the civil rights movement in 1967 seeking a universal franchise, the end of gerrymandering of electoral boundaries, the ending of discrimination against Catholics in the allocation of public sector housing and jobs and the disbandment of the 'B-Specials' would lead to further conflict as Civil Rights Association rallies were met with counter demonstrations organised by Ian Paisley and his supporters. (It would take almost fifty-years before Ian Paisley admitted in a televised interview on BBC on 13 January 2014 that the grievances of the Catholics of Northern Ireland were legitimate).

The steady slide into bloodshed, of then unimaginable magnitude, had begun. Lisburn would not be spared.

1950

Teachers at the Convent Grammar School included;
Catherine Kerrigan (Maths & Science and hockey).
Miss O'Neill (Geography & History). Her brother was parish priest in Hannahstown and her sister was the first principal of St Monica's School on the Ravenshill Road, Belfast.
Miss McGinley (English).
May Marrinan (Elocution, Drama & P.E.).
Pat Scott (Music) She lived at Bachelor's Walk, Lisburn.
Sister Cecilia Henry (Maths & Religious Education). Canon Boyle was her uncle.
Sister Fidelis (Irish & French).
Sister Theodore (French).
Sister Kofkta (?) (Music and Choral singing).
Sister Taracissius.
Miss Ann McSparran (Domestic Science).

John Grimley was employed as the convent groundsman/handyman and he tended the vegetable garden in front of the Convent Primary School.

The informative process for the Beatification of the Venerable Pierre Jean Antoine Galilee, founder of the Congregation of the Religious of the Sacred Heart of Mary, was formally opened in Rome in August. (Catholic Herald 25 August 1950)

The Feis Dal Mbuinne held in St Joseph's Hall and St Patrick's Youth Hall attracted entries of almost 1,800. (Irish Press 8 June 1950)

Hugh Kearney (24), Chapel Hill, Lisburn was electrocuted while working on a building site at Benson Street, Lisburn. Employed as a hodsman in the building of precast reinforced concrete houses he accidentally touched an electric cable after carrying bricks to the top of a ladder. (Irish Press 21 September 1950)

Rev. A. Scott was a curate in Lisburn at this time.

1951

Mr Brendan Fitzpatrick (son of the previous principal) was appointed as principal of St Patrick's National School. He was an enthusiastic sportsman and was a director of Belfast Celtic Football Club

A number of Catholic children from the Hilden/Low Road end of Lisburn attended Hilden Primary School, formerly a private National School established in the mid-nineteenth century by the Barbour family, owners of Hilden Mill, to educate the mill employees and their families. Provision was made for the Catholic children to be prepared for first Holy Communion, etc. Corporal punishment was a way of life in schools in this era and religious education was no exception so if pupils did not know the answer to a question or got the answer wrong they got a few whacks on the hand with either a cane or a 'leather'. During the annual visit by the Ecclesiastical Inspector (Rev. McNamara in the 1950s) the Protestant pupils were given a day off school. (Pat McHugh)

The head teacher was Mr Alexander Woodend, much respected and feared by pupils, parents and staff. A man of huge intellect, energy and presence he dominated any room he entered. Naturally therefore his nickname was simply 'the Wee Man'. He was a fierce disciplinarian and carried a concealed thin bamboo cane down the inside of his left trouser leg.

Only the brightest and best pupils were allowed to sit the 11 Plus exam. After the 11 Plus the selected few went to their chosen grammar school. The rest were split into two sub groups: the Protestant pupils went on to the state comprehensive and the Catholic pupils stayed at Hilden, marking time until they went briefly to the Lisburn Technical College at 15 (there was no Catholic secondary school at that time). Between 12 and 15 the 'last class' was shared by different age groups oldest at the back, youngest to the front.

In the 1950s members of the Catholic community in the Low Road area walked to church and it was usually only the old and infirm who took a bus to attend 8:00 a.m. Mass at St Patrick's. To facilitate those who used the bus service Rev. McAuley delayed the distribution of holy communion until after Mass to enable members of the congregation to get to the bus stop on time. (Unlike today when the majority of the congregation go forward to receive Holy Communion this was not always the case in the 1950s). (Hugh Rooney.)

1952

Mr. Peter O'Hagan was appointed to Lisburn Boys' School in 1952. His first classroom was 'The Big Hall' and every Friday afternoon all desks, chairs, etc. had to be moved out to accommodate the week-end functions. The small playground, referred to as the 'yard' was almost filled by an air raid shelter.

On Friday afternoons when the weather was suitable the senior boys and teachers walked from Chapel Hill to the Barbour Playing Fields on the Saintfield Road for football and games, returning to the school around four o'clock.

Rev. McAleese was a curate in Lisburn at this time.

The Portadown Catholic Dramatic Society were regular performers in St Joseph's Hall with production such as 'All Souls' Night and 'Quin's Secret' which was performed at the Feis Dal mBuinne fifth annual Festival in the hall. (portadownphotos.co.uk)

31 October A tragic fire in Lisburn provided an opportunity for political point scoring at Stormont.

Patrick Reynolds (Rollins per Ulster Standard, 7 November 1952) was at the cinema in Lisburn when a message was flashed on the screen for him to return home. His terraced house in Fairymount Square had been attacked with fireworks which resulted in the complete destruction of his home and all his belongings. To make matters worse he had been paid off work the previous day. Appeals were made by the British Legion in Sackville Street for bedding, clothes, etc.

At Stormont Mr Diamond MP asked the Minister of Health and Local Government whether he is aware that as a result of the discharge of a firework a house was burned and gutted in Lisburn on the night of the 31st October, rendering the tenant, Mr. Reynolds, an ex-Service man, his wife, and three children homeless and destitute; and if so, whether he can state the reasons why the Lisburn Council refuse to carry out their humanitarian duty to provide this family with alternative accommodation.

Captain O'Neill:

> *'The matter of the letting of council houses is not one in which I have any power to intervene. I have, however, brought the hon. Member's representations to the notice of the local housing authority for the area with a request that they may be given sympathetic consideration. The case has also been brought to the notice of the Northern Ireland Housing Trust.'*

Mr. Diamond:

> *'Is the Minister aware that this man, who is an ex-Service man, lost his home through no fault of his own and as a result of an accident, and that the Lisburn Urban Council has refused to carry out its duty of rehousing him, and by so doing is carrying out the traditional policy of bigoted, sectarian discrimination because he happens to be a member of the minority? May I ask further whether the Parliamentary Secretary is prepared publicly to endorse this treatment of former Service men and, if he is, let him say so in the House.'* (The Stormont Papers, Vol. 36 (1952,53.)

1953

Miss Mary Johnston presented a new missal to the church at Easter 1953. (Parish archives)

24 May Brother Joachim (Frank Lyttle) was ordained and celebrated his first Mass in St Patrick's. Crowds lined the streets to welcome him to the church.

1 September The Ministry finally approved the establishment of a grammar school at Rathmore House, Dunmurry. It opened on 1 September with 36 qualified boarding and day pupils, under the principalship of Mother Saint Brigid Galvin. Numbers increased and in 1955 the school took over huts which had been erected for use as offices by Messrs. Short and Harland during the war. When it opened as a school four air raid shelters and a drill hall from the war years still survived as did the house's original stables. Additional buildings were opened in 1960 and 1961.

Sister Jeanne d'Arc Lynam, later known as Sister Joan became principal in 1962/3. The school continued to flourish and further new buildings were opened in 1965 and 1973, with additional accommodation being created in the basement of the 1973 building in 1983 and 1990.

The school adapted to the changing needs of the times and in 1971 the preparatory school and boarding department of the grammar school closed while in 1974 the grammar school took in its first boys.

29 November There is a manuscript note on a leaf of a missal that Rev. Thomas McAuley, P.P. transferred to Reilly's Trench. (Parish archives.)

1954

In the Marian Year 1954 the parish organised a pilgrimage to Lourdes.

Throughout the 1950s the Catholics of Lisburn who contributed regularly to charitable causes included many from the Catholic business community in the town; P. Elmore, Jubilee Ave, Miss E. Armstrong, Railway St., Dr J. McHugh, Railway St., Mrs Robinson, Railway Hotel, Lisburn, Mr F. Elmore, Bow St., Miss A. & K. Adair, Causeway Ends Rd., Mr T. Brown, Market Sq., Mr M. Cunningham, Bridge St., Mr W. McConnell, Bridge St., Mr J. Marley, Dublin Rd., Mrs M. Gilmore, Dublin Rd., Mr McKeown, Blaris, Mrs Drake, Warren Gdns., Mrs Downey, Antrim Rd., Mrs Kearney, Gregg St., Mrs Clenaghan, Soldierstown, Mrs Mooney, Chapel Hill, Miss Kenny, Bow St., Mr Eastwood, Bridge St., Mrs Colgan, Pond Park, Mr. Gorman, Gregg St., Mr P. Brogan, Causeway End, Mr G. Kelly, Magheragall, Mr S. Drayne, Ballymacash House, Ballymacash, Miss Fullerton, Bridge St., Mr Luccido, Bridge St., Mr Hunter, Brookfield,

Antrim Rd., Mrs P. Hague, Chapel Hill, Miss M. Corr, Hill St., and Mrs B. Mullholland, Tonagh Pk. (Parish archives)

1955

Anna Mulholland was appointed teacher at Magheramesk School with eight pupils under her care. The school, one large classroom was heated by a coal fire at one end and an oil heater at the other end. During winter months when it was really cold children were called up in relays to warm themselves at the fire. The furniture consisted of long old-fashioned heavy desks with ink wells and tip-up seats. Lunch for the pupils was a small bottle of free milk with their sandwiches. (St. Aloysius Silver Jubilee booklet.)

The mid-1950s brought the new phenomena of rock 'n' roll music to Lisburn. Canon McAuley did not approve of the dancing associated with this music and banned the playing of rock 'n' roll music in St Joseph's Hall. It was usual to see signs in Catholic dance halls prohibiting jiving and jitterbugging.

20 November Rev. T.H. McAuley opened Lisburn Drama Festival in St Joseph's Hall. Among those groups performing were Ballyshannon Dramatic Circle, Portadown Catholic Drama Club, the Stella Maris Players, Belfast and the Dalboyne Players, Lisburn (Irish Press 21 November 1955.)

Among the projects supported by the Apostolic Works committee was a subscription for beds in Southern Rhodesia. (Parish archives)

1956

The women of the parish had formed an Apostolic Group making priests' vestments, embroidering altar cloths, etc. for the foreign missions. They met on a regular basis in the convent in Seymour Street.

During a women's mission in the late 1950s a rat emerged from the gratings in the floor of the church. There was pandemonium as the congregation climbed onto the pews.

20 April The 'Catholic Herald' newspaper, under the column 'Listen to This', advertised an Evening Service from the Oratory of the Sacred Heart of Mary Convent, Lisburn. Conducted by Fr Louis Comerton, assisted by Fr John Sloane, with the school choir it was to be broadcast on Sunday, at 7:45 p.m. on the North of Ireland Home Service.

During the 1950s and early 1960s St Patrick's operated the Parish Pools to help the parochial funds. Collectors went from door-to-door each week to collect one shilling from those parishioners who had agreed to participate in the Pools.

1957

The curates in St Patrick's at this time included Rev. D. Davey and Rev. J. Sloane.

1959

4 May 'Presented by the Parishioners to the Very Rev. T.H. Canon McAuley P.P. V.F. on the occasion of his election to the Chapter of the Diocese of Down and Connor is recorded in a missal held in the parish archives.

Canon McAuley owned a black Morris Minor car and Jim Gorman was his driver. Having parked the car in the garage at the parochial house Jim had then to walk home, often in the pouring rain.

1960

Because of health and safety concerns and pressure from various enforcing authorities Rev. McAuley embarked on major structural renovations to St Joseph's Hall. The hall had three floors and the upper floor, used as a schoolroom, presented a severe fire hazard as there was no external means of escape in the event of a fire on the floors below.

17 October Rev. McAuley wrote to the bishop informing him that major structural repairs costing £1,400 to Reilly's Trench church were required. Old buttresses had to be removed and replaced on new foundations, corners of the main walls had to be taken down and rebuilt and a new concrete base placed around the church. The walls had to be stripped back to the stone and re-plastered. He replaced the Stations of the Cross (at no cost to the parish as he noted). (Parish records Lisbreen House, Belfast.)

Rev. Thompson who was in charge of the Protestant Children's Home behind the old cemetery agreed to share the cost of the repairing the stone wall at the cemetery. The cost to Rev. McAuley was £173.15.00. (Diocesan records.)

The Boys' School had over 300 pupils and the teaching staff had increased to ten. The school was the winner of the Lisburn Schools' Under-12 League and cup 1960/61.

Over 100 male parishioners from St Patrick's attended a weekend Retreat at St Clement's, Ardglass, County Down conducted by the Redemptorist Fathers. These popular Retreats to Ardglass and later to St Clement's on Cavehill, Belfast were from Saturday to Sunday. Retreats were held at the old castle in Ardglass from 1945 to 1961 and then at Cavehill from 1961.

1962

Lisburn Boys' School went on a school trip to Dublin. (See framed photo in St Patrick's Pastoral Centre.)

Sr Joan Lynam, who had previously taught at the Convent Grammar School in Lisburn was appointed principal of Rathmore Grammar School. She held that post until she was succeeded in 1990 by Sr Ursula Canavan. During her time at the school the VIP visitors included in the early 1970s Margaret Thatcher when she was Education Secretary and Garret Fitzgerald who would later become Taoiseach in 1981.

On her retirement Sr Joan was awarded the OBE for services to education. (From Derriaghy to St. Anne's, Jim O'Hagan.)

1963

Rev. Bernard Magee, born 11 July 1924 and ordained 18 June 1950, had been a curate in St Malachy's Castlewellan (1957-1963) before being appointed to St Patrick's, Lisburn. He arrived at the time of a mission in the springtime of 1963.

One of his early initiatives was to form, for the first time, a parish committee. As the parish had three curates and the parish divided into three districts it was decided that each priest would appoint 15 parishioners from their districts. The interaction between parishioners and the clergy was positive and beneficial to both parties. It became known as the '45 Committee'.

1964

The former Convent primary school was replaced by a new school which was renamed St Joseph's Primary School.

There was an acute absence of any facilities for the young people in the parish and it was decided by Rev. McCaughan, using volunteer labour, to refurbish and extend the youth centre at the rear of the parochial house. Among those who assisted with the refurbishment were Frankie Watters and Danny Kearney.

(Frankie Watters had joined Lisburn Distillery Football Club from Banbridge Town at the start of the 1950s, making his debut on 31 January 1951. By November 1951 he was the established centre-half. He played throughout the decade and got one Irish League cap. He took part in 3 trophy wins:—- CAS, Irish Cup and City Cup. In 1957 he dropped down to the Seconds, making a few first team appearances at full-back over the next four years. In December 1958 he became temporary first team coach when Maurice Tadman left and by 1960/61 he was the reserve team coach. In his 11 season career he made 264 appearances but never scored a goal.)
(Lisburn Distillery History.)

Managed by a youth leader, Mr McLaughlin from Lurgan and a committee which included Hugh Rooney, this was a welcome provision for training and entertainment for the young people of the parish.

It was around this time that St Patrick's Gaelic Athletic Club was revived. One of the leading lights in reestablishing the club was Glenavy man, Gerry McAreavey and in the absence of a playing field in Lisburn the team used the GAA pitch at Glenavy. The new team turned out in a plain blue top and white shorts.

The club attracted players from both the Catholic and Protestant communities with some of the Protestants going on to play at county level. However as the 1960s progressed community relations turned sour with the Paisley orchestrated tricolour riots in 1964, the sectarian murders in Belfast in 1966, through to the civil rights protests and counter-protests. In this toxic mix of political and religious bigotry, in Lisburn as elsewhere, the communities coalesced as separate entities. The Protestant members of St Patrick's GAC began to leave, not due to pressure from their co-religionists or from other club members but from a bigoted element in the Catholic community in Lisburn.

During Sunday Masses a baby-sitting facility was provided in the adjoining St Joseph's Hall with volunteers including Mrs Eastwood taking care of the children.

26 September   Canon McAuley was in Lisburn courthouse as a complainant in a case concerning Arthur Gentle. Arthur, his wife and nine children were living in a caravan parked on church property, the tennis enclosure at Trinity Terrace. He was using it as a base for his scrap metal business which brought complaints from neighbours. When asked to leave he said he would only do so if the canon provided him with a house. Canon McAuley had no option but to take legal action but the case was dismissed as there was a dispute whether or not payments had been made to the Canon.

1965

Following the ending of the Second Vatican Council and the resulting decrees, the use of the vernacular was introduced in the Mass and the priest would no longer celebrate Mass with his back to the congregation. This resulted in the construction of new altars in many churches including St Patrick's. Other significant changes included the relaxation of penance during Lent and the changing of Friday abstinence regulations.

The church took a more lenient view of those who committed suicide in that those who took their own life were deemed to be not responsible for their actions and cremation which had previously been condemned by the church was now approved.

Priests and nuns were now permitted to wear lay dress.

Side altars were eliminated in new churches and became practically redundant in existing churches. Altar rails were to be removed and the practice of kneeling to receive Holy Communion with recipient's hands tucked under a snow white cloth would eventually be replaced with communicants standing and receiving communion in an outstretched hand. Many of the traditionalist priests and, it must be said, the laity found it difficult to come to terms with some of the new rules and regulations but gradually everything changed.

Rev. Finbar Glavin and Rev. C. Bready were curates in Lisburn at this time. Rev. Bready always wore his soutane when he went out in Lisburn. (Rev. B. Magee.)

August The Apostolic Works Committee in St Patrick's sent £34.15, as their contribution, to the Down and Connor Centre, located at Xavier House, 156 Cliftonville Avenue, Belfast, for the missionary church in the Punjab.

Little did they realise that forty years later parishioners at St Patrick's would include people from the Indian community and a priest from India would celebrate Mass in St Patrick's.

1966

1 March Rev. Ian Paisley who, agitating for a new bridge across the River Lagan in Belfast to be named Carson Bridge rather than Queen Elizabeth II Bridge, and had attracted a crowd of 4,000 inside and outside the Ulster Hall in Belfast, made a similar appeal in Lisburn's Orange Hall. Supported by Edward Carson, the son of Lord Carson he demanded that Lord Erskine, the governor of Northern Ireland 'must go' for objecting to naming the bridge Carson Bridge. He said that he foresaw Mass being said in St Anne's Cathedral (Belfast) if things are allowed to go the way they are. (Belfast Newsletter 2 March 1966.)

10 May Paisley was back in Lisburn Orange Hall addressing a meeting that was a portent not only for the Catholics of Lisburn but in Northern Ireland as a whole. He had organised a recruitment meeting for the new Ulster Protestant Volunteer movement. When the chairman of the meeting William Belshaw presented Rev. Paisley with a 1912 UVF cap badge Paisley said that the new volunteers would be guided by the UVF motto 'For God and Ulster'. (Belfast Newsletter 11 May 1966.)

September St Patrick's Intermediate School opened on the Ballinderry Road. Among the teachers was Miss Eileen Cooley who began her teaching career at the school in September 1966 when St Patrick's was a newly opened school of 220 pupils, 14 teaching staff and one caretaker. She was later appointed vice-principal.

1967

Canon Thomas McAuley celebrated the diamond jubilee of his ordination.

December The parish committee organised a bazaar, raising £770 to renovate the Sanctuary in St Patrick's.

1968

In June over 60 girls, from Lisburn's Convent School made a day trip to the home of Scotland's Robert Burns. At Alloway, the poet's home town, they saw the cottage where he was born and visited several places connected with him. (Lisburn Star June 1968.)

Lisburn Boys' Primary School in Chapel Hill closed in 1968 and pupils moved to a new school (St Aloysius Primary School) on the Ballinderry Road next to the local Catholic Secondary School (St Patrick's).

3 September On opening St Aloysius' had 330 pupils and eleven teachers - Mr O'Hagan, Mr McNulty, Mr Cassidy, Mr Jack Hoey, Mr Donnelly, Miss Hegarty, Miss McEvoy, Mrs Adams, Mr McCann and Mrs Harte. The first principal was Brendan Fitzpatrick. The school badge was designed by Mr Doherty formerly from Lisburn Boys' School.

The official opening and dedication was performed by Canon Thomas McAuley assisted by Rev. Bernard Magee. Some weeks later Rev. Charles Denvir celebrated the inaugural Mass in the school assembly hall.

The school soon became known as St Ally's. Teacher Peter O'Hagan had objected to the naming of the school because many would struggle with correctly spelling Aloysius.

When Rev. Denvir, a popular priest in the parish, organised fund raising bazaars in St Joseph's Hall his target was always £1,000. He was ably assisted in organising the bazaars by a number of parish stalwarts including Eileen Drayne who incidentally met her husband at function in St Joseph's Hall in 1945. Eileen was known by all the parishioners as she made her annual rounds to collect money for the Apostolic Society. She also took a keen interest in various charities including Combat Cancer, Save the Children and Meals on Wheels.

The Father Joachim Championship Cup for figure dancing at Lisburn Feis which ended on 5 June was won by McAleer School. (Irish Press 6 June 1968)

When Canon McAuley became ill and infirm Rev. Denvir became, de facto, the parish priest. Canon McAuley collapsed while saying 8:00 a.m. Mass. After announcing that he did not feel well and that he would not be able to continue he became unsteady. Patrick McHugh who had been sitting near the altar jumped over the altar rail and caught the Canon before he fell backwards and laid him on the floor.

He recalled that the Canon was wearing a green chasuble. The Canon was then removed to the sacristy and Rev. Magee who was in one of the country churches was contacted. He rushed back to St Patrick's and fearing the worst set about anointing the Canon. As priests are anointed on the palms of the hands when ordained it was appropriate to anoint on the back of the hands which Rev. Magee did. The Canon regained consciousness, looked at Rev. Magee and said, 'The back of the hand'. Even in his weakened condition he was going to ensure that proper procedure was followed. (Pat McHugh & Rev. B. Magee)

Minnie Fox, from Newtownbutler, County Fermanagh, was Canon McAuley's housekeeper.

December The parish committee organised a bazaar raising £650 which went towards the cost of changing the heating system in St Joseph's Hall from coke to oil.

THE TROUBLES

1969

A group of Catholic parents in Lisburn formed an action committee to oppose what they described as the 'dictatorial decision' of Bishop Most Rev. William Philbin to close the Convent grammar school. The nine-member committee, formed after a meeting of 250 parents, did not want the school to be amalgamated with Rathmore school and said that a 21-acre site for a new grammar school was available on the outskirts of Lisburn. They complained that at no stage had Dr. Philbin consulted the layity in Lisburn in the matter. (Irish Press 12 April 1969.)

14 August There was heightened tension in Lisburn following extensive rioting over a number of days in Derry and subsequent sectarian rioting in Belfast and other towns starting on 14 August, which is generally accepted as the start of the 'Troubles'.

16 August The AOH Hall in Linenhall Street, Lisburn was damaged by fire in what was widely believed to have been a sectarian attack.

24 August In the early hours of Sunday W.O. Welton & Sons' handkerchief factory, off the Hillsborough Road, Lisburn, which employed many Catholic workers, was destroyed in an arson attack. Hugh Boyd, the managing director, stated that the fire could not have been as a result of an electrical fault, leaving readers of the 'Ulster Star' to read between the lines. (Ulster Star 30 August 1969.)

Rev. Emmett Dagens, who had been ordained in 1958, was transferred from St. Joseph's, Bury to Lisburn. (Catholic Herald 2 October 1969.) He later took an interest in St Patrick's Gaelic Athletic Club. He celebrated the golden jubilee of his ordination at St Kieran's College, Kilkenny in August 2008.

Rev. Bernard Magee, who had been a curate in Lisburn from 1963, was transferred to St Patrick's, Donegall Street, Belfast where he served as a curate until 1978 and later as Administrator from 1978-1981. He later was appointed parish priest in St Macartan's, Loughinisland 1981-2000 and became priest-in-residence at St Malachy's, Castlewellan from 2000.

He arrived in Donegall Street barely two months after the cataclysmic events of August 1969 and half-way through his 12 years there remembered one night, along with Fr Blaney recalling by name 67 people who had been killed in their parish since his arrival including the New Lodge Six in February 1973. The second half of his ministry there was marked by the heinous crimes of the Shankill Butchers. He had ministered to the victims of the UVF atrocity, the McGurk's Bar bombing in December 1971 when 15 people lost their lives, the worst single atrocity of the Troubles in Northern Ireland until Omagh. He recalled that Mrs McGurk had been to confessions that evening and had taken the unusual step of introducing herself following her confession, something that he had never experienced with any penitent before. The next time he saw her was amid the rubble of what remained of McGurk's Bar when her body was being placed in an ambulance.

Canon Magee was one of three priests shot during the Troubles, critically injured in a sectarian murder bid in 1974. The other two were both killed administering the Last Rites: Fr Hugh Mullan in 1971 and Fr Noel Fitzpatrick 1972.

He and a friend, John Taylor, were shot near his father's home in the grounds of St Colmcille's Church, Ballyhackamore. Recalling the incident he said,

'That particular week I was on holidays but was in clerical dress because I had also visited my aunt in hospital. I think I took my father to Bangor and returned and stayed for tea, parking my car outside the church.

The police told me afterwards a car was stolen by the gunmen in North Road and driven to St Colmcille's where they got out and fired at me, first shooting me in the head and leg, and then John in the abdomen. There was some talk about me getting two shots in the head. I just don't know because there were two wounds in my head, an entry wound and an exit wound and yet the bullet is still in the brain.'

John, much older than Fr Magee, also recovered but is now deceased.

He had earlier that year in March 1974 given absolution to a 28-year-old police officer, Constable Thomas McClinton, a married father of one, who had been murdered by the IRA outside St Patrick's, Donegall Street Church.

> *'I gave him absolution and Fr Blaney anointed him and we stayed with him and gave him what care we could until the military ambulance came and took him away.'*

When transferred to the country parish at Loughinisland he was to experience more carnage when on the evening of Saturday, June 18, 1994, the 44th anniversary of his ordination, he was called from watching the Ireland-Italy World Cup match on TV with news that there had been an attack on 'The Heights Bar'.

At 10:10 p.m., two UVF men wearing boiler suits and balaclavas, and armed with assault rifles had walked into the pub and opened fire on the crowd. Six men were killed outright, and five other people were wounded. It was later claimed that members of the RUC had colluded with the UVF gunmen in the attack.

He, along with a Passionist priest who had just given a mission in the village attended the scene of the shooting and anointed the dead and dying.

('A Remarkably Priestly Life' - The Irish Catholic 2 May 2013.)

16 October

> IGOE - October 16, 1969 at Hospital, Eugene, dearly beloved husband of Delia Igoe - RIP. Funeral to-day (Saturday) at 3.00 pm from St Patrick's Church, Lisburn to Holy Trinity Cemetery. On his soul, sweet Jesus, have mercy. Very deeply regretted by his sorrowing wife and Family circle. House strictly private. (Irish News 18 October 1969)

Originally from Galway Eugene Igoe played a prominent role in the War of Independence as a member of the Royal Irish Constabulary.

One of Colonel Winter's (British Director of Intelligence) sub departments was an undercover team known officially as the Identification Branch of the Combined Intelligence Service (CIS).

Led by Head Constable Eugene Igoe, who reported directly to Deputy Police Adviser Ormonde Winter, the head of the CIS (National Archives, Kew), the unit comprised veteran RIC constables from outlying counties who could recognise leading IRA men by sight. The purpose of the unit was to identify provincial IRA members, especially those from the Western Region under Martial Law when they visited Dublin. Some put the numbers involved at about 30 whilst others estimated it as at least 50. Operating in mufti, Igoe and his team, known as the 'Igoe Gang', moved relatively freely about the city, and it took some time before Michael Collin's intelligence staff discerned the identity and purpose of the unit. (Michael Collins & The Anglo Irish War by J.B.E.Hittle.) They managed to arrest Charlie Dalton a member of Michael Collins 'Squad' (in reality not one but two squads). (National Archives, Kew)

These men were regarded as being the type who would be prepared to shoot IRA men on sight, and did, in fact, shoot a number of Volunteers who had arrived in Dublin from the country. Igoe and his men, in the main, waited around the various railway stations in the city attempting to identify known Volunteers. These Volunteers would be shadowed, and in a number of cases were killed or arrested.

This unit was quite successful in its operations to harass and hinder operations of the IRA/Irish Volunteers and was partly responsible for the British success in the war against the IRA in Dublin.

Eugene Igoe later adopted the name F.W. Willson and went to live in London. When he later came to live at Ballinderry near Lisburn he reverted to his original name but lived in fear of being assassinated by the IRA. When he was being buried in Holy Trinity cemetery there was still an element of secrecy. There is no record of his funeral in church records, there is no record of his burial plot and his grave remains unmarked. When he was being buried the sexton Tim McGrath sensed the secrecy and when no explanations were forthcoming he vowed to find out the reason. When he did find out about Igoe's background he confided that he had put an extra shovel full on top.

Work on the extension to the convent school estimated to cost £50,000 commenced.

5 & 6 December The parish committee held a bazaar to raise funds to modernise and renovate St Joseph's Hall.

1970

The Convent Boarding School closed in 1970 and the premises were vacated.

Magheramesk School closed. (St Aloysius Silver Jubilee booklet.)

St Joseph's Primary School became co-educational in 1970 when both boys and girls were admitted. This decision was influenced by the ongoing Troubles and sectarianism within Lisburn where boys walking from the other side of Lisburn to St Aloysius' Primary School were subject to taunts and attacks.
St Aloysius' also became co-educational.

1971

2 - 4 July Lisburn was targeted by the IRA in an incendiary bomb attack on shops in the town centre on Friday evening. J.C. Patterson's in Market Square suffered minor damage. Two devices in the Spinning Mill were extinguished but C&W Titterington's and McCormick's hardware store, both in Bow Street were extensively damaged. Reporting the incidents the 'Ulster Star' stated that the attacks had achieved the desired reaction of turning one section of the community against the other when Protestants and Catholics had been living in harmony.

That night a mob 'hell bent on revenge' marched to Chapel Hill to attack St Patrick's Church and St Joseph's Hall where the usual Friday night dance was taking place. The police, although outnumbered, blocked their way and came under a sustained attack until the early hours of Saturday morning but held their line. A rumour had been spread that a tricolour had been waved from a window at the front of St Joseph's Hall. A member of the parish committee denied this and explained that it was physically impossible as the windows at the front could not be opened.

The violence continued on Saturday evening into the early hours of Sunday. Catholic-owned premises including the Corner Bar, the Hayloft Bar, Elmore's fish shop and a confectioner's shop at the bottom of Chapel Hill were attacked and windows broken. Police reinforcements were drafted into the town and soldiers were deployed the protect the front and back of

St Patrick's church. The attack on the church was reminiscent of that fifty-one years earlier in 1920 and was compared by the 'Ulster Star' to the infamous Twenties.

The police made over twenty arrests.

The Feis, which had been held in St Joseph's Hall for twenty years had not been held the previous year because of a dispute among Irish dancing schools. (There may have been a gap in the Feis programme as records show that a Feis was held in St Joseph's in the 1930s). Gerry Traynor, a committee member of St. Patrick's Gaelic Athletic Club, along with Tony Magee took the initiative to bring the Feis back to St. Joseph's Hall. Gerry had won many medals for Irish dancing and was an All-Ireland champion dancer.

As arrangements had been made months in advance and despite the violence directed at the church and hall on Friday and Saturday nights the Feis went ahead as planned on Sunday. (Ulster Star 10 July 1971)

A large number of male parishioners attended St Patrick's Retreat at St Clement's Antrim Road, Belfast this year. (See framed photo in St. Patrick's Pastoral Centre)

During the 1970s selected Sunday newspapers were sold at a green kiosk at the side of the church next to the parochial house.

Following the introduction of internment 9-10 August 1971, when a large number of Catholics, suspected of being involved with the IRA, were arrested and imprisoned without trial, a former RAF airfield at Long Kesh outside Lisburn was pressed into use as a prison and the inmates were housed in Nissan huts. Later a small number of loyalists were arrested, many, as were the Catholics initially arrested, innocent. It has since been proven that this was to show that the authorities were acting 'impartially'. This later became known as Maze Prison.

A Capuchin priest Fr Joachim Lyttle, (Frankie Lyttle) a native of Lisburn, was appointed as chaplain at the prison. Previously he had served in Parow, a district of Cape Town, South Africa for five years and at Church Street Friary, Dublin.

Born on 17 January 1925, he became a Capuchin Friar on 3 October 1945 and was ordained on 24 May 1953. He was extremely well read and had a gift for eloquent speech and became well known for his compassion. His great love apart from reading was singing and during his time at Church Street, Dublin he conducted the choir.

During his time as chaplain at Long Kesh/Maze Prison he was respected by prisoners and prison authorities alike. He realised early on that the prisoners should put their time to good use and he set about collecting books to start a prison library and encouraged education as the key to a better future.

If there was a football match among the inmates it would not be unusual to see him running after the ball with his monk's garments flapping in the wind. (Richard McCauley Sinn Fein Publicity Office and former inmate - Irish News 30 Sept 2005)

In the area where Mass was celebrated in Long Kesh there were 'inappropriate pictures'. He ignored these 'pin-up' pictures and did not ask for them to be removed but after some time during a homily he said that he often thought he was in a British military camp because of the pictures on display. The pictures were removed immediately. (Irish News 30 September 2005.)

During this period and later Fr Joachim acted as an assistant priest in St Patrick's and was always well received when he celebrated Mass. In many ways he was a breath of fresh air and the congregation always listened intently to his homilies as he stood at the altar in his brown Capuchin robe and open-toed sandals. He had a particular talent as a confessor.

1972

This was to prove a significant year, not only for the Catholics of Lisburn but in Northern Ireland and would be marked as the worst year of the Troubles.

On 30 January thirteen men were shot dead and seventeen wounded by the Parachute Regiment in Derry leading to widespread anger within the Catholic community and encouraged many young men to join the IRA.

On 9 February William Craig formed an umbrella group of right wing unionists - Ulster Vanguard. The IRA conducted a murderous bombing campaign and in March alone eight people were killed and

230 injured by bombs placed in The Abercorn Restaurant and in Lower Donegall Street, Belfast.

The Prime Minister Edward Heath announced the suspension of the Stormont government on 24 March and introduced direct rule. This was considered by many Catholics to be a political victory and by most Protestants as a defeat and as such deepened sectarian divisions. The Catholics of Lisburn would not be immune as sectarian tensions were increased by Ian Paisley who portrayed the 'Church of Rome' as being behind the IRA.

13 February The Catholic population in Tonagh estate were somewhat apprehensive when 1,500 loyalists gathered at The Green. The newly created Vanguard Unionist Progressive Party, known as the Vanguard Party, had chosen Lisburn for its official launch. The choice of The Green, in what was perceived to be a predominately Catholic estate, seemed a somewhat strange location rather than the large Wallace Park nearer the town centre.

Closely affiliated with several loyalist paramilitary groups and the Orange Order it presented a threat not only to the Catholics of Lisburn but throughout Northern Ireland. Its leader William Craig, a former minister of Home Affairs, who arrived escorted by motor cycle outriders walked up and down lines of loyalists in paramilitary uniforms, referred to at Stormont as 'his so-called storm troopers'. Those present were asked to make certain pledges and while raising their right arms say, 'I do' three times. This and subsequent rallies had all the appearance of neo-nazi rallies.

At Lisburn Craig, in the first of a series of speeches of increasing bellicosity, proclaimed loyalist determination to maintain their British traditions and way of life and 'God help those who get in our way, for we mean business'. Capt. Austin Ardill, one of the deputy leaders of Vanguard stated that it was time to back the words 'No Surrender' with effective action. (Ulster Star 19 February 1972)

In a subsequent rally at Ormeau Park, Belfast (tickets were available at Lisburn Orange Hall at £1 each) Craig said, 'We must build up the dossiers on the men and women who are a menace to this country, because one day, ladies and gentlemen, if the politicians fail, it will be our duty to liquidate the enemy.' (The End of Stormont and impositions of Direct Rule in 1972 - Dr Marc Mulholland , St Catherine's College, Oxford.)

16 February The fears of the Catholic population of Lisburn were realized when after a 'Burning of Lundy' ceremony at the Bridge Street car park, where Rev. Ian Paisley applied a lighted torch to the effigy, a mob broke away from the 2,000 strong crowd at the bonfire to target Catholic-owned premises in Lisburn.

Among the places attacked were the old convent and the AOH Hall. The mob broke windows in the Corner Bar at the corner of Bow Street and Antrim Street before proceeding to Chapel Hill to stone St Patrick's Church and to break the windows of Caldwell's, another Catholic-owned public house. The local paper denied that stones had been thrown at the church.
(Ulster Star 19 February 1972.)

1 March St Patrick's Church held their annual dinner dance in the Woodlands Hotel. The 'Ulster Star' printed photos of some of the guests.
(Ulster Star 4 March 1972.)

28 March Tension among the Catholics of Lisburn increased when 1,000 people attended a Vanguard rally in the Smithfield market area. George Morrison, Country Grand Secretary and District Secretary of the Orange Order, a Lisburn councillor and a member of Vanguard called on a parades ban to be ignored and stated that at the 'Twelfth' he did not want to see picnics in the fields.

A couple of days later the IRA detonated a large car bomb near Smyth Patterson's department store in Market Square.

In April Lisburn Orange Hall was filled to capacity when a decision was taken to form a Lisburn branch of the Ulster Vanguard Clubs Association. Speaking at the event Rev. Martin Smyth, Grand Master of the Orange Order and deputy leader of the Vanguard party, endorsed the Vanguard's policy of a return of Stormont with full powers or an independent Ulster.
(Ulster Star 15 April 1972.)

22 April Over 100 loyalists marched through Lisburn en route to Long Kesh prison to join an anti-internment rally protesting about the internment without trial of Protestants. They were stopped by the police and army at the Moira Road. This triggered rioting and stones and bottles were thrown at the police. The rioting which went on into Sunday morning resulted in homes in Drumbeg Drive being attacked and a milk-float overturned and set on fire. A number of Catholic families lived in this area and nearby

Maralin Avenue. Sixteen people were arrested but later released. George Morrison stated that the disturbance was due to 'the provoking nature of the security forces in the early part of Saturday.'(Ulster Star 29 April 1972.)

May St Patrick's Gaelic Football Club held a dinner in the Greenan Lodge Hotel. (Ulster Star May 1972.)

4 June Gerald Murray (26) a Catholic married man from Killaney Avenue, Lisburn was shot by the UVF. He worked at Morans Music Company record shop at Annesley Street on the Antrim Road, Belfast and that night, after being out with his wife and brother for a few drinks, had returned to the shop just after midnight in the company van to check the telephone answering machine. As he was leaving the shop a number of shots were fired at him. He continued to walk towards the van saying that he had been hit and then collapsed. He had been shot in the chest. Three shots had hit the van and Mrs Murray was struck on the back of her head but was not seriously injured. She later told the inquest that her husband had never been threatened in any way. The police said that six rounds of .22 ammunition were found in Fleetwood Street, at the end of Annesley Street. (Lost Lives - David McKittrick, Seamus Kelters, Brian Feeney, Chris Thornton, David McVea, Mainstream Publishing.)

17/18 June The second annual Feis was held in St Joseph's Hall over the weekend. The dancing competitions attracted over 500 entries. The organising committee included Sean Adair and Gerry Traynor. Gerry was the first person in the parish to read from the scriptures as part of the Mass.

At the beginning of that week a famous landmark in Lisburn, the Top Hat Ballroom was destroyed in a bomb attack. Despite the mayhem in Lisburn in preceding days and months normal life went on when possible and the Feis continued the following weekend with singing and music sessions. (Ulster Star 24 June 1972.)

18 August Members of the Ulster Vanguard Movement included a party of women wearing armbands, blue uniforms and peaked caps as they marched in military fashion to a rally in Lisburn. (Irish Press 19 August 1972)

October A brawl erupted at closing time on Friday night when 25 UDA men stormed the Catholic-owned Corner House pub and tried to seize Catholic drinkers.

The attack was fought off, with at least one shot fired and the Protestants besieged the pub for four hours until British troops scattered the attackers and escorted out 30 trapped Catholics. Three people were injured. (Belfast UP)

17 October A group of about sixty, known as the Ulster Young Militants, the youth wing of the UDA, gathered in Bridge Street at 10:40 p.m. and attacked buildings with petrol bombs and broke the windows in various business premises, including the Catholic-owned McCready's Hayloft pub at 50 Bridge Street, which was badly damaged.

The mob steadily grew in strength to about one hundred and moved down Bow Street to the junction with Antrim Street where they attacked the Corner Bar which was closed at that time. They forced the door open and set fire to the premises. By now the mob had grown to two hundred and fifty.

A barrier was erected in Bow Street with building materials and the mob returned to Bridge Street where they ripped up flagstones. They then made their way to Linenhall Street where they attacked and extensively damaged the AOH Hall before setting it on fire. Also damaged was the Linfield shirt factory adjoining the Hibernians Hall. (Ulster Star, 21 October 1972 and Irish News 18 October 1972.)

St Patrick's Church and the Catholic-owned County Down Arms public house were also damaged by fire. (Belfast UPI 21 October 1972.)

1973

29 January James Trainor (23), a Catholic married with two children, from Lagan Walk was shot by the UDA/UFF.

James worked at the Speedline Garage on Kennedy Way in west Belfast and was alone when a car containing three men pulled into the forecourt. James went out and unhooked the petrol pump hose ready to deliver the petrol. He immediately realised that he was in danger, having recognised one of the occupants of the car or having seen one produce a revolver. He tried to escape but the gunman opened fire hitting him four times.

The police said that the killing appeared to have been an indiscriminate attack on 'whoever happened to be handy.' It was the second shooting in the Kennedy Way area within 24 hours. Earlier a Catholic man had been shot from a passing car and was seriously injured so James Trainor would have been aware of the risks faced working alone in this area.

This was the second time tragedy struck the Trainor family. James' father had been seriously injured a year earlier when a blast bomb was thrown at a Saracen army vehicle in Castle Street, Belfast. (Lost Lives - David McKittrick, Seamus Kelters, Brian Feeney, Chris Thornton, David McVea, Mainstream Publishing.)

May In an attempt to burn down the church two confessional boxes and a section of the roof were burned when incendiary devices exploded in St Patrick's Church at lunchtime. A number of wall mounted oil paintings, part of 'The Stations of the Cross' were damaged when acid was thrown at them. Previously the parochial house had come under a stone throwing attack and gravestones and surrounds had been vandalised in Holy Trinity cemetery.

Seamus Close who had joined the Alliance Party at the end of 1970 was elected to Lisburn Borough Council.

1974

2 March The Holy Trinity cemetery was attacked in the early hours of Saturday. Headstones were overturned and many, including a large celtic cross, smashed.

Windows were broken in Catholic homes in the area around the same time. Lisburn's mayor, John Gilchrist, described this attack as vandalism. At the end of March Kilrush cemetery also came under attack. Slogans including 'No Pope Here' and 'UDA' and 'UVF' were painted on headstones and others were smashed. (Lisburn Star, 8 & 29 March 1974.)

23 April The home of a Catholic family at Barley Hill, off the Low Road, was petrol bombed by individuals who arrived by car. One of the petrol bombs set the living room on fire. There were three people in the house at the time. (Ulster Star, 26 April 1974.)

15 May A strike was called by loyalists and unionists in protest to the signing of the Sunningdale Agreement in December 1973 which gave nationalists and the Irish Government a role in running Northern Ireland.

The Catholic community in Lisburn faced a particularly difficult time when the Ulster Workers Council, which included members of the UVF and the UDA, enforced an industrial stoppage by encouraging power station manual workers to go on strike. This was quickly followed by taking control of petrol and oil supplies.

Protestant working class support for the strike was substantial in Lisburn and when it became obvious that the security forces and government departments were inactive or ineffective in dealing with what was undoubtably a politically motivated strike, support grew within all Protestant classes including unionist politicians.

Road blocks manned by Protestant paramilitary groups, wearing masks and carrying cudgels, prevented people from going to work and intimidation became rife. Hijacked vehicles were often used to block the streets. (The May 1974 UWC Strike - A review by the Department of Commerce.)

George Morrison, District Secretary of Lisburn District Loyal Orange Lodge No 6, advised all members, along with other loyalists, to support the stand taken by the Ulster Workers Council. A rally of around 1,000 people gathered in Market Square, Lisburn on Wednesday 22 May to support the UWC strike.

Individuals on strike and those unable to get to work formed queues four deep outside the labour exchange in Bow Street. Families cooked meals during the short time electricity supplies were switched on and petrol supplies were limited to £1 per customer. Ration type books were printed for doctors and other essential services including civil servants making emergency benefit payments.

28 May Brian Faulkner, Chief Executive of the Northern Ireland Executive, along with his unionist colleagues resigned resulting in the collapse of the Northern Ireland Executive and the Sunningdale Agreement.

A loyalist victory parade to celebrate the collapse of the power sharing executive was organised by Lisburn District LOL No 6. Accompanied by five bands it made its way from the Longstone, past St Patrick's Church to a rally in Smithfield Square.

Lisburn was under the control of the UDA/UVF and the Catholic community was isolated as the police, army and the Westminster government had neither the policy or the ability to protect vulnerable Catholics.

Petrol bombs, hurled through the windows of two houses at Lisburn, drove two Catholic families into the street. Police said the top floor of one house was burned out but no one was hurt. (Belfast UPI.)

1975

Mr Peter O'Hagan was appointed principal of St Aloysius' Primary School on the Ballinderry Road on the retirement of Mr Brendan Fitzpatrick. His wife was a district midwife.

19 September Catholic workers were forced to leave a building site at the Lagan Valley Hospital. Five workers were injured when a bomb in a small cylinder, fixed with a time fuse, left under the corrugated hut where they took their tea break exploded. (Irish Press 20 September 1975.)

In 1975 St Patrick's Ladies Social Club had an active membership of almost one hundred members and about eighty non-members who joined in various activities organised by the club. Bus trips in June where a number of 49 seater buses were chartered were popular as was the Christmas dinner which cost £3 per person for members and £3.35 for non-members. One hundred and sixty attended the Christmas Dinner and there was a waiting lists held. Mrs Toner was president of the club, with Mrs Jean Fitzpatrick vice president. Betty McClinton was secretary, Marie McClinton treasurer, and committee members were Ann McKeown, Bridie Gawley, Mrs McGuiggan and Mrs Edith Donnelly. (Parish archives.)

1976

Sunday 25 January Two Lisburn Catholics, Raymond Mayes (33) and John Tennyson (27) were killed when the UDA bombed the AOH Hall in Conway Street, Lisburn.

John Patrick Tennyson from Crossan Walk, Old Warren Estate, married with three children, was having a quiet drink along with about twenty-five others when a bomb, estimated to contain 10 lbs of explosives was left on a window sill of the club. It exploded without warning killing him and Raymond Mayes. Five others were injured by shards of glass and rubble.

Joseph Raymond Mayes from Glebe Walk, was also married with three children.

Three men were seen running away towards Wallace Park after the explosion and it was later claimed that the UDA had carried out the bombing. At his funeral service Bishop Dr William Philbin said that 'individual assassinations and group and random massacres are horrifying the whole world and reducing this province to barbarism.'

A spokesman for the RUC said that the deaths marked a very bleak start to the new year with an average of more than one person per day being sent to an early grave. (Lost Lives - David McKittrick, Seamus Kelters, Brian Feeney, Chris Thornton, David McVea, Mainstream Publishing.)

9 March Two Catholic brothers, Myles (41) and Patrick Anthony (Tony) (43) O'Reilly, owners of the Golden Pheasant Inn on the Upper Ballynahinch Road, outside Lisburn, were killed by the UVF.

Three gunmen entered the isolated inn shortly after opening time and forced the owners and the 13 members of staff, which included women, girls and a six-year-old child who was also there, to the back of the building and into a storeroom. Myles and Tony were ordered to come out and to crawl up the stairs. Those in the storeroom heard three or four shots. These were the shots that brought the brothers' lives to an end. There was then an explosion in the building and those in the storeroom fled for their lives. A second explosion destroyed the building. The bodies of the two brothers were later found in the rubble of what had been the restaurant.

Both brothers were married. Myles left a widow and two children. Tony left a widow and eight children. The brothers who were married to two sisters were close friends of Mary McAleese who would later become President of Ireland. The murders took place on her wedding day.

Two men were jailed for this crime, one received two life sentences for the two murders and the other 18 years for a variety of lesser offences. There had been three gunmen present during the attack. The UVF man given the life sentence stated that the restaurant was regarded as 'a military target' and claimed that the brothers were members of the IRA who were getting money from America for the organisation. There was absolutely no credence given to these claims.

The families decided not to have the funeral service in St Patrick's Church in Lisburn and instead Requiem Mass was held in St Brigid's Church in

Derryvolgie Avenue, Belfast and the brothers were buried in Milltown Cemetery, Belfast. (Lost Lives - David McKittrick, Seamus Kelters, Brian Feeney, Chris Thornton, David McVea, Mainstream Publishing.)

10 September In a sectarian attack, Catholic Seamus Muldoon (29) from Donard Drive, Tonagh Estate was shot in the back as he cycled to work as a postman. He had been hit in the small of the back by 29 pellets from a shotgun blast He died ten days later in the Royal Victoria Hospital, Belfast on 21 September. His father told an inquest that his son did not belong to any organisation. A detective said that the motive for the murder was sectarian. The UDA/UFF were behind the shooting according to reliable loyalist sources. (Lost Lives - David McKittrick, Seamus Kelters, Brian Feeney, Chris Thornton, David McVea, Mainstream Publishing.)

St Patrick's Ladies Social Club organised a Christmas Dinner with over 100 attending.

1977

Under the guidance of Peter O'Hagan St Aloysius' became the Northern Ireland Primary Schools Netball Champions. They were to reach the finals again in 1982.

Peter O'Hagan was appointed as a member of the newly created South Eastern Education and Library Board (S.E.E.L.B.) and later became its chairman (St Aloysius Silver Jubilee booklet.)

22 September St Patrick's Ladies Social Club organised an event listed as 'Mina Dornan'. Mina was a Lisburn actress and part of the cast of the soap opera 'The McCooeys' radio show, broadcast on Saturday evenings. She was also registrar for births, deaths, and marriages at the town hall in Castle Street, Lisburn. In the McCooey's she played the part of Maggie the mother, Joseph Tomelty was the father and James Young played Derek the window cleaner.

1978

26 January St Patrick's Ladies Social Club organised an event when author Sheila St Clair was the guest speaker.

10 May The police at Castlereagh Barracks, the main interrogation centre, announced that Catholic Brian Maguire (27), a AUEW shop steward, from Ardane Gardens, Causeway End Road, had been found hanged in his cell by a torn-off sheet attached to a ventilation grill.

He had been arrested a 6:00 a.m. the previous day and was being questioned about the killing on 22 April 1978 of RUC photographer Millar McAllister who had been shot while off duty at his home at Woodland Park, Lisburn.

In Castlereagh at the same time was the UDA brigadier for south Belfast and a member of the UDA's inner council. He was being held in a cell opposite that of Brian Maguire. He claimed during a trial for the manslaughter of his father-in-law that the death of Brian Maguire had been used to intimidate him. He claimed that detectives asked him what he thought of their handiwork in the cell opposite. (Lost Lives - David McKittrick, Seamus Kelters, Brian Feeney, Chris Thornton, David McVea, Mainstream Publishing)

23 May Very Rev. Canon McAuley died.

Rev. Joseph Cunningham was appointed as parish priest of Blaris (Lisburn)

Born in St Paul's Parish on 20 April 1923, he studied in St Malachy's College from 1935-1940 and afterwards at Queen's University Belfast from 1940-1943 where he obtained a First Class Honours Degree in Classics. The following year while studying theology in St Patrick's College Maynooth he continued his studies of the classics and was awarded an MA by QUB. In Maynooth he obtained First Class Honours in the B.D. (1946) and was ordained on 22 June 1947. His post graduate studies were in the Gregorian University in Rome (1947-1950) and he was awarded a Doctorate in Canon Law.

15 June Calling in the House of Commons for a judicial inquiry into Brian Maguire's death Mr. Fitt MP asked the Secretary of State Roy Mason,

'In view of the solemn and binding undertaking given by the British Labour Government to the European Court of Human Rights that ill-treatment and maltreatment would no longer be carried out in interrogation centres in Northern Ireland, is my right Hon. Friend aware that the whole credibility of the government and, indeed, of the Labour and trade union movement is at

stake on this issue? Is he aware that the 78 people mentioned by Amnesty International—a respectable and respected organisation—have tried to take civil action in the courts against the detectives who beat them up in Castlereagh, and that the government and the authorities in Northern Ireland have refused to give the names of those involved? (Hansard HC deb 15 June 1978)

1979

St Patrick's Gaelic Athletic Club moved from their pitch at Causeway End Road when the field they had rented since 1971 was vested for housing and relocated to a new playing field near the Down Royal Inn on the Ballinderry Road.

In what was seen as a sectarian attack to prevent the club using the new playing field the pitch was sprayed with diesel oil and littered with broken glass. Sean Adair, St Patrick's GAC chairman, strongly condemned the attack in the local press. (St Patrick's GAC)

1980

Sister Denise (Kathleen McCartan) was appointed principal of St Joseph's Primary School. Previously a pupil in Castle Street convent she joined the Sisters of the Sacred Heart in 1950 and had been teaching in Liverpool before taking up the post in Lisburn. Rev. Joseph Cunningham visited the school on practically a daily basis, something not always appreciated by the principal.

Former pupil of St Joseph's, Cecilia Daly employed initially at Aldergrove airport moved to Nottingham after three years and provided weather forecasts for a number of local radio stations. She later moved to the London Weather Centre, providing forecasts for various BBC and independent local radio stations. In 1997, she began presenting weather forecasts for BBC Northern Ireland's 'Newsline' programme.

15 April The Catholic-owned Woodlands Hotel on the Belfast Road, Lisburn was one of three hotels in Northern Ireland bombed that day by the Provisional IRA. The bomb estimated at between 200 to 300 lbs. badly damaged the building and smashed windows in houses within a 200-yard radius. The hotel closed in 1985 and the site was used for a new housing development.

1981

18 February Rev. Charles A. Bready born 1916 who had been a curate in St Patrick's died suddenly. He had been parish priest in Loughinisland from 1971.

When the new Church of St Nicholas in Carrickfergus was blessed and dedicated by the Most Reverend William J. Philbin, Bishop of Down and Connor on Sunday 26 April 1981 among the celebrants were Rev. Archibald Kelly C.C. and Rev. Brendan Beagon C.C. from Lisburn parish.

Brother Joachim, the popular assistant priest in Lisburn, was presented with a trip to Rome by Lisburn parishioners. The prisoners in the Long Kesh/Maze Prison presented him with a leather wallet made in the prison along with some money. He was in Rome during the assassination attempt on Pope John Paul II in St Peter's Square on 13 May 1981.

In almost every local government district unemployment amongst Catholics is much higher than amongst Protestants, sometimes by a gigantic margin. In Lisburn Catholic male unemployment in 1981 was 22.1% and non-Catholic 8.8%. Catholic female unemployment was 15.8% and non-Catholic 9.6% ('The Economic Situation of Catholics and Protestants' by Bob Rowthorn and Naomi Wayne, from Northern Ireland - The Political Economy of Conflict.)

1985

8 November Catholic Kevin McPolin (26), a single man, was shot by the UFF.
   He was sitting in his car at 8:30 a.m. prior to starting work along with his brother renovating pensioners' bungalows at Drumbeg Drive in the Old Warren estate. He was shot through the windscreen by Michael Stone (UFF Milltown killer). Stone later told detectives, 'I fired one shot and as he slumped over I blasted him with the other one. I got back into our car and

we drove away.'

A shotgun had been used to murder Seamus Muldoon in Lisburn in 1976. (Lost Lives - David McKittrick, Seamus Kelters, Brian Feeney, Chris Thornton, David McVea, Mainstream Publishing)

Before his attack on mourners in Milltown cemetery on 16 March 1988 Stone shot dead Paddy Brady (SF) in November 1984, then he killed Kevin McPolin in 1985, then Dermot Hackett near Omagh in May 1987. Convicted for multiple murder in March 1989 Justice Higgins sentenced him to thirty years. He was released from prison in July 2000 under the terms of the Good Friday Agreement. (UTV News 24 July 2000.)

1986

31 March Tom King, the Secretary of State, banned the Apprentice Boys Easter Monday Parade. His decision was received with anger and resentment from loyalists, which they directed mostly towards the RUC. Rioting broke out in Portadown and other areas, police homes were attacked with petrol bombs, and 11 Catholic homes were petrol-bombed in Lisburn. (CAIN: Issues: Parades: Chronology 2:Historical Dates and Events.)

Between 9:00 and 10:00 p.m. on 31 March Lisburn loyalists launched attacks on Catholic-owned homes and property. Among the premises petrol bombed were houses in Glebe Walk, Beechland Drive, Donard Drive, and on Longstone Street a video shop and four cars parked outside Murdock's Bar were burned. Three shops at the entrance to Knockmore estate were damaged and three houses occupied by Catholics in the estate were petrol bombed. Commenting on the violence DUP councillor Rev. William Beattie said, 'The Roman Catholic community may well reap what they have sown and have no-one but themselves to blame.'

Men, wearing balaclavas, combat jackets and armed with batons, pickaxe handles and petrol bombs, unhindered by police or army, roamed the streets of Lisburn burning and destroying at will Catholic-owned property and the homes of policemen who had become a new target. The Fire Brigade was prevented from tackling fires when roads were blocked with burnt out cars. When fire officers were attempting to put out a fire in a petrol bombed house in Hertford Crescent one of the fire crew was dragged from the fire engine and beaten with batons. (Ulster Star 4 April 1986.)

Ursula McGurnaghan (15) a St Patrick's High School pupil won 1st prize in a Rotary Club competition with a 'Letter of Peace' addressed to US President Reagan. Also in April St Aloysius' Primary School as part of history studies organised an Antiques Show. The exhibits included a plaque which had belonged to Ryan Marsden's grandmother and was dated 15 November 1817. (Ulster Star 11 April 1986.)

Protestant and Catholic women formed 'Lisburn Women Together' aimed at defeating sectarianism in Lisburn. The group had little affect on those whose violence was excused by unionist politicians. The attacks continued as cars belonging to Catholic families were set on fire and families were forced to leave their homes in Ashmount Gardens and Longstone Street. The homes of police officers were also attacked. (Ulster Star 11 April 1986.)

When the home of former police reservist Fred Gracey was petrol bombed at 4:00 a.m. a Catholic neighbour heard the sound of breaking glass and was first on the scene to help rescue the Gracey family from their burning home. (Ulster Star 18 April 1986.)

Loyalists went on the rampage following the funeral of Keith White (20), the first Protestant killed by a plastic bullet fired by police since the sectarian violence began in 1969. He was struck in the head during a 31 March demonstration in Portadown against the Anglo-Irish Agreement which gave the Republic of Ireland a consultative role in the administration of Northern Ireland.

The 'Lisburn Star' of 25 April had a headline 'An Orgy of Violence'. Mr White's father's plea that there should be no retaliatory violence was ignored. Among the targets over the weekend 19/20 April was St Patrick's Church. The sacristy at the church was attacked on Saturday night in an attempt to burn down the church. Four police officers were injured on Chapel Hill as they sought to protect the church. (AP News Archive April 20, 1986.)

The fire failed to take hold, not before records held there were destroyed, and the area badly smoke damaged. Dr Joseph Cunningham said,

'While I certainly regret the burning of the church and would not like to see it again, it really is a minor event compared to others. The attacks on Catholic families have to be deplored, the majority of those people who were involved have told me that they are prepared to stay in Lisburn. That is an indication

of how the families are really treating the situation.' He praised the police and emergency services and said that a Protestant minister had visited the church and offered his condolences. (Ulster Star 25 April 1986.)

21 April In the early hours the AOH social club, off Longstone Street, was set on fire and was completely gutted. The damage was estimated at £250,000. The 'Lisburn Star' reported that the most disturbing aspect of the present troubles was the ferocity of the attacks on the Roman Catholic families and the police officers.

24 April On Thursday night over forty loyalists took control of the Manor estate and set about burning cars and terrorising families. The homes of two Catholic families in Jeremy Walk were petrol bombed and the occupants forced to leave. Mrs Celine Martin, a widow, was awakened at 11:00 p.m. when a petrol bomb smashed through a downstairs window. She was afraid to leave the burning house to face a jeering mob, that included women, outside her house. She hid in the bathroom and filled the bath with water and soaked towels to seal the door to prevent the smoke coming into the room. She was eventually rescued by the Fire Service, delayed by burned-out cars placed across the road. She had lived there peacefully with her neighbours for 23 years. Across the street Thomas Catney (68) and his son Jim escaped injury when their house was also petrol bombed. Around the corner in Craig Crescent another Catholic home was attacked. (Ulster Star 25 April 1986.)

Over 1,000 dancers attended the Eight Annual Lisburn Feis in St Joseph's Hall, organised by St Patrick's GAC. The Depo School of Dancing was awarded the top prize, the Centenary Shield. Special guests, Walter Williams and Jim Moffat from the Lisburn Arts Advisory Council presented a cheque on behalf of the council to the organisers. (Lisburn Star 20 June 1986.)

12 July Speaking at the field at Ballinderry Orange leader George Morrison called for the attacks on the homes of RUC officers to stop. He did not call for the attacks on Catholic homes to stop.

11 July The 'Ulster Star' reported that after five nights of violence up to 10 homes had been attacked, including that of a prison officer and a Protestant family in Begney Walk. Four Catholic homes were attacked on bonfire night, houses at Glebe Walk and Crossan Walk petrol bombed and the front windows of a house in Dromara Park had its front windows smashed and a house at Drumbeg Drive petrol bombed. Double glazing prevented a petrol bomb from exploding inside a house at Beechland Drive.

The Catholic homes attacked included one at Ballyknockan Park which was petrol bombed and a house on Hillhall Road attacked by stone throwers. (Ulster Star 18 July 1986.)

29 July As July drew to close four more Catholic homes were petrol bombed. A concrete brick was used to break a window in a house in Glebe Walk before a petrol bomb was thrown into the house. A home in Young Street was attacked but the petrol bomb did not explode. Petrol bombs were thrown at a home in Nicholson Gardens, in Hill Street estate, and at a home in Rushmore Grove. (Lisburn Star 1 August 1986)

Intimidation of Catholic families living in predominately Protestant housing estates in Lisburn, which had been ongoing since early 1986, reached a critical stage in August when dozens of families were forced to leave their homes. The intimidation had begun in some cases with the theft of clothing from a washing line, progressing to damage to cars, including the loosening of wheel nuts, to anti-Catholic graffiti and the breaking of windows and homes being petrol-bombed. The objective of the UDA was to ensure that estates such as Old Warren became exclusively Protestant. Many of these evictions went unreported by the local press.

The RUC said that there had been 43 petrol bomb attacks on property owned or occupied by Catholics in Lisburn and that the attacks had been organised and directed. A total of 124 people had been arrested and 77 petrol bombs recovered. Mr. Seamus Mallon SDLP claimed that 144 Catholic families in Lisburn had been either intimidated or attacked since the loyalist stoppage on 3 March. (Irish Press 20 August 1986)

August The UFF threatened Catholic workers in Lisburn's Department of Health and Social Services office in Bow House, Lisburn. (UTV News 21 August 1986.)

6 August The body of a middle-aged Catholic man who had been missing from his home at Roseville Gardens since the previous night was found on wasteland near the River Lagan. He was identified as 57-year-old Dermot Peter McCann. He had been drinking in a local pub and had gone home to feed his dog, saying that he would return later. He was attacked on his way back to the pub by two schoolboys aged 14 and 15. They were later arrested and convicted of his murder. The police said that they did not believe the motive to be sectarian although it was evident to the Catholic population of Lisburn that that was the case. The teenagers served their sentences in the Maze prison alongside loyalist prisoners. (Lost Lives - David McKittrick, Seamus Kelters, Brian Feeney, Chris Thornton, David McVea, Mainstream Publishing)

An RUC spokesman said that Peter McCann had been stabbed to death. (Irish Press 8 August 1986.)

8 August Catholic homes in Warren Park Gardens, Dundrod Drive, Glebe Walk and Drumbeg Drive were attacked. The previous night, Eastwoods, a Catholic-owned estate agent's premises in Bridge Street, had inflammable liquid poured over the door and set alight.

13 August Two children and their parents were asleep in their Mourneview Park home when petrol bombs were thrown into the living room. Later at 3:30 a.m. another Catholic family in Tonagh Park suffered a similar attack.

The Housing Executive reported that since April, 114 Lisburn families had been subjected to intimidation with 63 families having to move out of their homes. Councillor Paddy Ritchie stated that Catholic families were being driven out of mixed estates and over 100 transfer applications had been made to the Housing Executive. Councillor Peter O'Hagan said that it had reached the stage that on average three families were being petrol bombed every week. (Lisburn Star 15 August 1986)

21 August When John McMahon's home in Tonagh Park was petrol bombed at 3:30 a.m. his life and that of his wife, their three sons and a daughter were placed at risk. All managed to escape and despite serious damage to the ground floor he refused to leave the house. An anonymous Protestant, admiring his courage, donated £50 via the 'Ulster Star' to the family saying that he was appalled at the sectarian attacks on innocent families.

Mayor Walter Lilburn appealed for the madness to stop and said that he feared the Catholics in Lisburn, proud of its tradition of integrated housing, would be forced to retreat into sectarian ghettos. (Lisburn Star 22 August 1986.)

October The loyalists of Old Warren estate realised that they had destroyed the appearance of the estate which had burned out and derelict houses vacated by Catholic families. Tattered flags and bunting festooned the streets. Walls and empty houses were covered with graffiti. A clean up was ordered because 'if nothing is done to the area it won't be long before loyalists move out and others offered houses in the estate.' It was suggested that flags and bunting be replaced with strategically placed plaques.

19 October The attacks continued on Catholic-owned homes. In the early hours the garage of a house at Whitla Road was set on fire and in neighbouring Addis Avenue there was an attempt to set a car on fire. The police stated that they did not believe there was 'a serious sectarian motive behind the incidents' despite UVF slogans being daubed on the house and in the general area.

When Lisburn Borough Council was again adjourned to protest against the Anglo-Irish Agreement Councillor Patrick Ritchie stated that at a previous meeting a councillor had remarked that of 20 houses allocated by the Housing Executive 18 had gone to Catholics. Cllr. Ritchie asked why Catholics should not get houses in Lisburn when they were at the head of the points table. Mayor Walter Lilburn said that he was sorry Cllr. Ritchie had introduced sectarianism into the dispute.

Councillor William Belshaw urged all loyalists to support the family of George Seawright 'who had given up his freedom for the cause of Ulster.'

Seawright had been jailed for physically assaulting the Secretary of State for Northern Ireland at Belfast City Hall during an Anglo-Irish Agreement protest. He had previously referred to Catholics as 'fenian scum' and said that 'taxpayers money would be better spent on an incinerator and burning the lot of them. Their priests should be thrown in and burnt as well'. He later denied making making these comments which were widely reported by the press. (Lisburn Star 31 October 1986.)

7 November The 'Ulster Star' gave UDA leader John McMichael a platform to expound in a bizarre article that the blame for the intimidation of Catholic families in Lisburn was because of 'the influx of hard-line republicans from West Belfast'. He said that it was republicans who whipped up fear and sectarianism in the town where it previously did not exist. (History shows that the truth was somewhat different.)

Deploring the spread of housing from west Belfast to Twinbrook and Poleglass estates on the outskirts of Lisburn he said that Protestants were in fear of being overrun. He pointed out that Manor Drive in Lisburn appeared as a 'green area' on British army maps, (proving that the UDA had access to army maps), and said, 'I do not condone the intimidation of ordinary decent Roman Catholics but given the circumstances as those which currently exist that sort of thing is liable to happen.' There was always a but. Police later denied that they were aware of any republican activists in Lisburn.

14 November A Catholic woman and her daughters, aged seven and ten, were living in a flat at Woodside when it was petrol bombed. They had been living there for about three months after having been intimidated out of Old Warren estate. Her father who lived nearby was helping another Catholic family whose house in Beechland Drive had been attacked earlier when he learned that his daughter's home was on fire.

15 November Tensions heightened after a loyalist march to take over Hillsborough to protest against the Anglo-Irish Agreement was followed by a large demonstration in front of Belfast City Hall. Lisburn loyalists were prepared to mark the anniversary of the Anglo-Irish Agreement with further intimidation. The police discovered a crate of petrol bombs in the Ballymacash Road area. (Ulster Star 21 November 1986)

'Ulster Resistance' had been formed a few days earlier by Rev. Ian Paisley and Peter Robinson to 'take direct action as and when required' to end the Anglo-Irish Agreement.' (CAIN)

At the end of November the Northern Ireland Housing Executive provided an update on intimidation in Lisburn stating that in the past six months 178 families had to vacate their homes because of intimidation. (Ulster Star 28 November 1986)

David Trimble, chairman of Lisburn Ulster Club, who had previously been present when a tricolour was burned outside Lisburn's police station to protest about the Anglo-Irish Agreement suggested in December that Lisburn's streets should be renamed as a further protest. It was proposed that Chapel Hill be renamed as Carson's Hill. Two streets in nearby

Seymour Hill had been renamed after two UDA men killed by the IRA.
(Ulster Star 5 December 1986.)

6 December Catholic Paul Bradley (30) was badly beaten and horrifically injured in the Tavern Bar, Bridge Street, by a UDA gang.

Paul Bradley who lived in Tirowen Drive and had been employed as a bin man was drinking on his own when four men came into the bar after 9:00 p.m. and attacked him using a chair, pool cues and pint glasses. He was taken to the Lagan Valley Hospital where he died three days later from brain injuries and multiple skull fractures.

The UDA chairman Andy Tyrie was reported as saying that there had been a long-standing feud between Peter Bradley and some UDA members in Lisburn. Three Lisburn men were charged with his murder but charges were dropped when all those who had witnessed the assault declined to give evidence. (Lost Lives - David McKittrick, Seamus Kelters, Brian Feeney, Chris Thornton, David McVea, Mainstream Publishing.)

The mindset of the UDA in Lisburn was revealed in an interview conducted by a reporter for the New York Times with John McMichael, the Deputy Commander and leader of the UDA's South Belfast brigade.

'John McMichael is well known as the owner of the local pub (Admiral Benbow) and leader of the Protestant loyalist vigilante group here lately accused of burning the Roman Catholic nationalist minority from their homes. He professes absolute innocence of the months of residential gasoline bombings, a selective reign of terror that has been driving Catholic families away from this rare mixed community.

"The whole thing is territorial," Mr. McMichael said, "Lisburn has become another battle for territory in Northern Ireland."

Indeed it has, with more than 100 Catholic families having moved out in the last nine months after experiencing the intimidation of firebombings through their front windows as they slept in their beds.

"I personally don't like violence, but there is a war going on in Northern Ireland and I find it very difficult to condemn people," he said, speaking of his own people, the Protestant loyalist majority.

"We're a defensive community, always defending the border, always in a state of vigilance against the fear of the Fenian uprising," he said, referring to the anxiety that the minority Fenians, or Catholic nationalists, are more interested in union with the Irish Republic than even their own domestic peace.

Peter O'Hagan, the parochial school principal, denied this, insisting that nothing is more sacred to the minority population than to be left alone in peace in a place prized as a step above the sectarian ghettos. They sense that this is a new campaign to stamp out the relative integration of Lisburn, in line with the terrible precedent of 1920 when the Catholic minority was driven from the town after a sectarian shooting.

Catholic leaders like Mr O'Hagan condemn the modern IRA killings occurring elsewhere in the province even more strongly than does Mr McMichael. Where the school principal warns violence breeds violence, the publican stresses that force must be met by force.

"Every day, it's a struggle for territory," McMichael said of the simple act of residency and the modern movement of Catholic nationalists away from the ghetto that, he said, came to alarm some Protestants.

"Every house, every street, every farm which is taken over by an Irish Nationalist is a little bit less of Northern Ireland and a little bit more of Ireland. It must be very difficult for people outside of Northern Ireland to understand the behavior of people here, but basically the issue for us, the loyalists, is Northern Ireland either exists or it doesn't, and what you see is people marking out their territory."

At the age of 38, Mr McMichael is a man of many sides. He says he is drafting a proposal for political compromise between the two communities. His critics, however, say this is only his cover of moderation for the nasty midnight business of the loyalist thugs.

Police and government officials say the violence is mainly one-sided and seems directed against the British-Irish agreement, the latest attempt at pacifying the province, one that has incensed Mr McMichael and other loyalist leaders who stress that the pact has bypassed the views of the majority and so can never make true progress.

"Loyalists become very defensive, keep Catholic nationalists at arms length," Mr McMichael conceded. "They do that in a sense by discriminating to insure that they don't get their hands on the wheel of state. You get a Catch 22 situation because the more that happens the more Catholics feel that they're discriminated against, that they're alienated."

The answer, he said, is political negotiation and compromise - a possibility that critics of the UDA say could not in fact be lower on the paramilitary group's agenda, with firebombings still occurring.

"I've tried to develop politically, I hope," Mr McMichael said. "I don't want to make a career of this." (By Francis X. Clines, Special to the New York Times 23 December 1986.)

(John McMichael was killed by a bomb attached to his car outside his Hilden Court home, in Lisburn's loyalist Hilden estate on 22 December 1987. There were allegations that members within the UDA had colluded with the IRA in his death by passing on vital information about him and his activities, enabling the IRA to target his car. The Chief Constable of the RUC speculated that McMichael had been investigating UDA racketeering.

Cardinal Tomás Ó Fiaich, Archbishop of Armagh and Primate of Ireland described him as having been 'untiring, fresh and constructive and ready to cross the religious divide to find a solution for Northern Ireland'. John McMichael was buried at the New Blaris Cemetery in Lisburn.) (Wikipedia)

Lisburn Council of Churches showed a united front when they collected 5,700 signatures for a petition to oppose further cutbacks in the provision of acute services at the Lagan Valley Hospital. Rev. Dr. Joseph Cunningham represented the Catholic Church on the council. (Ulster Star 12 December 1986.)

1987

24 March Two Sinn Féin members on Lisburn Council had glasses of orange juice thrown over them at a council meeting when they refused to stand as a token of respect for those who have been recently murdered by the IRA. (Irish Press 25 March 1987.)

In the summer St Patrick's Gaelic Athletic Club decided to return to their playing field on the Ballinderry Road and tendered to have the pitch relaid. Brannigan groundwork contractors were successful and moved their plant and equipment onto the site. The machinery was vandalised and burned. Undeterred the club sought another contractor, the sportsground specialists Prunty Contracts. The pitch was completed to the highest standard and the grass was sown. Just when it was ready for the inaugural game a stolen JCB digger was driven on to the pitch, the bucket was lowered and the playing surface ripped up. The JCB was left in the middle of the pitch and set on fire.

Again this was a sectarian attack and the club sought compensation but the police were reluctant to sign off a compensation claim as there had to be proof that three or more individuals had been involved in the attack. The club nevertheless lodged a claim which after about eighteen months was settled at the eleventh hour. Prunty returned and relaid the pitch.

Matters did not end there. A club member had fabricated steel goalposts which could be slotted into position and had installed one goalpost and was engaged in spot welding the crossbar in the other one when he saw approximately fifteen masked men at the other end of the field. They came armed with Stihl saws and proceeded to cut the goal post into pieces. Fearing for his life he immediately drove from the pitch and went to the Down Royal Inn and about 3:00 p.m. made a 999 call to the police. The police arrived at about 7:00 p.m. and told the club representative, 'Look these people won't stop until they kill somebody and we can't give you round the clock protection out there to play your games'.

A few days later a club member was warned by a neighbour that plans were being made for further attacks but this time individual club members were to be targeted. The club chairman, Michael Lavery, decided in the light of recent murders of Catholics in Lisburn that the threat was real and called a halt to club activities at this location. The land was sold. St Patrick's GAC never played on their new pitch.

It would not be until 1998 when Kevin Madden, a County Antrim football star, was appointed as the club's development officer that the club was revitalised and began to attract new members. They later were granted the use of a playing field at Kirkwoods Road. (St Patrick's GAC & Ulster Star 4 May 1990 & Ireland's Professional Amateurs: A Sports Season at its Purest, Andy Mendlowitz.)

23 July William Richard Megrath, a Catholic (46), married with two children and a member of the Ulster Defence Regiment, was ambushed by the IRA on Stewartstown Road as he was on his way home to Jubilee Avenue, Lisburn from the Ford Motor Company at Finaghy Road North. The killers had hijacked a Ford Escort taxi at Slieve Gallion Drive in Andersonstown and fired at least seven 7.62 mm bullets, which are designed to kill with a single shot, at Mr Megrath.

He had been in the UDR for two years and made no secret of that fact in his workplace. He had served with the Royal Artillery from 1958 to 1964. The priest officiating at his funeral described the victim as 'respected, decent and quiet, a good family man, obliging and neighbourly.' He was buried with full military honours after Mass at St Patrick's Church, Lisburn. (Lost Lives - David McKittrick, Seamus Kelters, Brian Feeney, Chris Thornton, David McVea, Mainstream Publishing.)

1988

Bishop Cahal Daly of Down and Connor went specially to preach to the congregation in St Patrick's Church after six soldiers were blown up returning from a charity fun run in Lisburn. He stressed, in the wake of the outrage, that the IRA can claim no kind of recognition from the Catholic Church, which has in fact 'repeatedly and most solemnly' condemned the terrorist organisation.

The bishop denounced the murders 'in the strongest possible terms', saying;

> 'Such deeds not only expose innocent Catholics to grave fear and even physical danger. They also and above all do great spiritual harm to the Catholic community, because all sin not only wounds the individual who commits it, but also does a great wrong to the Christian community from within which it is perpetrated.
>
> But the Catholic community as such can in no way be held guilty of evils committed by a few who obstinately refuse to listen to the teaching of their Church. I am confident that Wednesday's multiple murder will not be allowed to disturb inter-community relations in Lisburn.'
>
> The stance of the Catholic Church on the IRA and its campaign of terror is plain, Bishop Daly pointed out. 'No-one can be a faithful Catholic and at the same time a member of the organisation which carries out these crimes'. (Catholic Herald 14 June 1988.)

The days that followed were tense throughout the community. A civic service was held the following Wednesday evening, when thousands of people gathered in the Market Street/Bow Street area to identify with the expression of sorrow and sympathy. Rev. H. Cromie insisted on the parish priest, Canon Joseph Cunningham, taking part in the Service, resulting in many of his parishioners attending, standing along Chapel Hill. ('Through Changing Scenes' The Very Reverend Howard Cromie.)

The Lisburn Leisure Centre was forced to remain shut for a time after the loyalist Protestant Action Force, a cover name of the UVF, issued a warning that they regarded Catholic staff working there as 'legitimate targets', inferring that they may have had a hand in the bombing. Lisburn mayor Councillor William Bleakes condemned the threats by the PAF. (Wikipedia.)

In mid-August a telephoned threat was made to Catholic staff working in the Department for Health and Social Services office in Lisburn. All the workers walked out. The action spread to every DHSS office in Northern Ireland. As office after office closed and 4,000 workers, Catholic and Protestant, stopped work the UDA, who had issued the threat, backed down.

Eamonn Haughey was appointed principal of St Patrick's High School in September 1988. Previously he had been head of history at the school for fifteen years.

Eileen Drayne was awarded a MBE in recognition of her efforts on behalf of 'Meals on Wheels'.

1989

January Lisburn mayor William Bleakes urged the council to rethink spending £20,000 on a floral effigy of King William to mark the tercentenary of the Glorious Revolution. The views of the Catholic ratepayers were not part of his consideration.

Sunday 8 January After a delayed 7:52 p.m. departure, a British Midland flight from Heathrow to Belfast experienced problems shortly after take-off. The left engine on the brand new Boeing 737-400 aircraft lost power, went on fire and caused severe vibration. The captain and his co-pilot however decided that the right engine was causing the problem and shut down that engine. (This was later blamed on Boeing's redesign of controls from the previous version of the 737 of which the pilots were apparently unfamiliar). The flight was diverted to East Midlands Airport but crashed just a 1/4 mile short of the runway. Among those of the 118 passengers on board who were killed were Jean Johnson, wife of Bernard Johnson and two of their children Daniel James and John Francis Martin. Their other son Kevin was on a ski trip organised by Rathmore Grammar School and returned to the devastating news.

The entire community in Lisburn was in grief and St Patrick's was packed to capacity an hour before the start of the Requiem Mass which was celebrated by Bishop Cathal Daly. The mother's coffin was flanked on each side by her sons' coffins. Both boys had been pupils at St Joseph's Primary School.

Hundreds followed the funeral cortege in a biting January wind to the

Holy Trinity cemetery. Bernard Johnson who lived at Priest's Lane, Blaris and was financial director of Warne Surgical Products paid tribute to the pilots for their efforts to land the plane. An active member of St Patrick's Church he was generous in charitable work and donated a six figure compensation payment to charity.

25 January At 8:00 a.m. David Dornan (26), from Carlisle Park, Ballynahinch, who was working on a building site on Knockmore Road as a mechanical digger driver was shot dead as he sat behind the wheel of his digger. The two killers were seen running towards the loyalist Rathvarna estate. He was taken to the Lagan Valley Hospital but was dead on arrival. Married with a young daughter, whose photograph he kept in his cab, he was described by workmates as a hard-working and decent young man. A 34-year-old Lisburn man was sentenced to five life terms for this and the murder of three Catholics, one in conjunction with two full-time UDR soldiers. (Lost Lives - David McKittrick, Seamus Kelters, Brian Feeney, Chris Thornton, David McVea, Mainstream Publishing)

This shooting had been a mistake by the UDA's intelligence section who had misinformed their bosses that the man hired to drive the digger was a Catholic. (Ten-Thirty-Three: The Inside Story of Britain's Secret Killing Machine in Northern Ireland-Nicholas Davies, Mainstream Publishing eBooks.)

Mr T. Patrick McClean was appointed principal of St Aloysius Primary School on the Ballinderry Road on the retirement of Peter O'Hagan.

Sunday morning Masses were at 6:45, 8:30, 10:00, 11:15 and 12:30 p.m.

Former parishioner Donna Traynor, whose father Gerry had played an active part in parish affairs, joined the BBC presenting news bulletins on BBC Radio Ulster. She would later become the anchor presenter on BBC Northern Ireland's flagship evening news programme, 'BBC Newsline'. As the duty news reader at the station, she was the first person to break the news of the Provisional IRA's ceasefire in 1994.

16 June St Patrick's Gaelic Athletic Club held the 11th Annual Lisburn Feis in St Joseph's Hall over the weekend. Sixteen Irish dancing schools participated in the event including the Lisburn based Depo School. All proceeds from the Feis including the 50p programme went towards the club's 'continuing grounds development programme'.

Sponsors included, Nesbitt's newsagency, 152 Longstone Street, Mooney's Maze Inn, Chapel Hill, David H. Coffey, Brogan's Pharmacy, Chapel Hill, Maureen's newsagency, Smithfield, Leonard Lavery, gent's hairdresser, 1a Warren Gardens, Kevin & Damien Johnston, Warren Park Stores, Drayne Farms, Elmore's, 81 Bow Street, Brian Agnew & Son Ltd, vehicle repairs, 45-51 Bachelors Walk, Kelly's, fruit and vegetables, 116-118 Longstone Street and James Thompson, funeral directors, 16 Longstone Street.

A special mention was made of the Lisburn Arts Advisory Council for their financial support and for printing the programme.

Dancing in the Depo School under twelve age group Four Hand Reel competition were; T. Gillen, A. Mullan, J. Moore, F. Hague, C. Braiden, D. Creaney and P McArdle. (11th Annual Lisburn Feis programme.)

24 June Catholic Liam McKee (36) was shot at his home in Donard Drive, Tonagh Estate by Ulster Freedom Fighters, a cover name for the UDA. Three or four gunmen broke into the family home around 12:40 a.m. using a sledgehammer to smash down the front door. He died when his bedroom door was blasted by a shotgun. His mother was slightly injured in the attack.

The family had lived alongside their Protestant neighbours at that address for around 40 years.

In March 1992 a 25-year-old UDR man from Lisburn was sentenced to life imprisonment for his murder. He had, without any evidence whatsoever, passed information to the UDA that Liam McKee had set up a part-time UDR soldier for assassination. He also made statements that he had passed on information about 14 other people, confirming the collusion that existed between the security forces and the loyalist murder gangs. (Lost Lives - David McKittrick, Seamus Kelters, Brian Feeney, Chris Thornton, David McVea, Mainstream Publishing)

11 September BBC NI News reported; 'Two UDR men appear in court on L. McGinn murder charge last month, one of men is also charged with killing Liam McKee, Lisburn, in June. Andrew Brown (25) and Andrew Smith (24), and third man Ed Johns named as accused.'

Gary Quinn (34) (former UFF) from Lisburn was convicted of four murders and two attempted murders. Ulster Television carried a film report on those killings between 1985 and 1990. He killed Loughlin McGinn (Aug

1989), Patrick Feeney (February 1989), David Dornan (January 1989), who was a Protestant, but Quinn thought he was a Catholic and Hugh Delaney (July 1988). (UTV News 11 December 1998)

1990

Former pupil of the Sacred Heart of Mary Convent Ursula Canavan, originally from Kilwarlin, was appointed as principal of Rathmore Grammar School.

After spending part of her novitiate in France Sister Ursula taught French in Lourdes Mount School, Ealing in west London. In 1980 she was principal of the Sacred Heart of Mary Grammar School in Holywood, County Down and retained that post when the school amalgamated with St Patrick's College, Knock before moving to the post at Rathmore. (From Derriaghy to St. Anne's, Jim O'Hagan.)

15 July Catholic Martin Hughes (34), single man, was shot in the driveway of his home at Huguenot Drive by UDA/UFF. His friend was seriously injured.

They had been returning to Martin Hughes' home just before midnight after an evening at the AOH Hall in Lisburn. His mother who was waiting up for his return home heard the shots as she sat watching television. The gunmen were reported to have escaped by car. In a BBC NI News report on 16 July the family called for no retaliation and denied the claim by the UFF that he was a member of the IRA.

At his funeral Mass in St Patrick's Church Bishop Cahal Daly said that Martin Hughes had been killed because of sectarian hatred of Catholics and that he was the 49th victim of loyalist sectarian murders in the diocese during his seven and a half years as bishop and it was the 39th such funeral at which he had officiated. (Lost Lives - David McKittrick, Seamus Kelters, Brian Feeney, Chris Thornton, David McVea, Mainstream Publishing.)

1991

2 June Rev. Hugh Maurice McAleese who had formerly served in Lisburn died. (History - Star of the Sea, Killyleagh.)

August The church of the Blessed Virgin Mary & St. Brigid at Magheramesk was subjected to a sectarian attack.

November The Magheramesk church was completely gutted in an arson attack. St Patrick's High School was also attacked by arsonists in November.

15 November Rev. Denis Newberry from St Patrick's along with the church's caretaker appeared in a BBC NI News film report from the destroyed church. (BBC DVD Number DO 1450.)

Rev. Newberry, a large man, was young and progressive when he came to St Patrick's. For a Mass on a Holy Thursday he had arranged for loaves and grapes to be displayed on a table at the rear of the church, some of which were to be brought forward as the gifts during the Mass. When it was time for the gifts to be presented he stood at the altar and waited, and waited. When the gifts were not brought forward he continued with the Mass. It was discovered later that Canon Cunningham had found the loaves and grapes and threw them into the porch. There was going to be no departure from tradition as long as he was in charge. (Pat McHugh)

Sunday 17 March Francis Paul Taggart, a Catholic (17), was murdered. He was the youngest of four children and lived at Beechland Drive and had started work as a storeman the previous year. He had been playing snooker with some friends and was taking a short cut home behind the Leisure Centre when he was attacked. A group of girls were reported to have watched the path while a number of young men carried out the murder.

On the day of the murder Nicholas Evans (23) met in Lisburn, in a chance encounter, five individuals whom he knew and he stopped to talk to them. One of the individuals left the group. Another, Jackie Allen, said he was going 'to do a Catholic tonight' and at this point he spotted Francis Taggart leaving a chip shop near to where they were then standing. Allen said that he was to be the victim and asked Evans if he would 'give a hand'. He agreed.

Evans and the four other members of the group followed Francis Taggart and then chased him. When they caught him they punched and kicked him. Allen stabbed the victim four or five times and passed the knife to Evans who said, 'no way'. According to Evans, Allen then said, 'you'd need to cause there'll be more than four of us that'll get you'. Evans took the knife and stabbed the victim twice in his stomach. Then another member of the group took the knife and stabbed the victim repeatedly.

A post mortem examination was carried out by Dr Carson, Deputy State Pathologist on 18 March 1991 stated that in total there were about 60 stab wounds, distributed mainly on the neck, chest and abdomen.

Evans later said that the killing was not on behalf of a paramilitary organisation but that it was just because the victim was a Catholic.

At Evan's trial LCJ Kerr ruled that Evans may not have been a member of any of the paramilitary organisations that were referred to in his interviews with the police, but that did not derogate from the fact that those who proposed and instigated the attack were members of those organisations and he well knew that.

Evans was sentenced for a term of twenty years. (Northern Ireland Courts and Tribunals Service www.courtsni.gov.uk/en-gb/.../documents/.../j_j_ker7184final.htm.)

26 August Martin Eamon Watters a Catholic (27), from Roseville Park, Low Road was the victim of a sectarian murder. He was attacked as he made his way home along the bank of the River Lagan in Lisburn in the early hours of the morning somewhat intoxicated. His body was discovered the following morning by a runner at about 7:00 a.m. He had been beaten to death.

In February 1994 four men, two of whom were members of the UVF, were convicted of his murder. One won an appeal against the murder conviction and the charge reduced to grievous bodily harm. They claimed that they had come across Martin Watters lying drunk on a bench and when they discovered that he was a Catholic they robbed him of £15 and beat him to death. Sometime later two of the murderers returned to the scene of their crime and dragged the body to the river and pushed it in.

Martin's best friend was Davy Johnston (30), a Protestant RUC officer. He was killed along with a colleague Roland Graham on 16 June 1997 while on foot patrol in Lurgan, County Armagh. Both men were shot in the back of the head from point-blank range.

(Within days Colin Duffy (IRA) was charged with the murder of the two officers. The charges were later withdrawn by the Director of Public Prosecutions for Northern Ireland, on the grounds that the evidence was insufficient to afford a reasonable prospect of conviction. Solicitor

Rosemary Nelson who represented Colin Duffy was murdered by loyalist paramilitaries on 15 March 1999.) (Lost Lives - David McKittrick, Seamus Kelters, Brian Feeney, Chris Thornton, David McVea, Mainstream Publishing and interview.)

1992

9 January Philip Campbell (28), a hard working individual was in his fast-food trailer on the Lisburn Road near the Moira/M1 motorway roundabout when an unmasked gunman fired a number of shots at him through the open door of his trailer. He was taken to Lagan Valley Hospital but died shortly after arriving at the hospital. The murder was carried out by the UDA/UFF.

He had operated this business at this location for several years and also worked evenings as a restaurant chef. Originally from Killeaton Crescent in the nearby parish of Derriaghy his mother, Pat Campbell through her work as a prominent peace campaigner, had close links with St Patrick's Church in Lisburn. Mrs Campbell continued her work as a peace campaigner despite the personal tragedy to hit the family and in June 1998 was one of a number of relatives of victims present at a garden party at Hillsborough Castle attended by Prince Charles where a symbolic tree of remembrance was planted. Davy Adams, a UDA man from Lisburn who was involved in the political side of loyalism and at the time a spokesman for the Ulster Democratic Party, also attended the ceremony and praised Mrs Campbell's spirit of forgiveness as 'a shining example to us all'. (Lost Lives - David McKittrick, Seamus Kelters, Brian Feeney, Chris Thornton, David McVea, Mainstream Publishing.)

30 January Catholic Paul Moran (32), married with one child, was shot outside a newsagent's shop in Longstone Street which he called at regularly on his way to work at Lisburn Hide Company. A masked gunman shot him twice at close range with a shotgun and ran off towards the nearby Manor estate. He was taken to the Lagan Valley Hospital but was dead on arrival.

The UDA/UFF tried to justify the killing by stating that he had been involved in the republican movement. At the inquest in November 1992 a RUC detective-inspector said that there was absolutely no substance in the allegation made by the UFF and Mr Moran was very well thought of in the community and had never come under adverse police attention. The coroner said that Paul Moran was shot because the UFF wanted to murder a

Catholic. (Lost Lives - David McKittrick, Seamus Kelters, Brian Feeney, Chris Thornton, David McVea, Mainstream Publishing)

1993

30 July UTV News carried a report of how in Lisburn a two pence coin in his pocket, saved a Catholic man's life when a bullet from a loyalist gunman hit it, then his gun jammed.

August Rev. Denis McKinley was transferred to Lisburn from Harryville, Ballymena. (Ballymenaparish.org.)

The church of Blessed Virgin Mary and St. Brigid at Magheramesk was rebuilt and opened in 1993.

Seamus Close, Alliance Party of Northern Ireland, became the mayor of Lisburn and the first Catholic elected to hold that office.

Eileen Drayne stood as an Alliance member in the Lisburn local council elections but was unsuccessful.

October In Lisburn the Taggart family, who's son was killed nearby by loyalists in March 1991, had their home petrol bombed, other Catholic homes were attacked in Lisburn, Derriaghy and Dromore. (UTV News 25 October 1993.)

1994

Because of demographic changes the number of pupils in St Aloysius School had settled at 320 resulting in empty classrooms which took on new roles as a library, a music and arts rooms. (St Aloysius Silver Jubilee booklet.)

11 July In July 1994 the IRA was edging its way towards announcing a cessation of military operations. A ceasefire would be declared on 31 August that year. It would come too late for Raymond Smallwood from Donard Drive who was shot as he left his home at 9:00 a.m. on 11 July 1994.

A prominent loyalist and spokesman for the UDA he was chairman of the Ulster Democratic Party and had secured his UDA credentials when he was involved in an attack on the Coalisland home of the former nationalist MP Bernadette McAliskey in 1981. She and her husband were both seriously injured in the attack. As driver of the getaway car Smallwood and his 'commando team' were unaware that the McAliskey's home was under surveillance by the 3rd Battalion, The Parachute Regiment and were promptly arrested. He received a 15 year jail sentence but only served half of the term. He then followed a political path, still talking violence, but thinking peace. He developed contact with Fr Alex Reid and Fr Gerry Reynolds from the Clonard Monastery off the Falls Road, Belfast, both of whom were pivotal in helping secure the peace process.

Raymond Smallwood was shot by IRA members who had the previous night taken over an elderly couple's house which overlooked Smallwood's front door. When he came out of his house at least one of the IRA gunmen ran down the street and fired several shotgun blasts at him. His wife Linda witnessed the murder. The IRA made their escape in a car which was later found abandoned behind the 'Traveller's Rest' public house at Milltown Road, Derriaghy.

His funeral was held on the 14 July and those attending included Alex Reid and Gerry Reynolds, the priests from Clonard monastery. Fr Reynolds led the entire gathering in prayer. Among the pall bearers at his funeral were Peter Robinson, DUP MP for East Belfast and his DUP colleague Sammy Wilson along with Fred Cobain an Ulster Unionist councillor.

1995

Professional footballer, Peter Kennedy, was named as the Ulster Footballer of the Year in 1995/96.

Married, with three children, Annie, Olivia and Peter, he was a Northern Irish football defender/midfielder. After his first spell in Northern Ireland he joined Notts County in August 1996 where he scored against Newcastle Town in the FA Cup, before moving onto Watford a season later. In his first season, he led Watford to promotion to Division One as their highest goal scorer. He scored two goals in quick succession in the derby with Luton, a hat-trick against Southend, and a splendid long-range effort against Sheffield Wednesday in the FA Cup. The following season was arguably the highlight of his career as he helped Watford gain promotion to the

Premier League in 1999. In the Premier League, he scored Watford's first goal of the season, a penalty. He left Watford at the end of the 2000/01 campaign and spent three seasons at Wigan, spending a period on loan at Derby County where he scored once against Ipswich Town. His final English club was Peterborough United, after which he returned to football in Northern Ireland. At the end of the 2007-08 season when his contract was not renewed by Portadown he left the club. He began training with Ballymena United FC but decided to retire from his footballing career to focus on becoming an accountant. After a year Peter came out of retirement and made a return to football by signing for Donegal Celtic FC who play in the IFA Championship. (Wikipedia.)

1996

9 September A 'mixed' marriage couple were awakened in the early hours of the morning to find their house in the Knockmore estate under attack by loyalists. This was the second attack on their home in two months. (rsf.ie/saoirse/record/sep1996.htm.)

1997

August Rev. Gabriel Lyons was appointed by Bishop Walsh, as a curate, to the Parish of Blaris.

September Damien Johnson started his professional football career as a midfielder with Portadown before moving to Blackburn Rovers where he made his debut in the League Cup on 30 September 1997. After a spell with Nottingham Forest he moved to Birmingham City in 2002 and was named captain for the 2006-7 season. He signed for Plymouth Argyle on 1 February 2010 but later that year joined Huddersfield Town and while there was nominated for the Player of the Year award. He was with newly promoted Fleetwood Town from 2012 to October 2013.

Damien made his senior international debut with Northern Ireland in May 1999. His last appearance was against the Czech Republic in Prague on 14 October 2009 and he announced his retirement from international football in July 2010. He had been capped 56 times for his country.

11 September A Catholic teenager needed nine stitches when a brick thrown through the window of a school-bus hit him between the eyes. The 15-year-old boy was one of more than 30 children travelling home from St Patrick's High School when their bus was attacked by a group of youths shouting sectarian slogans, some wearing Glasgow Rangers club scarves. A mother of one of the children on the bus said: 'The youths cheered when they saw that someone was hit and bleeding. This isn't the first time that they tried this but they missed every other day. All the kids are badly shaken and some of them are now even frightened to go to school.'

The teenager was taken to Lagan Valley Hospital where he received eight stitches to his nose and one to the ridge of his nose before being referred to the Ear, Nose and Throat unit at the Royal Victoria Hospital. (groups.google.com/.../d5303430511307bc%3Fq%3D%2522James%2BWi...)

28 September Loyalists taking part in the weekly picket of the Catholic Church at Harryville, Ballymena, said that they would extend the protest to include Catholic chapels at Ballycastle, Dervock, and Lisburn. They said that they would continue their protest until the Orange Order was allowed to parade in the Catholic village of Dunloy, County Antrim. (CAIN Chronology of the Conflict 1997)

1998

Very Rev. Sean Rogan was appointed as parish priest. One of his objectives was to completely refurbish and reroof St Patrick's Church.

In St Patrick's many of the oil paintings of the Stations of the Cross were damaged by acid in a sectarian attack inside the church in the 1970s.

The donors of the Stations of the Cross had plaques fixed to the wall;

Pray For;
1   John and Ellen Hamilton
2   Arthur and Ellen Ferris
3   William and Jane Cullen
4   James and Teresa Savage & family
5   John and Ruth Loughran
6   John and Ann McKenna

7   Henry and Ann Mulholland
8   No plaque
9   James Alice and Patrick Gallery [Patrick Gallery died on 12 March 1892 at his
    brother's home on Dublin Road. He had been employed by Barbour Threads and spent
    several years at their factory in Paterson, New Jersey, USA as book keeper and
    confidential clerk.]
10 The deceased relatives of Emily and Louise Mulholland
11 Brigid, Susanna and Bernard Campbell
12 James and Mary Burke
13 Doctor Aneas McFaull and Mary McFaull
14 Rose McFaull and Eliza Campbell.

These plaques were removed during the renovation of the church by Rev.
Sean Rogan and not replaced. They were however retained by a parishioner
in the hope that in the future the plaques would be replaced in memory of
those who made the donations and had asked for family members to be
remembered in prayers.

July Among the ten Catholic churches attacked in July was St Joseph's
Church, Magheragall which was razed to the ground in a sectarian arson
attack at the time of the Drumcree crisis when Orangemen were refused
permission to parade down the nationalist Garvaghy Road in Portadown.
On Sunday 9 July 1995 the Royal Ulster Constabulary, in line with a
determination made by the Parades Commission, prevented the Orange
Order march from returning to Portadown via this route after its annual
service at Drumcree church. A two-day stand off at Drumcree triggered
widespread attacks on the Catholic community in various parts of Northern
Ireland. The protests at Drumcree would continue each year until 2001 and
each year generated violence in loyalist areas.
    Caretaker Paddy Higgins and his wife Eilish were awakened about
midnight by a telephone call from a Protestant neighbour to tell them that
the church was on fire. Rushing to the church he found that the double doors
had been forced open and the wooden gallery at the back of the church was
burning fiercely. Unable to gain access he went to the sacristy entrance and
was successful in saving vestments, a chalice and even a couple of Stations
of the Cross paintings. By the time the fire brigade arrived from Lisburn
the fire had engulfed the roof and the seats and the wooden floor were in
flames. All they could do was to prevent the fire spreading to the

schoolhouse close to the altar side of the church. Only the four walls of the church were left standing.

William (86) and Kathleen (68) Mayers who lived beside the church escaped serious injury or death when large propane gas cylinders used to provide heating in the church fortunately did not explode.

Later when the church was being rebuilt it was discovered that the windows behind the altar had been sealed up, (now restored) and intriguingly a 6 foot by 3 foot pit at the altar which had previously been covered by the wooden flooring was discovered.

The disused two-room schoolhouse was used for Mass while the church was rebuilt and then demolished to make space for a much needed car park. A new vestibule was added to the church and the sacristy extended.

The church roof space is now home to a maternity bat roost which is monitored by the Department of the Environment. (Patrick Higgins)

St Colman's Catholic Church, at nearby Lambeg, was attacked by arsonists for the fourth time in the last four years. There was looting by loyalists in Lisburn during serious rioting in the Longstone Street area of the town. (7 July 1998 - rsf.ie/saoirse/record/jul1998.htm).

Also in July St Joseph's primary school in Lisburn came under attack from loyalist mobs who threw paint and petrol bombs at the school. (homepage.eircom.net/~eirenua/iris/236.htm)

Social Democratic and Labour Party (SDLP) councillor Peter O'Hagan became the first nationalist Mayor of Lisburn. (Peter O'Hagan died on 23 December 2009.)

1999

March Brian Magee turned professional boxer winning his first contest with a knock-out inside two rounds. He had competed as an amateur for Ireland in the 1996 Summer Olympics and won the Ulster Senior Title every year from 1995 to 1998.

He won the vacant IBO intercontinental super middleweight title in 2001 defeating Neil Linford before going on to win the IBO world super middleweight title which he defended successfully eight times. In July 2011

he captured the interim WBA super middleweight title in Costa Rica. In December 2012 he was unsuccessful in a bid for the same title in Denmark. In 2013, still not ready to hang up his gloves, Brian opened Magee Health and Fitness Gym on the Blackstaff Road, Belfast.
(www.mageehealthandfitness.com)

June Work began on the demolition of St Joseph's Hall. The footprint of the old hall was used for car parking space.

11 July Arsonists try to burn down St Patrick's Church in Derriaghy and St Patrick's Church in Lisburn. The police received a report at 03:28 a.m. that the church at Derriaghy had been attacked. At around 03:30 a.m. two wooden pallets were placed against the doors of the church at Chapel Hill, and set alight with firelighters. The blaze caused scorch damage to the doors and a stained glass window was broken.

Rev. Sean Rogan, who attended the mother of the three murdered Quinn children last year, described how the smell of smoke at his chapel after the arson attack reminded him of the Ballymoney attack.
[Three children, Richard, Mark and Jason aged 11, 9 and 7, born to a Catholic mother and living in the Protestant Carnany estate in Ballymoney died when their home was petrol bombed by members of the UVF on 12 July 1998 after a week of protests by Orangemen demanding access to the mainly nationalist Garvaghy Road, Portadown, as part of their annual march to Drumcree church.]

He said:

> *'One year to the day from the murder of the three Quinn children by loyalists, St Patrick's suffered an arson attack in the early hours of Sunday 11 July. This day last year I got a call to attend the boys' mother Chrissie in hospital. The smell of smoke then was the same today when I was alerted to the blaze at the church by the police. It seems so ironic that this happened on the anniversary of the boys' death. One year on and nothing seems to have changed.'* (www.anphoblacht.com/contents/5124)

Over the past few years, three other Catholic churches in the parish were attacked. The Church of the Blessed Virgin Mary and St Brigid and St Joseph's Church have both been burned to the ground (the former has since been rebuilt). Various arson attacks have also been made on St Colman's Church at Reilly's Trench.

21st Century

2000

VIOLENCE RETURNS

The Good Friday Agreement in 1998 called for the transfer of selected powers from London to Belfast and the establishment of a Northern Ireland Assembly and Executive Committee in which unionists and nationalist parties would share power. Additionally it created a North-South Ministerial Council to allow the political leaders on both sides of the border to cooperate on cross-border issues. Significantly it would bring Sinn Féin into government for the first time. The decommissioning of paramilitary weapons and explosives and police reform became a major issue with unionists arguing that Sinn Féin could not assume ministerial posts until such time the IRA had surrendered its weapons and that the name of the Royal Ulster Constabulary should not be changed.

On 11 February 2000 London suspended the devolved government which had David Trimble (UUP) as First Minister and Seamus Mallon (SDLP) as Deputy First Minister when Trimble threatened to resign to protest to the delay by the IRA in decommissioning its weapons and explosives. As the IRA prevaricated on decommissioning unionist tensions increased and when on 1 July David Trimble resigned violence again returned to the streets of Lisburn with upsurges in sectarian violence continuing over the next three years.

16 April On Thursday of Holy Week Eileen Drayne travelled to St Patrick's Cathedral in Armagh and received Maundy Money from Queen Elizabeth.

Eileen was a long serving member of Magheragall Women's Institute.

Rev. Eamon Magorrian was appointed as curate at St Patrick's in March. Born in 1940 in Castlewellan he was ordained in 1967 in St Patrick's Carlow College, a seminary for the priesthood. He served in St Patrick's,

Donegall Street, Belfast, Armoy, St Peter's and St Agnes' in Belfast. Prior to Lisburn he had served at the Cistercian Bolton Abbey, Athy, County Kildare with its guest house and a 300 acre working dairy farm. He recalled that the Cistercian community lived by the sweat of their brows. In Lisburn, at the rear of the parochial house he kept a half-dozen chickens, not for fresh eggs but as a hobby. It was known for an urban fox to try to steal one of his chickens. He also enjoyed reading and in particular studying the books of the Old Testament. Readily accepted by the parishioners he was highly regarded as a sincere and devout priest.

14 August A Catholic man in his 50s was assaulted in the living room of his home on the Hillhall Road.

18 August A number of paint bombs were thrown at a house belonging to a Catholic at Beechland Way.

29 August A Lisburn a man in his 30s was taken to hospital after being shot in the leg at Church Lane. (www.freewebs.com/saoirse/record/record23.htm.)

22 September Cardinal Seán Brady was invited as Guest of Honour at Friends' School, Lisburn Speech Day. Taking as his theme that there is more that unites us than divides us he said: 'A situation where people simply exist in a state of separation, doing no harm to one another, and interacting only when absolutely necessary in the public sphere, is far from satisfactory.' (Archdiocese of Armagh .org.)

REDEDICATION OF ST PATRICK'S CHURCH

17 December A ceremony was held in St Patrick's to dedicate the altar and to celebrate the reopening of the church after extensive structural repairs and internal redesign undertaken by Very Rev. Sean Rogan P.P.

The principal celebrant was The Most Rev. Patrick J. Walsh D.D., Bishop of Down and Connor and the concelebrants were - V. Rev. Sean Rogan P.P., V. Rev. Canon J. Cunningham. V. Rev. P. O'Neill P.P., V. Rev. J. Donaghy P.P., Rev. M. Browne C.Ss.R., Rev. E. Magorrian C.C.

Master of Ceremonies was V. Rev. Hugh P. Kennedy P.P. with Rev. G. Lyons C.C.

After Mass Isabel McArdle, as the parish's oldest member, then 94, was invited onto the altar and presented Bishop Walsh with a gift as a memento of the occasion. She was photographed with the Bishop and Rev. Rogan.

The redesign included the removal and sale of the large ornate wooden pulpit, the marble altar rails and the side sections of the reredos.

Eilis O Baoill who designed the new crucifix wrote;

> Using the figure from the old crucifix that was made more than 100 years ago I designed a new cross based on the Celtic cross form. The figure itself has been restored to natural lime wood with a colour stain and gold leaf highlights, the warm tones of the wood compliments the colour of the new ash cross but is distinctly different.
>
> The traditional centre of the Celtic circle has been replaced with a glass etching in the form of a passion flower which reflects the passion flowers on the reredos. At the heart of the real flowers there are three stamen and these come to represent the Blessed Trinity as well as serving to form a stylised shamrock-appropriate for St. Patrick.

Richard Hurley wrote;

> The altar is carved from one piece of Coombe Brune stone, quarried in the south of France. It embodies a cross shaped 'cut out' running through the lower part of the stone. The ambo is also carved from Coombe Brune stone.
>
> The Chair is constructed in Austrian oak with a logo - Christus Pax Nostra (Christ our Peace) with the Dove - influenced by a logo on a grill in the Baptistry of Constantine chapel adjacent to the Basilica of San Giovanni in Laterano, Rome. (Booklet produced for the Solemn re-opening & Dedication of the Altar, 17 December 2000.)

A glaring omission in the refurbishment of the church was the lack of provision of toilet facilities for the congregation.

During Rev. Rogan's tenure as parish priest he sold off a large proportion of the church's land portifolio in Lisburn. Property to the right of the church on Chapel Hill was sold. Land at Trinity Terrace was sold and despite vociferous objections from the Pastoral Committee part of the ground set aside for the Catholic Holy Trinity cemetery was sold for housing. The committee had been reminded by Rev. Rogan that their role was advisory only and they could not make any executive decisions.

This fire-sale of church land in Lisburn coincided with the payment of hundreds of thousands of pounds to settle numerous claims relating to sexual abuse by Catholic priests in Ireland. This sale of land was before the property crash when land was being sold for astronomical sums. It is claimed that land sold by the church at Trinity Terrace for £75,000 was sold on within a few days for £175,000.

Rev. Gabriel Lyons, chairman of St Patrick's Youth Club organised a cross generation millennium celebration in the Youth Club which included the display of old vestments and old photographs. A buffet meal was provided.

Sister Denise retired from post of principal of St Joseph's Primary School. During her time as principal the tennis courts which had once been used by the convent were sold by the parish to the Education & Library Board and the space used as a playground for the primary school children.

2001

21 February On Wednesday a pipe bomb exploded in a garden of a home in the Knockmore estate on the Moira Road around 5:20 a.m. The Catholic occupants escaped injury after this second attack in three days near the UDA controlled Old Warren estate. (IN, RUC.)

27 May On Sunday Magheragall church reopened after reconstruction following the arson attack in 1998.

10 July An elderly and disabled Catholic woman, Mrs Geraldine Ewing, died just hours after six loyalists forced their way into her Lisburn home where she had lived for 21 years and ordered her and her family to leave or be 'burnt out'. The family consisted of her two sons, one of whom was physically and mentally handicapped and her disabled brother.

Commenting on the intimidation Rev. Sean Rogan said: 'In any society that calls itself civilised, these people were the most vulnerable, the most weak and disabled. They are the people who should be most protected, looked after and most cared for.'

SDLP councillor Peter O'Hagan said: ' I am positive from my contacts with Mrs Ewing's relatives that the family were living in fear. The invasion of their home was the final straw for them. They have first suffered the indignity of having to leave their home, and now for their mother to die is too much for any family to bear.' Mrs Ewing's brother said: 'Geraldine had some heart trouble and the loyalist threats caused the heart attack, she was naturally very stressed by what had happened. If the loyalists hadn't have come and smashed the house up and told her to get out she would still be alive.' A spokesperson for the Housing Executive confirmed that the family had previously asked for their home to be secured after intimidation from loyalists. (IN, AN) (Lost Lives - David McKittrick, Seamus Kelters, Brian Feeney, Chris Thornton, David McVea, Mainstream Publishing.)

16 August Arsonists broke into St Peter's Catholic Church in Stoneyford, near Lisburn, and started a fire. A retired fireman entered the building and brought the fire under control. Loyalists from the Lisburn area were believed to have been responsible for the attack. (CAIN Chronology of the Conflict 2001.)

15 September A house in Donard Drive was attacked with a petrol bomb at approximately 11:00 p.m. The house was unoccupied at the time and the kitchen was extensively damaged by fire. (CAIN Chronology of the Conflict 2001.)

Catholics staying at Hillsborough Castle, including Catholic secretaries of state attended Sunday Mass in Reilly's Trench Church.

The 2001 Census, in relation to community background, shows that the population of the Lisburn council area was 108,694 of whom 36,251 (33.35%) gave their religion, or religion brought up in, as Catholic. (Source NISRA 2001 Census.)

2002

13 January On Sunday loyalists carried out arson attacks on St Bride's Primary School in south Belfast and on St Patrick's High School in Lisburn. Both schools suffered substantial damage. A fire started shortly before 10:00 p.m. extensively damaged a mobile classroom at St Patrick's High School on the Ballinderry Road. (IN, CW, BBC, RUC/PSNI)

8 June A house in Lisburn was petrol bombed at about 1:55 a.m. on Saturday. Minor damage was caused at the rear of the house in Tonagh

Drive. A neighbour extinguished the fire and said a petrol bomb had ignited at the rear door. (BBC News)

August Rev. Gabriel Lyons was transferred from St Patrick's to St Mary's on the Hill, Glengormley, Newtownabbey.

1 September On Sunday two stained glass windows in St Patrick's church were smashed in an unsuccessful attempt to gain access to the building. In the sectarian attack ornamental lights were smashed and plants in the garden around the church were pulled out of the ground and scattered around the building.

Rev. Rogan said: 'Nearly every Sunday morning I have to clean up broken glass from bottles thrown at the chapel the night before. All four Catholic churches in the Lisburn area have been burned down in the past and only six weeks ago Saint Joseph's had sectarian graffiti daubed on it.' (Irish News 2 September 2002)

28 October Loyalists were blamed for attempting to ram a stolen car through the main door of St Patrick's High School before setting it on fire.

At around 4:00 a.m. a green Volkswagon Polo, stolen in the Tonagh Drive area of Lisburn, was driven into the school grounds on the Ballinderry Road and reversed towards the front door of the school at high speed. The car was only stopped from causing serious damage by a metal handrail at the entrance. The vehicle was then set alight and the school suffered minor scorch damage. Several windows were also smashed during the incident.

Commenting on the attack Rev. Sean Rogan said that this was the second attack on the school in as many weeks and the attack was 'a very sad state of affairs. Had they gone a few feet just to the left of the handrail they would have got right into the school...and we would have had St. Patrick's school burned to the ground,' Fr Rogan said, 'We are very upset at what is happening.' (UTV News 28 October 2002.)

Rev. Rogan said that there were four Catholic churches in the area, and in recent years two had been burned out, and another badly damaged. He said that the churches had been hit by gunfire and vandals had caused thousands of pounds worth of damage to church property.

In an open letter to 'The Irish News' Father Patrick McCafferty from Lisburn called upon the Archbishop of Dublin, Cardinal Desmond Connell, to resign over the Church's handling of child sex abuse allegations in Ireland.

He accused church leaders of being 'guilty of the most stunning arrogance and breathtaking indifference to real human anguish'.

He said that the Cardinal Connell and other senior bishops were 'not fit to lead the people of God' and should follow the lead of Cardinal Bernard Law, the Archbishop of Boston, who quit last week.

There have been a series of calls for the resignation of Cardinal Connell who admitted earlier this year that he had made mistakes in dealing with complaints of abuse. The calls to step down were made shortly after a television documentary was broadcast, which detailed circumstances and responses to alleged child abuse offenders within the Church.

In a frank exposition of his views, Father McCafferty wrote that the Catholic Church had shown 'wicked contempt for survivors of clerical abuse'.

He said that when he had tried to highlight it through the pulpit he had been regarded as a 'troublemaker by certain ecclesiastical grandees'.

He added:

> *'These men, who moved paedophiles around from parish to parish, who later on refused to listen to stories of immense and incalculable harm visited upon little ones, have absolutely no excuse. I hope they all resign now. Just as there is no role for paedophiles in the priesthood, so there is no place for such individuals as Cardinal Law [and others] in the role of shepherding the people of God.'*

Meanwhile the Vatican announced the approval of the revised US bishops' policy that allows 'due process' for priests accused of molesting children.

'The Holy See is fully supportive of the bishops' efforts to combat and to prevent such evil,' Cardinal Giovanni Re said in a statement.

'The universal law of the Church has always recognised this crime as one of the most serious offences which sacred ministers can commit, and has determined that they be punished with the most severe penalties, not excluding – if the case so requires – dismissal from the clerical state.' (Irish News 16 December 2002.)

November Lisburn City Council carried out a survey as part of its community safety audit but, in an apparent attempt to play down the problem of sectarian attacks and harassment, questions about experiences of sectarian violence were restricted to the mainly Catholic area of Colin.

In a reply to a survey question about its policies designed to respond to or challenge sectarian harassment and violence Lisburn City Council cited policies relating to harassment of staff and mentioned flag flying, kerb painting, sectarian graffiti and interface areas as the main areas of concern. (ofmdfmni.gov.uk/violence)

NEW COMMUNITIES JOIN THE PARISH OF BLARIS

2003

Migration from Kerala in southwest India to Northern Ireland during the early 2000s increased as hospitals recruited health care professionals. In 2003 representatives from the Lagan Valley Hospital, Lisburn visited Kerala to recruit doctors, nurses and health care workers.

A major change took place in Lisburn in 2003 with the arrival of members of the Syro Malabar Catholic Community, and their families, from Kerala to work in the Lagan Valley Hospital.

These new neighbours came from strong church-going backgrounds and looked for an identity with their homeland to help them make the huge adjustment to living in a new country with different languages, different customs, different weather and different ways of being church. Many just brought back the gift of the Gospel that Irish missionaries brought out to their forebears. (www.catholicbishops.ie/...DirectoryOfMigrantLedChurchesAndChaplain...)

Rev. Fr Sony Palathara CMI had celebrated the first Malayalam Mass in the Clonard Monastery on 11 October 2002. Since then the community continued the Mass every month, and celebrated Christmas and New Year. Every year the community conducted retreats for adults, youth and children by popular retreat teams from Kerala.

April Lisburn councillor David Archer jnr boycotted the beginning of council sessions because the opening prayer was led by the lord mayor's chaplain Rev. Sean Rogan.

Archer, (27), a one-time secretary to Lagan Valley MP Jeffrey Donaldson, claimed that there was nothing bigoted in his stance, insisting he was following Orange Order rules. Anti-agreement Archer and some DUP councillors refused to stay in the council chamber for prayers led by Catholic mayor Betty Campbell's chaplain.

Perplexed Rev. Rogan said that his brief sermon was merely a Bible passage on reconciliation followed by the Lord's Prayer which was 'Common to Christians of all denominations'. (Newspaper article from The People, London, England.)

May Poland became a member of the European Union allowing its citizens to take up employment in the UK. The flow of individuals from Poland to the UK to seek better paid work took the British government by surprise as Poland experienced one of its largest emigration flows in its post war history. Many Polish citizens took up employment opportunities in Lisburn and the surrounding area. Many from a Catholic background added to the congregation of St Patrick's Church.

July

Ulster Unionist Party councillors of Lisburn voted to have 'no Catholic about the place' by excluding all Catholic Sinn Féin, SDLP and Alliance Party members from council positions within the city at last week's AGM. The UUP connived with the DUP to ensure that unionists secured all positions.

In doing so, the UUP abandoned established local protocol and ignored their commitment to creating Lisburn as 'a city for all', a slogan that had figured large in the borough's successful campaign to gain city status a year ago. The slogan was later changed to 'a city for life'. (anphoblacht.com/contents 10273.)

Dr Seamus Quinn was appointed as principal at St Patrick's High School, now St Patrick's Academy. Dr Quinn formed part of the Northern Ireland Commission for Catholic Education Working Group on post primary transfer.

Five of the staff, Gerry Heaney, Josephine Murray, Mary Smith, Eamonn Haughey and Eileen Cooley who had spent their entire teaching careers at St Patrick's retired in June 2003. (Lisburn Star 4 June 2003)

August Jean McConville, whose body was accidently found by a member of the public while he was walking on Shelling Hill beach, County Louth, was buried beside her husband in Holy Trinity cemetery, Lisburn.

In 1972, Jean McConville was abducted and murdered by the Provisional IRA and secretly buried on this beach. Witnesses to her abduction claimed that she had given aid to a wounded British soldier, but the IRA subsequently claimed that she had been passing information on republican activities to British security forces. Police Ombudsman Nuala O'Loan stated that, after an investigation by her office, there is no evidence that Mrs McConville gave information to the police, the military or the security service.

The crime remains unsolved.

(en.wikipedia.org/wiki/Murder_of_Jean_McConville.)

20 November On Thursday Catholic James McMahon (21) was badly beaten at Hancock Street by UDA using baseball bats. He died later in hospital.

A major police investigation with follow-up searches ensued in an effort to find his killers. Later in the evening that James McMahon was murdered Darren Kenneth Grant and Anthony Madden, along with another man went to the home of Mr Foster in the nearby Hillhall estate and left items in his attic. A police search of the house revealed a deadly arsenal consisting of six sub-machine guns and magazines, approximately 2,000 rounds of ammunition, three pipe bombs, a blank firing weapon, an accelerant powder and weapons cleaning materials. There were also pick axe and sledge hammer handles.

At their trial Justice Weir stated; 'Had there been evidence that either of you intended to personally use any of these weapons or direct others to do so then the sentences imposed would have been significantly more severe.' Both men were sentenced to eight years' imprisonment on each count to run concurrently with eighteen months' probation supervision to commence upon release from prison. (Northern Ireland Courts and Tribunal Service - www.courtsni.gov.uk/en-GB/.../PublishedByYear/.../j_j_WEIF5412.htm.)

It will take 'many floods of water to wash away the stain and the shame' of the sectarian murder of a Catholic man on the banks of the River Lagan, mourners heard yesterday.

Parish priest Fr Sean Rogan and Auxiliary Bishop of Down and Connor Anthony Farquhar concelebrated Requiem Mass for 21-year-old James McMahon who was attacked by a loyalist gang last week. Mourners, the majority of whom were young people, who filled St Patrick's Church were told that the community had been 'robbed' of one of its youngest members.

The eldest of five children, James McMahon had been set upon by a masked gang armed with baseball bats as he walked home with friends along Hancock Street. He died in the Royal Victoria Hospital, Belfast the following afternoon and was the first Catholic to be killed by loyalists in more than a year.

As family and friends carried his coffin through Lisburn they paused for a moment close to the spot where he was attacked.

Fr Rogan told the congregation, which included senior police officers, the murder victim's mother had requested that his organs be donated.

'What a contrast. This woman interested in giving life - so starkly opposite to the actions of those masked individuals who were dealing in death. Deirdre we salute you for your bravery, for your thoughtfulness, for your generosity. You are an example to us all.'

The parish priest said all humans were 'made in the image and likeness of God' and therefore everyone had a responsibility to respect and protect the sacredness of life.

Bishop Anthony Farquhar branded Mr McMahon's death a 'brutal and callous' murder which had disgusted the community.

'The repeated threats to human life, young and old, have filled us with tension and anxiety, but when they spill over into killing then we experience a more profound sense of shock at the evil which is being perpetrated,' he said. 'The motivation for murder, be it domestic, political, sectarian, or perhaps just casual should never lessen the sense of shock', the bishop added.

'Frequently people look at the situation and compare it with 30, 20, 10 years ago. Some will mutter that things are still bad; others will tell us how much has improved.

'Some see a glass half empty, some see a glass half full. Today, however, we are starkly reminded that whatever else, the glass still holds the dregs of bitterness and hatred.'

Mr McMahon's brothers Christopher and Ryan gave readings and Bishop Farquhar praised the victim's family for their dignity during a time of great pain. He spoke of the need for love and forgiveness and an obligation to protect the dignity of human life 'particularly the most vulnerable and defenceless'.

Mr McMahon is survived by his mother Deirdre, sisters Maria and Kathleen and brothers Christopher and Ryan. (Maeve Connolly, Irish News, 26 November 2003)

2004

24 June The issue of Catholic representation on Lisburn Council was raised by Sinn Féin councillor Paul Butler at a council meeting when he stated that the practice of institutionalised sectarian discrimination was being continued when Sinn Féin and the SDLP were once again excluded from all senior positions on the council. (The previous year none of the council's seven nationalist councillors had been appointed as committee chairs or other senior posts.) The DUP and Ulster Unionists were elected to all the top positions. DUP Councillor Paul Porter stated that Sinn Féin would have to accept the democratic process.

Newry and Mourne District Council at a meeting on 1 November stated; 'This Council is disappointed at the decision by Lisburn Council to exclude Nationalists from the positions of Chairs, Vice Chairs of Council Committees and membership of outside bodies at its Annual General Meeting on 24 June 2004.

This decision by Lisburn Council is contrary to the spirit of the Good Friday Agreement in advocating the principle of partnership politics. The only way local Councils can serve the people they represent effectively is if they are committed to partnership, equality and mutual respect. These principles are particularly important in Local Government which must be seen to represent everyone.' (www.newryandmourne.gov.uk)

2005

25 March The annual Good Friday 'Carrying of the Cross' march of witness was held in Lisburn. Led by the Lisburn City Centre Ministers, the procession made its way along Bow Street to Market Square for a short act of worship at 1:00 p.m. The Rev. Brian Gibson, Minister of Railway Street

Presbyterian Church, welcomed those assembled (about 300 people) and the Very Rev. Sean Rogan - St Patrick's Church, introduced the opening hymn, 'Amazing Grace'.

2 April The pontiff, Pope John Paul II, died on Saturday and his Requiem Mass was celebrated in St Peter's Basilica, Rome on 8 April.

At St Patrick's Church the usual morning Mass at 10:00 a.m. was cancelled and instead Mass was celebrated at 7:30 a.m. and 12:00 noon to give worshippers an opportunity to both attend church and watch television coverage of the Pope's funeral.

On Thursday morning children from Catholic schools in Lisburn attended a special Mass in memory of the Pope in St Patrick's. This was celebrated at 11:00 a.m. and pupils of St Patrick's High School, St Joseph's and St Aloysius' Primaries took part in the Scripture readings, Prayers of Intercession and the Presentation of the Gifts.

19 April Rev. Sean Rogan, P.P. erected the Papal Flag at St Patrick's Church to celebrate the election of Cardinal Joseph Ratzinger as Pope Benedict XV1.

7 June On the Feast of St Colman, Bishop Patrick Walsh celebrated Mass at St Colman's Church, Reilly's Trench to mark its 200th anniversary.

Among the congregation were the Rev. William Nixon from the Church of Ireland in Hillsborough and Presbyterian Minister the Rev. John Deveney. After unveiling a plaque, Bishop Walsh planted a tree near the Mass Tree which was used by Catholics between the loss of the original building and the opening of the 'new' church in 1805.

Rev. Rogan said he was delighted to receive a letter from the Marquis of Downshire.

'To think that now six generations on, the Marquis sends us his best wishes on the 200th anniversary of our church is quite remarkable' he said. (Lisburn Star 10 June 2005.)

August Rev. Hugh P. Kennedy was appointed as parish priest when Rev Rogan was transferred to Downpatrick.

A member of the family which owned Belfast's famous Kennedy Bakery he was educated at St Malachy's and Queen's University and studied in Rome and Paris before entering the Seminary in Maynooth. He was due to be ordained by Pope Paul II in Rome in 1981 but his ordination was brought forward because of a need for new clergy within the Diocese of Down and Connor. His first parish was Castlewellan and he then moved to Glenravel at Martinstown, County Antrim before undertaking a three year Master's Degree in Theology in Paris. He returned to St Paul's Church on the Falls Road before completing his Doctorate at Maynooth where he spent four years. On completion he was appointed to St Bernadette's in Rosetta, Belfast before moving to the Sacred Heart Church in the Oldpark, Belfast where he spent eight years before being appointed to St Patrick's in Lisburn. He was also Bishop Patrick Walsh's official Master of Ceremonies and Chief Chaplin to the Order of Malta in Ireland.

10 August The walls of St Patrick's Church were daubed with sectarian slogans in orange paint; 'UDA' and 'Taigs Out'. Windows were smashed and bottles broken on the walls.

25 September Father Joachim Lyttle O.F.M., who had been ill for some years, died peacefully at Letterkenny Hospital. He had returned to Ards and Ard Mhuire in Creeslough, to the Friary where he had been ordained. Even though confined to a wheelchair but would often conduct the church choir at the Ards Monastery on Sundays.

Bishops Philip Boyce and Seamus Hegarty, his Brothers and neighbouring priests attended his funeral Mass at Ards Monastery. It was recorded that rain fell and autumn coloured leaves around the Friary drifted silently down from the trees as his funeral cortege made its way to the cemetery.

In line with the Down & Connor Diocesan policy for the protection of children, young people and vulnerable adults and those who work with them a Parish Safeguarding Committee was established, chaired by Gerald McGoldrick, deputy chair, Maria McDonald and Rev. D. McCaughan, Geraldine Clenaghan, Una Tracey, Pat Catney and Marie Allen.

The household survey for Tonagh showed that 37% of the estate is Protestant, 28% are Catholic and 28% are mixed religion households. Data from the 2005 Northern Ireland Life and Times Survey showed that 12% of people are married to someone who is not of the same religion, which means that Tonagh has more than twice the rate of mixed households compared with Northern Ireland as a whole. Most people living in Tonagh described the estate as 'mixed' and expressed their desire to continue to live in a mixed area (89%), whilst mixed households (97%) and Catholics (88%) were more likely to define the estate in this way, than Protestants (85%). (Shared Social Housing - A study of mixed housing in Tonagh, Lisburn, Housing Executive.)

2006

January The first Syro Malabar rite Mass was celebrated in St Patrick's, Lisburn.

27 January Lisburn boxer John Rodgers, a member of St Patrick's parish was honoured at a special ceremony at the National Stadium in Dublin when he was entered in the Irish Amateur Boxing Association's Hall of Fame.

He became the Ulster Junior Lightweight Champion and was the Ulster Senior Lightweight Champion when he was picked to go to the European Cup in Warsaw, Poland in 1966 where he won a bronze medal. He represented Northern Ireland at the Commonwealth Games in Edinburgh in 1970 and participated at the 1972 Olympics in Munich when eleven Israeli athletes and coaches, a West German police officer, and five terrorists were killed in what became known as the 'Munich Massacre.' He met Muhammad Ali when he was training in Dublin for the 1972 Olympics.

John was also the first Irishman to take part in the World Amateur Championships which were held in Havana, Cuba in 1973 where he met and shook hands with Cuban leader, Fidel Castro. (Ulster Star 3 March 2006.)

3 March St Coleman's Church, Reilly's Trench, hosted the Maze Women's World day of Prayer service organised by Mrs Kathleen McClure. A cross-community event it was attended by Maze Presbyterian, Hillsborough Presbyterian, Saint Malachy - Hillsborough, All Saints' - Eglantine, St. Matthew - Broomhedge, St. James's - Lower Kilwarlin, St. John's - Upper Kilwarlin, Moravian Church - Kilwarlin, Priesthill Methodist and Broomhedge Methodist.

16 August Rev. Hugh Kennedy who had been parish priest of Lisburn for just 12 months, was appointed Administrator of St Peter's Cathedral, Albert Street, Belfast to succeed Monsignor Thomas Toner. Rev. Kennedy was replaced by the Very Rev. Dermot McCaughan formerly parish priest in Hannahstown parish.

A Service of Installation for Rev. McCaughan, led by Bishop Farquhar assisted by Rev. Eamon Magorrian and Assistant Priest Rev. Edward Magee, was held in St Patrick's on 3 November.

Rev. Dermot McCaughan, Broughshane Road was ordained in Holy Family Church on 9 June 1974 and said his first Mass in All Saint's Church, Ballymena, the next day. Later transferred to Hannahstown he had been the last parish priest to live in the old parochial house before it was demolished.

Originally from Ballymena he was educated at St MacNissi's College, Garron Tower, in the Glens of Antrim (1960-1967). He then attended Maynooth College, County Kildare, graduating in French in 1970 and Theology in 1973. Following his ordination in Holy Family Church, Antrim Road, Belfast, in June 1974, he assisted at Holy Rosary and St Bernadette's, Belfast (1974-1978). He was Chaplain to the City Hospital and Nazareth Lodge, Belfast (1978-1982); Somerton Road, Belfast (1982-1983); St Mary's, Greencastle on the Shore Road (1983-1988); St Anne's, Dunmurry (1988-1994). In August 1994, he was appointed parish priest at Hannahstown with pastoral oversight of St Joseph's Church, Hannahstown and St Peter's Church (The Rock) Stoneyford. His Lisburn parish area consists of four churches: St Patrick's - Lisburn, St Colman's - Reilly's Trench, St Joseph's - Magheragall and Blessed Virgin Mary & St Brigid's - Magheramesk. He will be assisted by the Rev. Eamon Magorrian, curate and the Rev. Edward McGee, assistant priest. Rev. Dr. Eddie Magee who assists in Lisburn parish at weekends is a lecturer at St Mary's College, Belfast and was appointed to the post of spokesperson for the Diocese of Down and Connor. In many media interviews he is seen as representing the views of the Catholic Church in Ireland.

19 August

Rev. McCaughan took his first Mass at St Patrick's Church last Saturday evening. Since his arrival in Lisburn last week he says that he has found the people to be 'genuinely very welcoming' and stressed that it was his intention to, 'build on the great work carried out by his predecessor Father Hugh Kennedy in the field of inter-church relations'. (Lisburn Star August 2006.)

November Seamus Close announced that he was retiring from politics.

Mr Close had been one of the most senior figures in Northern Ireland politics for many years, having served as Alliance Chairman from 1981 until 1982 and as Party Deputy Leader for ten years from 1991 until 2001. He was a key negotiator in the Brooke-Mayhew Talks 1991-92 and served on the Northern Ireland Forum for Peace and Reconciliation 1994-95. He was a Member of the Legislative Assembly (MLA) for Lagan Valley from 1998 to 2007. He served as Lisburn's mayor 1993/4.

He was a member of the key Alliance delegations in successive talks about the future of Northern Ireland, culminating in the Belfast Agreement in 1998.

In 1997 he was awarded the OBE and in 2001 he was nominated as Parliamentarian of the Year. In 2010 became an Honorary Freeman of the City of Lisburn.

2007

Fiona McCausland, who grew up in Lisburn and helps run the Welcome House, said local people were adamant that the migrants must feel this was their home. 'We made it clear to them that, if they wanted to send their kids to the local Catholic primary school, there would be no hassle. Some Polish communities in Northern Ireland that reside in loyalist areas send their kids to state schools; they fear that the uniform of a Catholic school might mark them out for sectarian attack. We were determined not to let that happen on the Old Warren estate. The community here liaised with the local Catholic primary school to ensure that those Polish families who wanted to could send their kids to St Aloysius's.' (The Observer 18 February 2007.)

6 April The annual Good Friday 'Carrying of the Cross' march of witness was held in Lisburn on Friday afternoon. The Very Rev. Dermot McCaughan, Lisburn's recently installed parish priest, welcomed the large crowd. (Lisburn.com.)

18 June Improving relationships in Lisburn were demonstrated when President Mary McAleese and her husband Martin visited Lisburn Council and all members turned out to greet them. The President later called with her uncle Patrick Dorrian who had been an Alliance councillor in Lisburn in the mid 1970s. He remarked to her and her husband how impressed he was with the way the situation in Lisburn had progressed.

Referring to a recent visit to Messines in Belgium along with DUP MLA Alderman Edwin Poots the President reminded her audience that during the First World War soldiers of the 36th Ulster Division and the 16th Irish Division had fought and died together and how important it was for her to have the two jurisdiction represented there. (Ulster Star 22 June 2007)

September The parochial house beside the church, which had been built following the destruction of the previous one during the "Burnings" in 1920, was demolished. The site was cleared and a new parochial house built further back from the road allowing space for a church car park.

2008

21 March The annual Good Friday 'Carrying of the Cross' march of witness was held in Lisburn city centre on Friday. The procession gathered at the lower end of Bow Street then made its way to Market Square for a short act of worship led by the Lisburn City Centre Ministers. Taking part in the procession and act of worship were: Rev. Kenneth McGrath (Lisburn Cathedral), Rev. John Brackenridge (First Lisburn), Fr Dermot McCaughan (St Patrick's), Pastor George Hilary (Lisburn Christian Fellowship), Rev. Brian Anderson (Seymour Street), Rev. Brian Gibson (Railway Street), Rev. Dianne Matchett (Christ Church) and Rev. Paul Dundas (Christ Church). (Lisburn.com.)

2009

25 January The funeral took place of much-loved and respected north Antrim priest Father Ernest McCaughan who passed away on Sunday, aged 83.

Among those gathered to pay their respects to Father McCaughan was Cardinal Cahal Daly, Bishop of Down & Connor, Noel Treanor and Bishops Patrick Walsh and Anthony Farquhar. Father McCaughan had been the parish priest in Saintfield and Carrickmannon and in Portglenone in the eighties and nineties.

He was ordained to the priesthood on 22 June 1952 having studied at St

Malachy's College, Queen's University Belfast and St Patrick's Maynooth and served in Crossgar until 1961.

For the next 20 years he was curate in Newcastle, Lisburn and St Paul's in Belfast before being appointed parish priest in Saintfield and Carrickmannon. (Ballymoney Times 28 January 2009.)

Speaking about the decision of Lisburn Council to erect a UDR memorial outside the Lisburn Museum and Irish Linen Center in the centre of Lisburn Sinn Féin MLA Paul Butler said, 'Sinn Féin is opposed to the Commission's decision. Many nationalists will be disappointed that the Planning Service has given approval for this monument. Catholics in Lisburn are totally opposed to their rates being used to honour a regiment that was heavily involved in the killing of Catholics. The UDR monument, which will be erected on Council-owned land, with the approval of Lisburn Council's unionist majority, will stand as an indictment of the sectarian and exclusively unionist agenda the council has followed for decades.' (Cain.ulst.ac.uk)

(Two, more than life size, statues of UDR soldiers, one male and the other female [Greenfinch], are depicted operating a vehicle checkpoint. The statues stand on top of a large granite plinth which contains a bronze plaque. The entire memorial is 19 feet in height.)

This was seen as the ultimate insult to the McKee family in Lisburn whose son Liam was murdered by a full-time member of the UDR in Lisburn who had set up at least 14 other Catholics for assassination and the many Catholic murdered by members of the UDR.

15 February Parishioners were invited to view the newly built Pastoral Centre. Bishop Noel Treanor celebrated 12:00 o'clock Mass and later visited the Centre.

10 April The annual Good Friday 'Carrying of the Cross march of witness' was held in Lisburn on Friday. The procession gathered at the lower end of Bow Street then made its way along Bow Street for a short act of worship at 12:45 p.m. led by the City Centre Ministers from Seymour Street Methodist, First Lisburn and Railway Street Presbyterian, St Patrick's Roman Catholic Church, Lisburn Cathedral, Christ Church Parish and Lisburn Christian Fellowship.

2 June St Aloysius' Primary School and Nursery celebrated 40 years with a Mass of Thanksgiving. The main celebrant was Most Rev. Donald McKeown, auxiliary bishop of Down and Connor. (Diocesan records.)

28 November The Pastoral Centre was officially opened with a Gala Concert. The event, officiated by Bishop Noel Treanor, was marked by a cross community gala concert compered by BBC television presenter and former parishioner Donna Traynor.

Local talent performing on the night included Sean Crummey, Starburst Theatre School, Depo-McGuigan's Irish dancers, Pat Catney, Cleland Memorial Pipe Band and Fusion Theatre featuring 'Songs from the Shows', Hillsborough Drama Group and the Lisburn Youth Dancers. Among the distinguished guests was Lisburn Deputy Mayor Alderman Paul Porter.

Rev. McCaughan said the new Centre would provide 'an excellent social facility which is by no means exclusive to the parishioners of St Patrick's. I am delighted to see that drama, theatre and youth groups are among those from all communities in the city of Lisburn that are already making excellent use of the centre'. (Irish Catholic 18 Dec 2009.)

The Centre has since achieved its objective to be inclusive, with the Protestant and Catholic communities together enjoying various functions. As part of the Orange Order's outreach programme a presentation on the history of the Order was well received in the Centre. The ethnic minorities also make good use of the facilities in the Centre.

Mr. Pat Catney was appointed manager of the Pastoral Centre.

2010

Bishop Noel Treanor, Fr Magorrian C.C. and Fr McCaughan P.P. celebrated the confirmation ceremony for students in St Patrick's Church. (Irish Catholic 3 March 2010)

The annual Good Friday 'Carrying of the Cross March of Witness' was held in Lisburn. Following the Blessing by Rev. Dermot McCaughan, refreshments were served in First Lisburn Presbyterian Church where there was an opportunity to receive prayer or take time for quiet reflection. (Lisburn.com)

Commenting on attendance at Mass Fr Edward McGee said: 'My own experience of Mass in my home parish of Lisburn is that attendance was very good, and there was a good crowd at the Easter Sunday ceremony celebrated by Bishop Treanor in St Peter's Church in Belfast. Anecdotally parishioners say they prefer Easter ceremonies even over Christmas because it is less commercialised and allows people to be more reflective.' (The Irish Catholic 9 April 2010)

There was mixed reaction to a planned boycott of Sunday Mass call made by Catholic pensioner and women's rights campaigner Jennifer Sleeman, from Clonakilty, west Cork. She called on women 'to let the Vatican and the Irish Church know that women are tired of being treated as second-class citizens'. Lisburn priest Father Edward McGee said he did not see any drop in numbers at his service. He said the boycott call was a way for people to voice their concerns about the Church and that people needed reassurances that their concerns were being addressed. (Motherwell Times 26 September 2010)

2011

7 March Bishop Jose Colin Mendoza Bagaforo from the Archdiocese of Cotabato in the Philippines visited Lisburn and celebrated a special Mass for the Filipino community in St Patrick's. The Mass was followed by a reception for the bishop in the Pastoral Centre where he was entertained by Irish dancers and songs by Pat Catney, the Centre's manager.

The Filipino community continue to play an important part in parish life and Lorenzo, the son of Lauro (Larry) and Rosa Cuteo became the first Filipino altar boy in St Patrick's. Lorenzo attended St Aloysius' school in Lisburn. Lauro himself scored another first when he was accepted, in 2011, as the first Filipino member of the Knights of St Columbanus in Ireland. (Lauro & Rosa Cueto 2013)

Rev. Pat O'Connell, a Redemptorist from Rathgar in Dublin administers to the Filipino community.

In due course the strength of the Syro Malabar Indian community increased and people settled not only in Belfast but in other areas of Northern Ireland including Lisburn, Bangor, Antrim, Portadown, Enniskillen and Derry. To help the members in these areas Masses were held there. Priests, Rev. Fr Mathew Arakkaparambil and Rev. Fr Paul Njaliath from Dublin, helped the community for their spiritual needs. In 2010 Rev. Fr Joseph Karukayil was appointed in the diocese of Derry. He extended his service to other parts of Northern Ireland.

When the then migrant bishop Rt. Rev. Dr Gregory Karotemprayil CMI visited the community in the year 2005, arrangements were made with the Down and Connor bishop Rt. Rev. Dr Patrick Walsh and bishop Rt. Rev. Dr Donal McKeown to appoint a Malayalee priest for the community. The process of appointing the priest took many years until Rev. Dr Fr. Anthony Perumayan was appointed as a curate in St Paul's Church, Belfast. He arrived Belfast on 7 Jan 2011 and took charge officially during the initiation ceremony led by bishop Dr Donal McKeown on 16 January 2011. (www.smcbelfast.org/hostory.html)

22 April On Good Friday the 'Carrying of the Cross march of Witness' in Bow Street was held on Friday.

May Pat Catney was elected to serve on Lisburn City Council as a member of the Social Democratic and Labour Party, a position previously held by the late Peter O'Hagan. Pat, was the former owner/manager of Belfast's famous Kitchen Bar which was demolished to make way for the Victoria Centre shopping complex.

June Martin Barlow, a partner in Lisburn-based graphic design consultancy 2b:creative, won an international competition to design the graphic identity for the 50th International Eucharistic Congress of the Roman Catholic Church, held in Dublin. In recognition of his achievement Martin was invited to the Vatican where he had a private meeting with Pope Benedict XIV. He was accompanied by Archbishop Diarmuid Martin from Dublin.

September Police were called to deal with three separate security alerts which caused disruption across the province. At a second alert in Lisburn, a suspicious object was found by police after they were told a device had been thrown at a house in the city. According to one councillor, two Ulster flags were found pinned to the door of a Catholic chapel close to the scene of the alert on Sunday morning.

SDLP councillor Patrick Catney said he believed those responsible for both incidents were not from the local area. (Belfast Telegraph 27 September 2011.)

November Rev. Patrick McCafferty, who had called on former Archbishop of Dublin, Desmond Connell to resign over clerical sex abuse, claimed that a fellow cleric, James Martin Donaghy, attempted to have sex with him on the night before the accused cleric's ordination into the Catholic Church.

He was giving evidence against a 53-year-old former priest of Lady Wallace Drive, Lisburn who denied a total of 26 charges involving the alleged sex abuse and indecent assault of three males, Rev. McCafferty, another trainee priest and a former altar boy, between June 1983 and December 2000. (Belfast Telegraph, 17 November 2011.)

4 December Canon Joseph Cunningham, (born 20 April 1923, ordained 22 June 1947), died peacefully at Our Lady's Home after a long illness.

Requiem Mass and Divine Office was celebrated in St Patrick's Church on 7 December with Bishops Treanor and Farquhar officiating. His remains were laid to rest in Holy Trinity cemetery.

Funeral Homily for Canon Joseph Cunningham
By Bishop Anthony Farquhar

..............'One of the difficulties, however, for the sick, the elderly, the infirm is that we have no choice as to how we will be tested. As that Mass for the Sick was being celebrated last Sunday, the Canon was making his transition from a long period of struggle between ill-health with the quest for independence to death itself – a struggle which he himself had fully participated only in the early years of his illness.

Canon Cunningham insisted with ever greater precision than usual that there would be no panegyric at his funeral. So I speak today in more general terms about those whom I mentioned – Jesus, Mary , John the Baptist, all manifested a resignation and calm in the face of suffering and were able to achieve this through their humility.

I shall not betray the Canon's wishes, suffice it to say that I experienced his talent as a teacher when he taught me at A-level for a year in a classroom on my own. What could have been a burdensome situation for me and an even more frustrating one for him was made quite congenial through his humility. I have often reflected that one of the sadder aspects of clerical longevity is that younger priests never have the opportunity of witnessing the genuine humility that can accompany immensity of talent shown by colleagues when they were in their prime.

In both parishes of Drumbo and here in Blaris the Canon left (and probably inherited) a legacy of prayer and worship which would eventually find their way into a new Church and a renovated Church – neither of which may have been in keeping with the architectural or liturgical style which he would have favoured. For there are people who enjoy change for change's sake; there are those too who try to preserve all that is best in Tradition. Maybe it is suitable that his final struggle and death were accompanied by the Church's call to Tradition in Translation.

Today we are reminded that innovation is at its most powerful when accompanied by humility and it is frequently this combination that transcends difference in age, tradition or denomination, through the security that comes from the knowledge that one is dealing with a person of principles. This engenders its own form of respect.

The life and death of each of us has its influence on others.

Canon Cunningham elicited goodness in others – in the early years of his ill-health in hospital, Alice herself no longer in the best of health, paralleled in the nursing and medical care of Our Lady's Home at Beechmount.

At last Sunday's Mass for the Sick there are probably few if any of the elderly or infirm who will be called upon to face the difficulties faced by Canon Cunningham. Without, as I say, wandering into the realms of panegyric I suggest that we today pray that we will acquire a calm and sense of balance in whatever awaits us.

I hope I have followed his personal wishes. Why no panegyric? Partly because of humility but more than that. Despite his immense talents, the Canon had an awareness of his own failings and limitations. I suspect that he felt that the instant canonisation of the deceased in a funeral homily detracted from and obstructed the path to the fulfilment of one of the central reasons for our funeral liturgy – that of intercession and prayer for the dead.

So in that spirit, let us pray,'

'Eternal rest grant unto him O Lord and let perpetual light shine upon him forever. May his soul and the souls of all the faithful departed through the mercy of God rest in peace. Amen.'

He is remembered as a traditionalist, conservative, intellectual and autocratic individual who did not like change. He celebrated Mass in Latin privately each morning and only celebrated the early Mass on Sunday and refused to celebrate Saturday evening Mass, which some attended in lieu of Sunday Mass, to show his disapproval. He initially refused to give Holy Communion to those who did not wish to have the Host placed on their tongue put presented the clasped open palm of their hand. He finally conceded but to show his displeasure of the new practice he exerted so much pressure on the communion wafer when placing it on the palm of the hand that it was crushed to pieces.

Canon Cunningham would inevitably finish his sermons with, 'And that's all I will say about that.' During his time in the parish when parishioners were being forced from their homes by sectarian mobs and were being murdered on the streets of Lisburn he never once made reference to their plight during his homilies.

The old parochial house had two entrances, one used by the parish priest and the other by the curates. Canon Cunningham had the heating controls in his side of the house and he decided when the heating should be turned on and off. There was an internal door connecting the two parts of the house and he would regularly go into the curates side turning off lights, etc. The constant intrusion led to curates placing locks on their doors. When Canon Cunningham was away for a few days Rev. Johnny Murray arranged for the connecting door to be bricked up. No one at the time suspected that Canon Cunningham may have been displaying the early symptoms of Alzheimer's disease.

2012

February Ex-priest James Donaghy (he had stepped down from the priesthood in 2004 and had never served in Blaris parish) was sentenced to 10 years in prison following his conviction on 23 sex abuse charges. The jury had deliberated for ten-and-a-half hours over three days. (www.bbc.co.news/uk-northern -ireland -16991435).

Rev. Patrick McCafferty, one of those subjected to the abuse was transferred to Mary Immaculate Refuge of Sinners Presbytery, 52 Lower Rathmines Road, Dublin. (Diocesan Clergy - Diocese of Down and Connor.)

Two joint Easter events were planned by ministers from Lisburn city centre churches - Seymour Street Methodist, First Lisburn and Railway Street Presbyterian, St Patrick's Roman Catholic Church, Lisburn Cathedral, Christ Church Parish and Lisburn Christian Fellowship. The annual Good Friday 'Carrying of the Cross march of Witness' was held in Lisburn on Friday April 6.

8 April A 'Joint Dawn Service' will be held in Castle Gardens on Sunday at 7:00 a.m. (entrance through Cathedral Halls) followed by breakfast in Lisburn Cathedral Church Hall. (Ulster Star 4 April 2012.)

Cecilia Daly, BBC N.I. weather girl, brought glorious sunshine to St Joseph's Primary School, Lisburn when she officially opened a range of brand new facilities on site. The new improvements to the school include the entrance foyer, state of the art disabled facilities, outdoor play areas, a new primary one classroom, a mobile classroom with toilets, an after-school cabin, a parents' cabin, a new car park, beautiful awnings and a new greenhouse.

About 200 young people attended a youth congress in St Mary's University College, Belfast on Sunday, which was organised by the Diocese of Down and Connor in preparation for the International Eucharistic Congress. Buses from Newcastle, Lisburn, Portstewart and Portaferry gathered young people from across the diocese for the day.

'It was a superb day and the great strength was that it brought together all the youth initiatives of the diocese and I think that will be the legacy of the Eucharistic Congress - gathering people together,' said Fr Eddie McGee. (Irish Catholic 18 April 2012.)

August St Joseph's Parent Teacher Association was awarded a £10,000 grant by the Big Lottery Fund to provide safety surfacing in the school grounds.

October St Patrick's Gaelic Athletic Association (GAA), no longer an exclusively Catholic club, was granted a ten-year lease on a seven-acre site at Kirkwoods Road, Lisburn. The land beside Thiepval Barracks and owned by the Ministry of Defence had been used by the club for a number of years but without a long-term lease it had not been possible to provide changing facilities. Lisburn council has promised a grant towards the cost of the new building. The GAA club will be required to make an annual payment of £3,000 to the Ministry of Defence. Among those who helped broker the deal were Jeffery Donaldson DUP MP and Alasdair McDonnell leader of the SDLP. (The Sunday Times 7 October 2012.)

An important aspect in the Filipino community is the celebration of a monthly Mass in Filipino. The Mass is celebrated by Rev. Donal Bennett from Drumcree parish in Portadown. He celebrated his Golden Jubilee since his ordination in 2011. Along with his brother Terry, also a member of the St Columban's Missionary Society based in Navan, County Meath he had retired from the missionary ministry in the Philippines. He now has special responsibility of ministering to people from the Philippines who are living in Northern Ireland.

8 December Rev. Donal Bennett celebrated Mass in St Patrick's to mark the first anniversary since his retirement from the missions and the congregation included people from the Filipino community from Belfast, Portadown and other areas.

December A housing row erupted in Lisburn after anti-Catholic graffiti was daubed over homes in a former British Army estate used to house army personnel and their families. The houses were set to be refurbished by Clanmil Housing Association to provide much-needed social housing. 'West Belfast Not Welcome' and 'All Taigs Are Targets' were just some of the offensive anti-Catholic slogans painted on garages, doors and windows the length of Mountview Drive by a group claiming to be 'UYM', or Ulster Young Militants, the youth wing of the UDA.

The disturbing news comes just three months after the 'Andersonstown News' reported that a West Belfast family were forced from Finch Gardens, an Oaklee Homes Group development near Lisburn's Pond Park Road, where they had been living for three years. They fled after being besieged by flags and then receiving a greeting card in the post referring to them as 'Fenian Scum' and signed by 'All Your Friends in Loyalist Lisburn'. (Belfast Media Group 7 December 2012.)

2013

6 March Nida Casino was appointed as the first Filipino eucharistic minister in St Patrick's. Nida had previously lived in East Sussex where she was also involved in church life there. She is also part of the team of volunteers who clean the church.

There are approximately thirty Filipino families living in Lisburn forming a tightly knit community centred on the church and making extensive use of the Pastoral Centre for social activities. The majority are employed in the nursing profession working in the Lagan Valley Hospital and the Belfast hospitals, Royal Victoria, Musgrave, City and Ulster at Dundonald. Others work in care homes, fast food outlets, KFC and Subway and Tesco supermarket.

They have formed 'Couples for Christ - Families in the Holy Spirit renewing the face of the earth.'

The Filipino community have experienced racial intimidation in Lisburn but are welcomed within the church and as Nida Casino said, 'People who don't know you will smile at you and you know that you are accepted.'

April Rev. Dermot McCaughan commenced a project to refurbish the organ in St Patrick's Church. The work was contracted to the Pipe Organ Preservation Co. and the organ is to be substantially rebuilt retaining only the casework and 5 ranks from the present Evans & Barr instrument. It is to be enlarged from 15 to 45 stops incorporating pipes from another organ by the same builder together with a new 3 manual console with 60 drawstops.

The existing organ has a plaque with the maker's name; Evans & Barr Ltd., Belfast and Dublin 1935. Another plaque with the name Rushworth & Dreaper, Liverpool with the date 1981 would seem to indicate that this firm of organ builders had carried out repairs at that time.

19 May To celebrate the birthday of Christ Church, Hillborough Road, Lisburn a 'Pentecost Prayer Walk' organised by the Lisburn City Centre Churches, was held on Sunday evening. Following a short service in Christ Church led by the rector, the Rev. Paul Dundas – members of the seven participating Lisburn city centre churches stopped for prayer outside St Patrick's Roman Catholic Church, First Lisburn Presbyterian Church, Lisburn Cathedral, Railway Street Presbyterian Church, Seymour Street Methodist Church and finished at Lisburn Christian Fellowship, where refreshments were served. Rev. Dermot McCaughan P.P. represented St. Patrick's Church.

The Syro Malabar Catholics in Lisburn, while attending the regular Masses in St Patrick's hold their own Mass on the last Saturday of each month at 3:00 p.m. in the church. The influence of the Indian community is reflected in the number of altar servers from that community. Mr. Cyril Jose and Mr.

Manoj Alex act as representatives for the Syro Malabar community in Lisburn. (http://smcbelfast.org/belfast.html)

Rev. Dermot McCaughan installed an automated bell chiming system to replace the traditional ringing of the church bell using a rope. The loudspeaker produces a similar sound to the existing bell and the change generally went unnoticed in the parish. The most significant change is that the bell rings out the Angelus each day.

Handrails were erected on each side of the main altar to help Rev. Eamon Magorrian climb the steps to the altar.

Rev. Dermot McCaughan provided a fitting memorial in Holy Trinity cemetery to those babies who had been still-born or died shortly after birth and buried in a previously unmarked part of the cemetery. In the bottom right hand side of the cemetery a Norwegian blue pearl granite plinth provides the base for a gold painted figure representing Jesus along with two small children. *'Let the little children come to me'* is inscribed in gold on the base. The block of granite, sourced in Norway was sent to China to be cut and gloss polished before being installed.

William Campbell, the gardener who maintains not only the cemetery but the grounds at St Patrick's church, created a beautiful garden with ornamental shrubs as a backdrop to the statue. The area in front of the statue is marked with small, similar granite posts and box shrubs.

June St Joseph's Primary School's PTA won the top prize in the annual Northern Ireland PTA Awards held at Stormont. Winner in the 'Changing the Life of the School' category for its greenhouse project Maria Geough, Denise Broderick, Gemma Plumb and Kieran Corrigan were presented with a cheque for £500.

July A number of Catholic families who had moved into a newly built development at Ballymacoss were intimidated from their homes. Catholics homes were daubed with red, white and blue paint and the area was festooned with union flags and bunting. The nearby entrance to Ballymacash housing estate is flanked by two large hand painted union flags, one proclaiming 'Loyalist Ballymacash'.

Rev. Eddie Magee was involved in a number of media interviews relating to tensions over Orange Order parades past St Patrick's Church in Donegall Street, Belfast in the previous year when a band stopped outside the church and marched around in circles playing, what was perceived to be, a sectarian song. In the smoke and mirrors of Northern Ireland politics the Orange Order later stated that an invitation had been issued to Bishop Noel Treanor to attend an exhibition at Schomberg House 'to develop mutual understanding'.

However a spokesman for Roman Catholic Bishop of Down and Connor, Noel Treanor, yesterday told BBC's Sunday Sequence programme that in recent weeks 'the portrayal and presentation of this invitation to a Covenant exhibition has morphed or changed into what some people believe is that Bishop Treanor has refused or rebuffed or even deferred face-to-face talks with the Orange Order'. Father Eddie McGee added that this was 'entirely inaccurate' as he said Bishop Treanor 'has not received any invitation to face-to-face talks around parades'.

'He has received no private communication from the Orange Order so there's no invitation to defer,' he said.

The Down and Connor cleric said at the time the invitation was issued, the parish priest of St Patrick's, (Belfast) Fr Michael Sheehan, 'was engaged in discussions' around parading.

'He responded to that open letter, and deferred a public visit to the Covenant exhibition to a later stage but he welcomed the opportunity for discussions around parading. The deferral was in no way to indicate there was a closure to ongoing dialogue.'

9 November Typhoon Haiyan one of the largest and most destructive storms of the century struck the Philippines devastating Tacloban City. In the past events elsewhere often had a direct affect the Catholic community in Lisburn now a calamity on the other side of the world impacted on Lisburn's Catholic Filipino community. They immediately organised fund raising appeals for the hundreds of thousands of people displaced by the 150 mph winds and the floodwaters. The entire community of Lisburn responded and appeals for shoes and clothing brought a quick response. The Pastoral Centre was used as a collection point for hundreds of bags of clothing and brand new sheets which were then shipped out to the Philippines. In addition over £8,000 contributed by the parishioners of the Parish of Blaris and the people of Lisburn was contributed directly to missionaries working in the disaster zones.

This was a further example of how the communities of Lisburn came together in a spirit of generosity to help those less fortunate.

December A webcam installed in St Patrick's became operational allowing parishioners, especially the sick and housebound to view Sunday, weekday and funeral Masses online.

Maureen Irvine retired as principal of Holy Trinity Nursery School after 33 years with the school. She had qualified as a teacher at St Mary's, Belfast and her first post was with St Oliver Plunkett's Primary School, Glen Road, Belfast before taking up her post at Holy Trinity in 1980.

24 December St Patrick's was filled to capacity for Christmas Eve Mass which was celebrated by Rev. Eamon Magorrian in the absence of the parish priest who was recovering from minor surgery.

EPILOGUE

This book began as an exercise to collate as much information as possible about the Parish of Blaris. As facts and details were discovered it was necessary to place them in context with events taking place both at national and local level. The book evolved to become, not only a history of the Parish of Blaris, but a social history of Lisburn and the surrounding district within the present parish boundary. It has also proved to be an interesting study in community relations over a four-hundred year period.

The Catholic community in Lisburn from the outset was a community set apart, not only initially by legislation but by prevailing attitudes which were to change little over the years. Protestant ascendancy was key to the division between the two communities and initially every effort to provide Catholics with equal rights to their fellow citizens was vociferously opposed. This spilled over into political matters providing further cause for division. The toxic mix of religion and politics would lead to regular outbreaks of sectarian violence.

It would be wrong however to view the people of Lisburn as constantly at loggerheads over religion and politics. This account lists many occasions when both communities worked well together and demonstrates that the Catholics of Lisburn played an important part in the economic and social life of the town and continue to do so to the present day.

So what led to the sectarian divide that caused such friction that would lead to people being killed because of their religion?

In examining the history of Lisburn it is evident that the vast majority of disturbances in Lisburn were fermented by individuals often seeking to exploit, for their own advantage, the political or religious issues of the day. It was relatively easy for individuals to stir up tension by playing on the inherent fears around unionist v nationalist politics and Protestant v Catholic religion by claiming that only they could prevent the fears being realised. The perceived enemy was demonized and killings, once started, would be accepted as a legitimate course of action and would be difficult to stop. It is only when the killing stops and sanity returns that people step back to see what has, or more the case, has not been achieved that the question is asked, what was it all about? The communities of Lisburn have expanded in recent times to include other nationalities and all tend to live largely separate lives and do so peacefully as long as they are left to live in peace.

Lisburn is in many ways like a fine red wine. There may be a sectarian sediment in the bottle but the longer the bottle is stored the more the sediment will settle and as long as the contents are not agitated it will remain a fine wine that can be enjoyed by everyone.

ACKNOWLEDGEMENTS

First and foremost my thanks goes to the parishioners and clergy of the Parish of Blaris, past and present, who helped with my research, provided anecdotes and photographs. It has not been possible to include all the photographs in the book but they have been added to the parish archives.

Eileen Murphy, now retired from the Diocesan Office, Lissue House, must also get a mention for making available documents relating to the parish and for providing tea and buns while I examined the archive. Further afield Fr. George Hayes, Vice-Rector of the Irish College in Rome gets my sincere thanks for taking time out of his busy schedule to facilitate my visit and in the absence of the resident archivist to locate letters sent from the parish to the Vatican.

The staff who go about their work quietly and efficiently in the Public Record Office of Northern Ireland, the Belfast Newspaper Library, Lisburn Library, the Linenhall Library and The National Archives of Ireland in Dublin and who provide such a valuable research service get my thanks.

My sincere gratitude goes to Dr. Éamon Phoenix for reading the manuscript, for his helpful suggestions regarding historical context and for his professional advice. Equally my gratitude goes to Ray Mullan of the Community Relations Council, who also took time to read the manuscript, for his valuable assistance and recommendations.

Last, but certainly not least, I must acknowledge the financial support provided by Lisburn Arts Advisory Committee to make this project possible.

Index